Corpus Data across Languages and Disciplines

ŁÓDŹ
STUDIES IN LANGUAGE

Edited by
Barbara Lewandowska-Tomaszczyk

Vol. 28

PETER LANG
Frankfurt am Main · Berlin · Bern · Bruxelles · New York · Oxford · Warszawa · Wien

Piotr Pęzik (ed.)

Corpus Data across Languages and Disciplines

PETER LANG
Internationaler Verlag der Wissenschaften

Bibliographic Information published by the Deutsche Nationalbibliothek
The Deutsche Nationalbibliothek lists this publication in the Deutsche Nationalbibliografie; detailed bibliographic data is available in the internet at http://dnb.d-nb.de.

ISSN 1437-5281
ISBN 978-3-631-62547-7

www.peterlang.de

Table of Contents

Introduction

Piotr Pęzik

Over the recent years corpus tools and methodologies have gained widespread recognition in various areas of theoretical and applied linguistics. Data lodged in corpora is used across languages and disciplines as distinct as historical linguistics, language didactics, discourse analysis, machine translation and search engine development to name but a few. The biennial PALC conference has been organized for the last 14 years at the University of Łódź to help a wide community of researchers, language professionals and practitioners keep up to date with new corpus theories and methodologies as well as language-related applications of computational tools and resources. Over the years the list of PALC conference participants has included hundreds of linguists, lexicographers, translators, foreign and native language teachers, methodologists, journalists and media discourse analysts, computer scientists working in the field of language processing, and many other scholars and practitioners of different disciplines and backgrounds.

More than 30 papers were presented at the *8th Practical Applications in Language and Computers* conference organized held in Łódź in 2011 with plenary lectures delivered by Bas Aarts, Raymond Hickey, Rafał Molencki, Maciej Piasecki and Anatol Stefanowitsch. The present volume contains a selection of those papers, which can be categorized into six broad corpus applications topical areas: l*anguage teaching*, *historical linguistics*, *media and political discourse*, *grammar and phraseology*, *computational tools* and *translation studies*.

Language teaching and learning

In the opening paper *Bas Aarts, Dan Clayton and Sean Wallis* introduce a corpus-based platform used in the process of teaching the grammar of English to secondary school students in Britain. *Štindlová, Rosen, Hana and Škodová* investigate the usefulness of error annotation in a learner corpus of Czech, while *Piotr Pęzik* provides and overview of the **PEL**CRA **LE**arner **C**orpus and some of the text mining tools developed within this project. The paper by *Jersus Colmenares* investigates the treatment of collocations in EFL textbooks used in Venezuela, and *Jacek Waliński* presents an online collaborative assessment environment developed within the CEFcult project.

Corpora in historical linguistics

In the first paper of this section *Anna Cichosz* describes the use of a parallel Latin-Old English corpus in word order studies, while *Joanna Kopaczyk* explores the use of repetitive patterns in early Scots legal and administrative texts.

Media and political discourse

Silvia de Candia, Mikołaj Deckert and Marco Venuti investigate the role of so-called *accessed voice* in British, Italian and Polish TV news reports using a comparable multilingual corpus of TV news transcripts. *Katarzyna Fronczak-Bartnikowska* conducts a corpus-based analysis of the discourse of the recent U.S. presidential election campaign. *Barbara Lewandowska-Tomaszczyk and Frauke Zeller* discuss the contribution of corpus linguistics methods to the analysis of computer-mediated communication within the *Transforming Audiences, Transforming Societies* COST Action IS0906.

Grammar and phraseology

Stanisław Goźdź-Roszkowski opens this section with a paper exploring the use of epistemic semantic sequences in academic legal discourse. *Marcin Grygiel* uses the Web as a corpus to investigate the status of affirmation modality in Serbian, while *Renata Novotná's* paper is a comparison of the Polish equivalents of the Czech preposition *na*. The last paper in this section contributed by Milena Hebal-Jezierska analyses the phraseological profile of the lexemes used by Czechs to describe foreigners living in their country.

Tools and services

Karlheinz Moerth and Matej Durco describe their efforts to build a multipurpose corpus research service. Anelia Belogaý et al. present a suite of web-based tools and services for the management of digital contents and legal documents. Finally, Marcin Miłkowski overviews the quality assessment features of *LanguageTool*, an open-source proofreading package.

Translation and localization

The last section of this volume comprises five papers dealing with translation and localization problems. *Belinda Maia and Rui Sousa-Silva* evaluate the contribution of the Google Translate service to the world of professional translation. *Łukasz Grabowski* compares corpora of translational and non-translational literary Polish in search of evidence for translation universals. *Natalia Quinteiro* and *Gabriel Quiroz* analyze the level of phraseological equivalence in the English translation of *Años de Soledad*. Monika Czarnecka examines the use of CAT tools by Polish translators and Anna Bączkowska's concluding paper explores the problem of signals of power in audio-visual translation.

Acknowledgments

This volume would not have been possible without the support and advice of professor Barbara Lewandowska-Tomaszczyk. Many thanks are also due to the members of the PALC 2011 committee including Anna Cichosz, Stanisław Goźdź-Roszkowski, Łukasz Dróżdż and Mikołaj Deckert, who offered their time to help with the organization of the conference. The preparation of this publication was co-financed by the Committee of Linguistics of the Polish Academy of Sciences.

Piotr Pęzik

Creating Corpus-Driven Teaching and Learning Resources for Secondary School Grammar Teaching

Bas Aarts, Dan Clayton and Sean Wallis

Abstract

In this article we describe a project at the Survey of English Usage, University College London which aims to build a web-based teaching and learning platform for teachers and students in secondary schools. The platform will consist of an interactive structured English language course with lesson modules, exercises, projects, etc. which dynamically access the parsed British Component of the *International Corpus of English* (ICE-GB). We will show how the corpus can be used in delivering lesson materials in secondary school classrooms.

Keywords

Grammar, grammar teaching, corpora, language teaching in schools

Introduction

The English language plays a very important role in the British National Curriculum (NC). Great demands are made of teachers at secondary schools to teach complex linguistic and grammatical concepts, as laid down in the NC. They have understandable difficulties with this, given the very limited linguistic training they have received at teacher training college. The teachers' students also have difficulties with learning complex grammatical concepts, because typically, in the tradition of grammar teaching, invented examples are used. Students find these difficult to relate to real linguistic settings and almost impossible to apply to their own language production. Regarding the lack of expertise in grammar teaching Hudson and Walmsley write:

> Most younger teachers know very little grammar and are suspicious of explicit grammar teaching. Not surprisingly, therefore, new recruits entering teacher-training courses typically either know very little grammar (Williamson and Hardman 1995) or have no confidence in their knowledge, presumably because they have picked it up in an unsystematic way (Cajkler and Hislam 2002). This situation raises obvious problems for the implementation of the official programme.
>
> (Hudson and Walmsley 2005: 616)

To address these problems for teachers and students we decided to create specific tools for the teaching and learning of the English language based on the existing research of the Survey of English Usage (SEU) at University College London (UCL).

The project

Our goals in this project were to create a web-based teaching and learning platform for supporting the teaching of English grammar in secondary schools. The impetus was a recent review of secondary school grammar teaching, published by the British government in 2007, which concluded that teaching should make use of formal and informal English in different settings, and that grammar teaching must be driven by real examples. Another impetus was the article by Hudson and Walmsley already quoted above. They say:

> In the education system, the quality of government documents, the quality of teaching about language, and specifically the training of future teachers of English are all areas where standards could be raised by improving the quality of input from linguistics.
>
> (Hudson and Walmsley ibid.: 619)

We took these observations to heart and constructed a web-based platform consisting of an interactive structured English language course, tailored to the goals of the British National Curriculum (Key Stages 3-5). It consists of lesson modules dynamically accessing a parsed corpus of English. The aims of the platform are to:

- translate our rich corpus resources into effective English language teaching tools and curriculum materials for teachers to use in the classroom, and
- provide pupils with high-quality web-based learning materials in both classroom and self-directed modes.

There has been a long tradition in language teaching of using artificial, made-up examples to illustrate grammatical phenomena to school children. In the past this was a necessity, because no alternative resources were available. However, as the British government report from 2007 observes, students and teachers find the artificiality of these examples a barrier to their ability to get to grips with how grammar applies to real life. To quote a recent undergraduate textbook:

> Invented sentences like the ones so often used in textbooks are just sterile fragments of that wonderfully rich language they are supposed to be identifying.
>
> (Börjars and Burridge 2001: 9)

In our web-based platform we overcome this problem by dynamically sourcing examples of English language phenomena in real settings from an underlying corpus. As noted above, our corpus is fully-parsed, and contains a very wide range of real contemporary English, both written and spoken, including informal conversations, formal speeches, spontaneous commentaries, interviews, radio discussions, academic, instructional and private writing (see Table 1). The spoken material has been transcribed word-for-word, and the audio data are available from the same web database. Hitherto our resources have only been used for academic research. We now make our research output available to a wider audience, specifically secondary schools.

Table 1.1: The structure of the 1 million word ICE-GB corpus (500 "texts" of 2,000 words)

Spoken (300)	**Dialogues** (180)	**Private** (100)	Conversations (90) Telephone calls (10)
		Public (80)	Class Lessons (20) Broadcast Discussions (20) Broadcast Interviews (10) Parliamentary Debates (10) Cross-examinations (10) Business Transactions (10)
	Monologues (120)	**Unscripted** (70)	Commentaries (20) Unscripted Speeches (30) Demonstrations (10) Legal Presentations (10)
		Scripted (50)	Broadcast News (20) Broadcast Talks (20) Non-broadcast Talks (10)
Written (200)	**Non-printed** (50)	**Student Writing** (20)	Student Essays (10) Exam Scripts (10)
		Letters (30)	Social Letters (15) Business Letters (15)
	Printed (150)	**Academic** (40)	Humanities (10) Social Sciences (10) Natural Sciences (10) Technology (10)
		Popular (40)	Humanities (10) Social Sciences (10) Natural Sciences (10) Technology (10)
		Reportage (20)	Press reports (20)
		Instructional (20)	Administrative Writing (10) Skills/hobbies (10)
		Persuasive (10)	Editorials (10)
		Creative (20)	Novels (20)

The dynamic selection of real language examples of grammatical phenomena has many potential benefits:

- Since the source material is independent from the teaching modules (the system design is modular and extensible), modules can easily be revised;

- A great deal of context and contextual information is available (e.g. the setting in which a conversation is conducted, who the speakers are, etc.), as well as audio material;
- Material can be selected for a particular student group or purpose (e.g. to teach students the features of formal English).

The main beneficiaries of the project will be teachers and students of the English language in the local community, but we have a longer-term aim of producing a resource that is available across the world. Teachers will benefit from the availability of pre-written, but flexible and adaptable, courses and modules for building their own course plans. They will be able to access corpus materials, including texts and audio recordings.

Students will benefit through the acquisition of grammatical concepts being made relevant to them through lessons and interactive hands-on exercises.

We have found particular advantages in providing genuine, attested examples of language use for the exercises. Our exercise materials demonstrate that linguistic rules 'work'. Repetition helps the student learn these rules, and with multiple examples populating exercises the student acquires the rules to improve their scores. They can see that these rules are applicable to their own and others' language.

We also aim to improve support in other ways.

- Teachers can monitor students' progress, and can support their homework and their self-study.
- Teachers can decide on course modules and then select specific text genres to teach (formal/informal, spoken/written, etc.). They can also select material written by different authors in different periods and opt for different complexities of analysis.
- Teachers can select source materials and determine a set of possible lessons and exercises.

The entire platform will be available over the internet from UCL and requires no additional software at the user's end, aside from standard internet browser programs. This will enable the community in general, and teachers and students of English in particular, to gain access to the system.

Project highlights

In this section we showcase a few of the features of the new resource. We summarise these in terms of the seven 'zones' we have created, as shown in Figure 1 below.

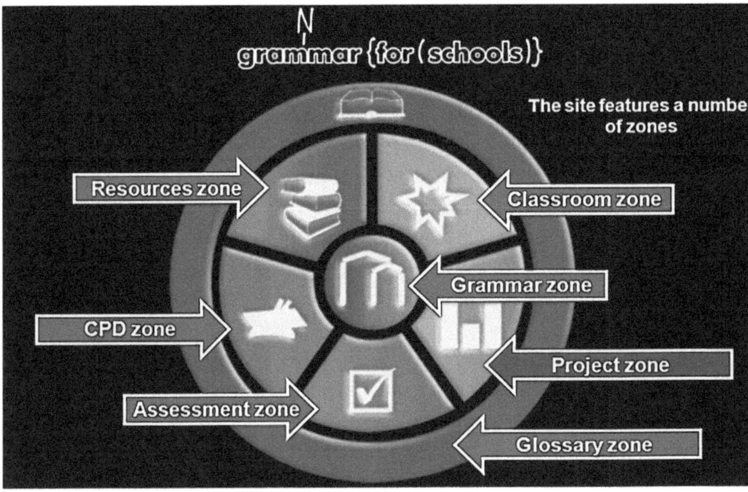

Figure 1.1: The Grammar for Schools Home Page

These zones intentionally overlap to some degree.

The Grammar Zone

The Grammar Zone is at the heart of the site and provides a comprehensive overview of the main areas of grammar, such as word classes, phrases and clauses, and how they are linked. The zone offers a concise, but complete, overview of the grammar of English. Figure 2 shows an example of a grammar lesson. We have developed technology for turning lessons on the site into a slideshow. These are not static PowerPoint projections, but can dynamically include examples taken from the corpus, exercises, videos and games.

The Grammar Zone is organised through the *Grammar topics* menu (see Figure 2). Teachers and students can look at introductory explanations which feature interactive examples and self-testing tasks, before moving on to specific activities and lessons designed to highlight a particular area of grammar. For example, teachers can choose to look at 'time and tense' and find activities which help students be more consistent in their use of tenses when they write, or they can look for modal verbs and connect this topic with work students can do on the power of persuasive language.

The Classroom Zone

The Classroom Zone is the area for classroom activities, lesson plans and even whole schemes of work for teachers to use in 3-4 week periods of teaching. It is organised under two broad headings which allow teachers to find the most relevant resource(s) to suit their class very quickly.

Firstly, we have *teaching topics*, which are areas of work which should be familiar to most teachers. In here users will find four areas: writing, reading, spoken language and investigating language. Each of these topics contains subtopics, such as 'writing to inform', 'writing to persuade', 'analysing language choices' and 'analysing speech', which will contain activities and lessons for that particular area.

Teachers will also find some ready-made units of work with suggestions about how to approach particular topics such as 'analysing spoken language', 'text messages' and 'the language of poetry'. These mini-schemes of work are designed to let students follow a path through a topic over a series of lessons. But teachers can also mix and match, selecting particular activities to use with one ability range and others to use with different students. For an example of a lesson plan on 'Martian Grammar', see Figure 3.

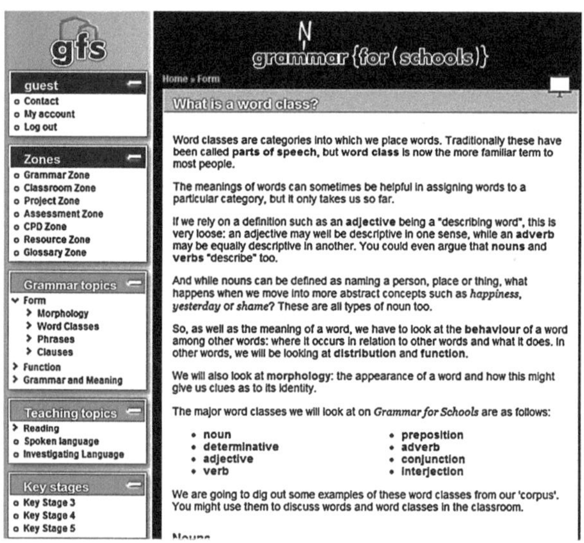

Figure 1.2: An example of a grammar lesson in the classroom zone. The teacher can explore the site using the navigation menus on the left hand side of the display (shown expanded). Page content can be presented as a slide show (top right icon).

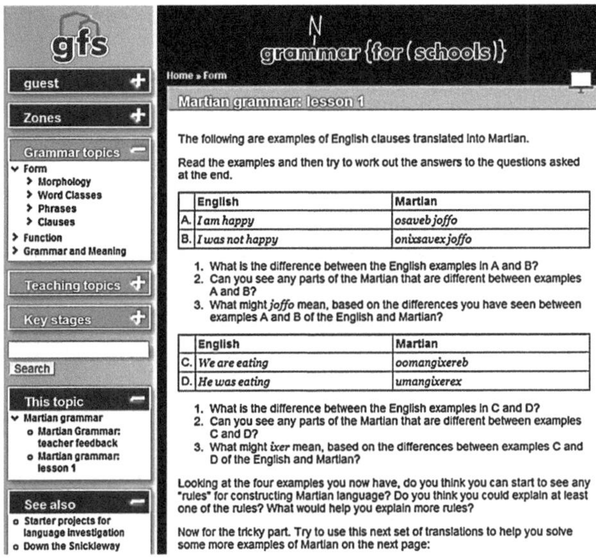

Figure 1.3: An example of a lesson – this time on 'Martian grammar'.

The Project Zone

The Project Zone is designed for investigative approaches to language. It encourages teachers and students to carry out investigations into a range of different language areas, such as using corpora to study grammatical patterns or to evaluate the language styles of men and women, exploring variations between Jamaican English and Standard English, or gathering media resources about different attitudes to language use.

The Project Zone explains some of the basics of using a corpus, provides links to other corpora and sets up investigations for students to carry out in class and for coursework projects. Some of the projects are specifically designed to work with existing British A-level English Language specifications while others are designed to encourage younger students to start thinking in a way that helps them solve linguistic problems and set up suitable methodologies, a new approach for many English students.

The Assessment Zone

The Assessment Zone is designed to provide an area where students can test their own knowledge of grammar and the English language in general. The interactive exercises are grouped here under grammar topics. For example Figure 4 below shows an exercise on Verb Phrases.

As we noted, examples are drawn from ICE-GB and other sources. We are currently looking at ways to use the scores from the Assessment Zone as a means of tracking student progress across key strands and substrands of the National Curriculum Standards.

The Continuous Professional Development (CPD) Zone

This is where teachers can access extended notes about particular lessons and activities. The idea behind the CPD Zone is that it will provide material that will allow teachers to become more confident in their understanding of grammar and how it might be made more relevant to their students.

Along with lesson notes, ideas for schemes of work and approaches to different grammar and teaching topics, the CPD Zone also includes discussion pages where arguments and debates about grammar and how it is taught are addressed. For example, the material on usage takes a look at conflicting positions on dialects of English and their place in the classroom.

The Resource Zone

The Resource Zone provides extra support material for teachers and students, for example links to other language sites, databases of articles and suggestions for further reading.

The Glossary Zone

The Glossary Zone complements the Grammar Zone by providing a 'quick grammar help' facility on grammatical terms (see Figure 5). Glossary entries are automatically cross referenced and indexed. Teachers can click on words they are unsure of in the browsing view and pull down a quick glossary definition.

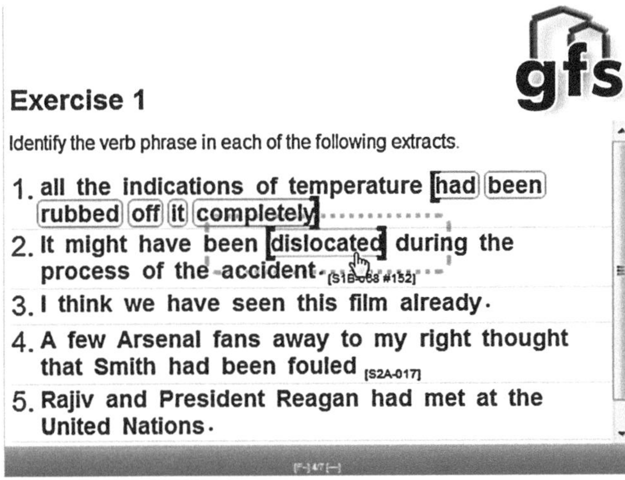

Figure 1.4: *In this slideshow exercise from the Assessment Zone the student must select the words forming the verb phrase in each snippet. Note the references to the corpus in brackets.*

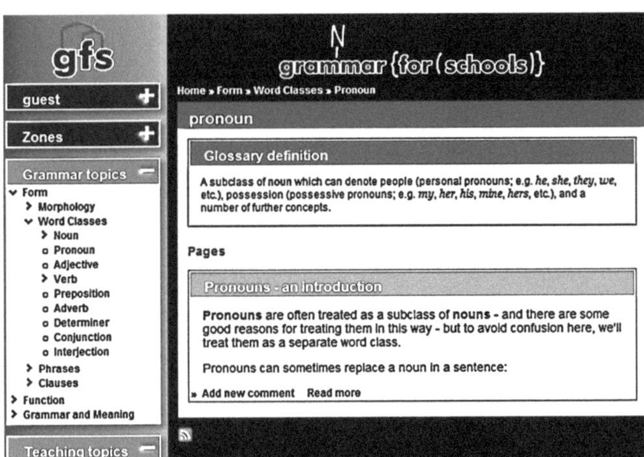

Figure 1.5: *Glossary Zone definitions pop up all over the site. Here, a teacher reviewing lesson plans on pronouns is given a helpful definition as a reminder of the purpose of the material.*

Conclusion

The resources that the Grammar for Schools site will offer once it is completed will, we believe, mark a sea change in the way that grammar is taught in schools. Teachers will be able to move from the static print-based texts that have been in use for centuries to dynamic materials available online. This will make grammar teaching and learning not only a worthwhile, but also an enjoyable and exciting experience.

References

Börjars, K. and K. Burridge (2001). *Introducing English Grammar*, Arnold: London.

Cajkler, W. and J. Hislam (2002). "Trainee Teachers' Grammatical Knowledge: The Tension Between Public Expectation and Individual Competence." *Language Awareness* II. 161-177.

Hudson, R. and J. Walmsley (2005). "The English Patient: English Grammar and Teaching in the Twentieth Century." *Journal of Linguistics* 43 (3), 593-622.

Williamson, J. and F. Hardman (1995) "Time for Refilling the Bath? A Study of Primary Student-teachers' Grammatical Knowledge." *Language and Education* 9, 117-134.

CzeSL – an Error Tagged Corpus of Czech as a Second Language

Barbora Štindlová, Alexandr Rosen, Jirka Hana and Svatava Škodová

Abstract

Using an error-annotated learner corpus as the basis, the goal of this paper is two-fold: (i) to evaluate the practicality of the annotation scheme by computing inter-annotator agreement on a non-trivial sample of data, and (ii) to find out whether the application of automated linguistic annotation tools (taggers, spell checkers and grammar checkers) on the learner text is viable as a substitute for manual annotation.

Keywords

Learner corpus, error annotation, second language acquisition

Introduction

Texts produced by non-native speakers are a precious source of information about the acquisition of a language by the learners and about second language acquisition in general. Collections of such texts – learner corpora – can be annotated in a way similar to other corpora with morphosyntactic categories or syntactic structure. However, their most interesting aspect is examples of deviant use, which can be corrected and assigned a tag specifying the type of error. Annotation of this kind is a challenging task, even more so for a language such as Czech, with its rich inflection, derivation, agreement, and a largely information-structure-driven constituent order.

The present work is based on a project aimed at building a learner corpus with errors manually corrected and labelled within a three-level annotation scheme. Manual annotation is supplemented by morphosyntactic tags assigned to the hand-corrected input by a tagger, and by additional error tags, whenever they can be derived automatically. Options to provide corrections and error annotations in a fully automatic way are being investigated.

The paper is organized as follows: first, Section 2 presents our learner corpus project in more detail; then Section 3 describes our annotation scheme and its evaluation by computing inter-annotator agreement using data from a trial annotation; finally, Section 4 presents the results of experiments in applying two taggers and a spell checker to the uncorrected text.

Learner corpus of Czech (CzeSL)

The learner corpus of Czech as a Second Language (CzeSL)[1] is built as a part of the Acquisition Corpora of Czech (AKCES), a research programme pursued at Charles University in Prague since 2005 (Šebesta 2010). Intended to reach the size of up to two million running words, the corpus is focused on the language of non-native speakers of Czech, consisting of three main groups: (1) speakers of Slavic languages, (2) speakers of distant non-Indo-European languages, (3) speakers of other Indo-European languages. A separate subcorpus, built along slightly different guidelines, covers the language of Czech pupils with Romani background (Bedřichová et al. 2011).

Although written texts prevail, each subcorpus has its oral part. A large portion of the written parts consists of short essays, collected as manuscripts and transcribed into an electronic format, preserving specific features of hand-written texts, such as self-corrections or emoticons (Štindlová 2011, 106). Manuscripts are used for their availability and also because the authors cannot check them easily by automatic proofreading tools. The rest of the written texts are Bachelors' and Masters' theses, written in Czech by non-native students.

The data being collected cover all language levels according to the Common European Framework of Reference for Languages (CEFRL), from real beginners (A1 level) to advanced learners (level B2 and higher), with a balanced mix of levels as much as possible. While most other learner corpora include texts elicited only as a part of written or oral examination, we use texts produced during all range of situations throughout the language-learning process, such as homework and texts produced during the class.

Each text is equipped with metadata records, some of them relate to the respondent (including sociological data about the learner, such as age, gender, first language, proficiency level in Czech, knowledge of other languages, duration and conditions of language acquisition), while other specify the character of the text and circumstances of its production (availability of reference tools, type of elicitation, temporal and size restrictions etc.).

The finished corpus will be used in the education of teachers of Czech as a foreign language, as a source of knowledge about interlanguage and second language acquisition, and ultimately as a source of data for the compilation of teaching materials and optimization of the learning process (Štindlová 2011).

---

1 The corpus is one of the tasks of the project *Innovation of Education in the Field of Czech as a Second Language* (project no. CZ.1.07/2.2.00/07.0259), a part of the operational programme *Education for Competiveness*, funded by the European Structural Funds (ESF) and the Czech government. The annotation tool was also partially funded by grant no. P406/10/P328 of the Grant Agency of the Czech Republic. The project team consists of partners from the Technical University in Liberec and Charles University in Prague.

The annotation scheme

The annotation scheme for CzeSL was designed to reflect the goals of the project and the specifics of Czech.[2] Rather than focusing on a narrow domain of learner language as the annotation target (such as spelling or lexical errors), the corpus is intended as open to as many research goals as possible using a multilevel annotation scheme, supporting successive emendation. As a compromise between several theoretically motivated levels and practical concerns about the process of annotation, the scheme offers two levels of annotation. This enables the annotators to register anomalies in isolated forms separately from the annotation of context-based phenomena but saves them from difficult theoretical dilemmas.

Levels of annotation are represented as a graph consisting of a set of interlinked parallel paths, where a path is a sequence of word forms corresponding to a sentence at a given level – see Fig. 2.1, glossed in (1). Each word in the input text is represented at every level, unless it is split, joined (as kdy by in Fig. 1), deleted or added by the annotator. Whenever a word form is emended, the type of error can be specified as a label at the link connecting the incorrect form at a lower level with its emended form at a higher level (such as incorInfl or incorBase for morphological errors in inflectional endings and stems, stylColl as a stylistic marker, wbdOther as a word boundary error, and agr as an error in agreement). These labelled relations can inter-link any number of potentially non-contiguous words across the neighbouring levels. Multiple words can thus be identified as a single segment, while any of the participating word forms can retain their 1:1 links with their counterparts at other levels.

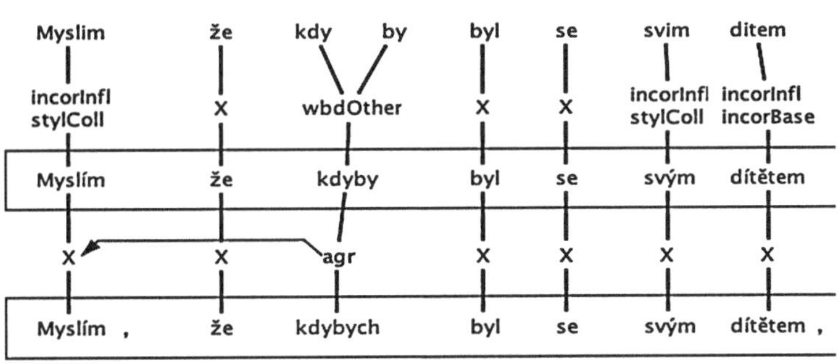

Figure 2.1: Example of the three-level error annotation scheme

2 See Hana et al. (2010) and Štindlová et al. (in press) for a more detailed description of the annotation scheme.

(1) Myslím,že kdybych byl se svým dítětem, ...
think$_{1stSg}$ that if$_{1stSg}$ was$_{masc}$ with my child,
'I think that if I were with my child, …

At Level 0 (L0), the level of the transcribed input, the words represent the original strings of graphemes. At L1, the level of orthographical and morphological emendation, only individual forms are treated. The result is a string consisting of correct Czech forms, even though the sentence may not be correct as a whole. A formally correct form may be corrected if the author clearly misspelled the form she intended to use, creating an unintended homograph. All other types of errors (such as errors in agreement) are emended at L2.

Manual annotation is supported by the purpose-built annotation tool *feat* (http://ufal.mff.cuni.cz/~hana/feat.html) and followed by automatic post-processing, providing additional information about lemma, POS and morphological categories for correct and emended forms, with error types not assigned manually (by comparing the original and corrected strings), and with formal error description: type of a spelling alternation, missing/redundant expression, inappropriate word order. In the future, we plan to automatically tag errors in verb prefixes, inflectional endings, spelling, palatalization, metathesis, etc. Table 1 shows the number of different error tags. Options to perform a fully automatic annotation are investigated in Section 4 below.

Table 2.1: Manually and automatically assigned error tags at L1 and L2

Error tags	L1 only	L2 only	L1 and L2	Total
Manual	8	11	3	22
Automatic	1	6	0	7
Total	9	17	3	29

Evaluation of the error mark-up

There is no widely accepted metric evaluating the consistency of annotation of learner corpora. In the current annotation practice of non-native speakers' corpora, it is common to have ill-formed texts tagged by a single annotator, despite problems in reliability and evaluation. A .general shift towards multiple annotation of learner corpora is imminent – cf. Tetreault and Chodorow (2008), Rozovskaya and Roth (2010), Meurers (2011).

Inter-annotator agreement (IAA)

The manual annotation of CzeSL was evaluated using the metric κ (kappa, Cohen 1960), widely accepted as the standard measure of inter-annotator agreement, especially for tagged corpora. It is calculated as:

$$\kappa = \frac{P(A) - P(E)}{1 - P(E)}$$

where P(A) is the observed agreement among the annotators, and P(E) is the expected agreement, i.e., P(E) is the probability that the coders agree by chance. The values of κ are within the interval [−1, 1], where κ = 1 means perfect agreement, κ = 0 agreement equal to chance, and κ = −1 "perfect" disagreement.

In the evaluation, we use the scale proposed by Rietveld and van Hout (1993), where the values 0.21–0.40 indicate fair agreement, 0.41–0.60 moderate agreement, and 0.61–0.80 substantial agreement. Values below 0.20 indicate slight agreement, whereas those above 0.81 are almost perfect.

Sample data

The data for the annotation were selected from a database compiled for CzeSL. The sample consists of 74 texts totalling 9848 tokens. Most of them were written by native speakers of Russian; the texts are classified according to the CEFRL scale as A2 or B1.

Method

The sample was annotated by 14 annotators. They were split into two groups: Annotators A and Annotators B. Each group annotated the whole sample independently. On average each annotator processed 1475 words in 11 texts.

On L1, the annotators chose from 8 tags for morphological, orthographical and word-boundary errors, and "non-Czech" expressions. On L2, syntactic, morphosyntactic, lexical and stylistic errors were captured by 15 tags. Stylistically marked expressions could be assigned additional tags at both levels.[3] The results of inter-annotator agreement for the domain categories (incor, wbd, fw and styl)[4] were summed up, without distinguishing the particular error subtypes.

---

3 The numbers of tags given here correspond to a slightly outdated taxonomy and differ from the current state, presented in Section 3.

4 The error taxonomy is hierarchical – error types are partitioned into domains, which are further divided into more specific subcategories, tagged manually or automatically. For example, the domain of complex verb form errors on L2 can be further specified as errors in analytical verb forms (*cvf*), modal verbs (*mod*), verbo-nominal predicates, passive or resultative form (*vnp*).

Results

Table 2 below summarizes the distribution of selected error tags. The column "Only A" shows counts for each tag used by annotators in group A but not by those in group B. Similarly for the next column. The following column shows cases when both groups agreed. The last column gives the agreement measure κ.

Table 2.2: Inter-annotator agreement on selected tags

Tag	Type of error	Only A	Only B	A and B	κ
incorSum	*incorStem+incorInfl*	168	130	894	0.84
incorStem	Incorrect stem	167	165	559	0.61
incorInfl	Incorrect inflection	173	130	250	0.75
wbdSum	Incorrect word boundary	14	21	45	0.72
fwSum	*fw+fwFab+fwNc*	25	17	18	0.46
fw	"Non-Czech" expression	4	6	1	0.17
fwFab	Author' coinage	23	13	3	0.14
fwNc	Foreign/unidentified form	10	9	3	0.24
***stylColl* L1**	Colloquial style at L1	10	2	2	0.25
agr	Agreement violation	82	99	110	0.54
dep	Errors in expressing syntactic dependency	99	118	87	0.43
neg	Incorrectly expressed negation	11	9	9	0.47
***stylColl* L2**	Colloquial style at L2	14	14	10	0.42
lex	Lexical or phraseology error	107	131	74	0.37
rflx	Incorrect reflexive expression	6	11	3	0.26
use	Improper use of tense, aspect etc.	60	74	19	0.21
vbx	Ill-formed complex verb forms	20	9	3	0.17
ref	Incorrect pronominal references	14	17	3	0.16
sec	Secondary (consequent) error	45	18	4	0.11

The table shows that on L1 the annotators tend to agree in the domain categories *incorSum*, *wbdSum* and *fwSum*, i.e., for incorrect morphology, for improper word boundaries and for "non-Czech" expressions in general (κ > 0.8, κ > 0.6, and κ > 0.4, respectively). IAA was lower (κ < 0.4) for categories with a fuzzy interpretation, where a target hypothesis is difficult to establish, such as subcategories of *fw*, used to tag attempts to coin a new Czech lexeme (*fwFab*), or foreign/unidentified strings of words (*fwNc*). Even the choice between the two subcategories was problematic (accounting for 26% of the total number of cases where the two annotators differed in the use of these two tags). This is true especially in cases where an annotator is not able identify the origin of the lexeme.

On L2 the annotators agree (κ > 0.4) in agreement errors (*agr*) and errors in expressing syntactic dependency (*dep*), and also in the well-defined category of errors in negation (*neg*). However, pronominal references (*ref*), secondary (consequent) errors (*sec*) and surprisingly also analytical verb forms and complex predicates (*vbx*), show a very low level of IAA, even though they are identifiable by formal linguistic criteria. In all these three cases, the distribution of tags and the annotators' feedback suggest that the annotation manual fails to provide enough guidance in distinguishing between the error types *ref* vs. *agr* and *ref* vs. *dep* (in either case the disagreement represents 19% of all the inconsistent uses of the tag *ref*), and at the same time does not specify the formal aspect of using this tag. The use of tags for lexical and usage errors is highly dependent on the annotator's judgment, and the results are low as expected.

Error tags depend on emendation

Analysis of the tagged data shows that the disagreement in using error tags is not necessarily caused by an annotator's fault, but could rather be dependent on the choice of the emended form, both on the current and the preceding level. For example, from the 181 cases of different use of the tag *agr*, 70 cases (39%) have a different L2 emendation. See (2) for an example.

(2) R0:	a kdyz stratil manzel
R2: annotator A	a když ztratí$_{agr}$ manžela$_{dep}$
	'and when she loses her husband'
annotator B	a když se ztratil manžel
	'and when the husband got lost'

From the remaining 111 disagreements in the use of the tag *agr*, 28 cases (15%) differ in the emendation already on L1.

In all these cases, tagging is correct vis-a-vis the selected emendation. Currently, we investigate the impact of emendation on error annotation at the individual levels, but we can already support the requirement of explicit target interpretation in the annotation scheme (Lüdeling, 2008). The scheme can thus be verified by the calculation of IAA in the distribution of the tags, depending on the final hypothesis (cf, i.a., Meurers, 2011).

Outline of the possible causes of the annotators disagreement

We can identify the following causes of the annotators' disagreements:

- Invalid or imprecise annotation scheme: Generally, the annotators' disagreement can be caused by the annotation scheme itself: if it includes invalid tags or misses some necessary tags, or if the definition of a tag misleads the annotator. In the case of trial tagging of a sample of CzeSL data, it was problematic in several points, such as poorly distinguished subtypes of word boundary error (*wbd*), fuzzy definition of the error in pronominal reference (*ref*), also in contrast to the *agr* and *dep* types, or an imprecise boundary between the wrong choice of verbal tense (*use*) and the error in the analytical verb form (*vbx*).

- Insufficient screening and training of the annotators: The level of screening and training process has a significant effect on the IAA rate. Higher IAA was demonstrated for annotators exposed to extensive and detailed pre-annotation training. It would be interesting to test what kind of impact the annotators' exposure to Czech as a foreign language has on the consistency of their annotation.
- Different target hypotheses: Some annotations require a considerable amount of interpretation, while each annotator can have his/her own interpretation because of age, gender, education, etc. Moreover, in the case of multilevel annotation, annotators can differ also on intermediate levels, even though their target hypothesis might be identical. However, the annotation scheme of CzeSL, supporting emendation on both levels, makes the reasons for the possible disagreements explicit.

Automatic processing of learner texts

Despite the benefits of annotators' insight and judgment, manual annotation is tedious and costly. On the other hand, automatic tools are more error-prone and cannot produce the sort of sophisticated annotation envisaged in the present project. Aware of these pros and cons, we are still interested in how far we could get without manual annotation. Due to the lack of methods targeting learner texts, we confronted some 'native Czech' tools (two taggers and a spell checker) with ill-formed input.

The two taggers are based on different concepts: *Morče* (Votrubec, 2006) uses a morphological analyser, preferring lexical and morphological diagnostics over syntactic context, while *TnT* (Brants, 2000) has the opposite strategy while using lexicon extracted from training data. Both taggers were trained on the same tagset and include a method to handle unknown words. Because of the different strategies the taggers use to tag correct input, they respond differently to various types of deviations. A mutual comparison of their results is thus as interesting as their evaluation against a golden standard, which – in the case of ill-formed input – is a difficult concept anyway.

Identifying all errors would involve comparing manual annotations at L2 form-by-form with the original text at L0. In the current absence of such data, we used data obtained from the easier task of comparing L0 to L1, where all erroneous forms are emended to a closest correct version, disregarding context.

Table 3 presents data extracted from a sample of 93 texts including 12,681 word tokens, with 1,323 tokens (8.9%) identified as ill-formed by the morphological analyser. The two taggers agreed on the same tag in 405 cases, i.e. in 28.8% of the total of ill-formed tokens, and disagreed in 918 cases (71.2%). The figures are additionally split by 12 morphological categories constituting the tag. Column 1 (L0m x L0t) shows in which categories the two taggers disagree at L0 for the 918 tokens, where their tags do not match at least in one category. Agreement is significantly lower between categories largely determined by syntactic context (POS, Gender, Number, Case) as opposed to those determined lexically. Columns 2 (L0m x L1) and 3 (L0t x L1) show agreement rates of tags assigned by *Morče* and *TnT*, respectively, to all tokens at L0[5] in comparison with tags assigned by *Morče* to the corresponding tokens at L1.[6] *Morče* shows better results overall and in most categories. Columns 4 and 5 show agreement rates for an ill-formed subset of the sample used in Columns 2 and 3. Interestingly, *TnT* shows significantly better results, except in the categories of Person and Tense.

Table 2.3: Tags on L0 and L1 – percentages of agreement

	L0m x L0t	L0m x L1	L0t x L1	L0m x L1	L0t x L1
No. of tokens	918	2589	2589	314	314
Entire tag	0	84.1	79.0	19.1	26.1
POS	39.2	89.6	88.7	43.9	52.5
SubPOS	37.1	89.2	87.9	42.0	49.7
Gender	23.9	88.8	88.2	36.0	46.5
Number	36.9	91.1	91.2	49.0	63.1
Case	31.2	89.0	86.5	43.0	51.3
Possessive Gender	98.6	99.8	99.9	98.4	99.7
Possessive Number	99.5	99.8	99.7	99.0	99.7
Person	68.1	96.3	94.2	81.8	76.1
Tense	70.6	96.7	95.3	83.1	77.4
Grade	78.3	96.4	96.9	75.2	81.5
Negation	74.4	95.3	93.8	73.9	74.2
Voice	70.6	96.7	95.5	83.1	78.7

The difference between the two taggers is also reflected in the share of different POS categories assigned to ill-formed words. Table 4 shows that *Morče* has a more even distribution, but strongly disprefers all verbal categories.

5 The size of the sample is smaller than in the previous comparison at L0 only due to a more demanding procedure to obtain the data at L1.

6 The reason why *Morče* was used to tag L1 is because it is currently the best tagger of Czech and we were only interested in the cross-tagger comparison on the ill-formed input at L0.

Table 2.4: Numbers of tags assigned to ill-formed words

POS	*Morče*	*TnT*	POS	*Morče*	*TnT*
adjective	158	94	particle	8	–
adverb	118	21	finite verb	32	129
gradable adverb	31	11	infinitive	7	41
Noun	499	441	l-participle	10	119
preposition	10	–	passive participle	1	29

To sum up, the comparison of the two taggers confirms the assumption that the differences in their strategies will have a significant effect on the interpretation of faulty forms. A more general observation concerns the comparison of the success rate of the two taggers on the ill-formed input: *TnT* loses ground in a context with many errors but outperforms *Morče* on faulty forms, while *Morče* strongly disprefers verbs and works better in general.

Next, a spell checker was used to test whether automatic emendation is possible. In fact, Korektor (Richter, 2010) has some functionalities of a grammar checker, using a sophisticated combination of lexicon, morphology and a syntax model. Moreover, the same core can be used as a spell checker, proofreader and diacritics assigner.

The tool was tested on a subset of the 918 ill-formed words in the sample, namely on those where the annotators came up with an identical emendation – there were 786 such forms, assumed as "truth". Korektor was used in three different scenarios. The diacritics assigner mode was right in 552 cases (70.2%), the proofreader mode in 639 cases (80.5%), and the diacritics assigner followed by proofreader in 644 cases (81.9%). Even though L1 data are not the optimal benchmark, this tool seems to be useful as an aid to the annotator, or even as a way to obtain large quantities of annotated (emended) texts at the cost of a higher error rate.

Conclusion

It is no simple task to design an annotation scheme for a learner corpus and to maintain consistency in the annotated texts, both in a way that would reflect most demands of the corpus users. One of the main reasons is that annotating learner texts tends to be a highly specific enterprise, and even seemingly similar projects do not offer enough guidance – solutions are often too specific to a language or to the project concept and user requirements. On the other hand, annotation itself is quite rewarding due to the plentiful feedback about all aspects of the task and, of course, about the learners' interlanguage.

More specifically, our experience shows the rules for tagging morphosyntactic errors (labelled in the annotated texts as incorStem, incorInfl, agr and dep) are relatively easy to formalize and it is thus possible to obtain a high inter-annotator agreement for such errors. However, we were unable to obtain a similarly robust annotation of semantic errors, which are much more dependent on subjective judgement. It is even unclear whether it is desirable to aim to standardize their annotation.

The pilot study, where two POS taggers and a spell checker were applied to ill-formed input, confirmed the viability of a fully automatic annotation as an alternative to manual annotation, when the demand for large data is higher than concerns about the error rate. It remains to be seen to what extent the comparison of results of multiple taggers, based on different tagging strategies, can lead to usable interpretations of faulty forms.

Acknowledgments

The authors wish to express thanks to other members of the project team, namely Karel Šebesta, Milena Hnátková, Tomáš Jelínek, Vladimír Petkevič, and Hana Skoumalová.

References

Bedřichová, Z., Šormová, K. and K. Šebesta (2011). "ROMI – první rozsáhlá databanka romského etnolektu češtiny." [ROMI – the First Large Database of Romani ethnolect of Czech]. Lidé města. 2011, n. 13/1. Available at: http://lidemesta.cz/index.php?id=769

Brants, T. (2000). TnT – "A Statistical Part-of-Speech Tagger." In Proceedings of the Sixth Applied Natural Language Processing Conference ANLP-2000, Seattle, WA.

Cohen, J. (1960). "A Coefficient of Agreement for Nominal Scales." Educational and Psychological Measurement, 1960, 20 (1): 37–46.

Díaz-Negrillo, A., Meurers, D., Valera, S. and H. Wunsch (2010). Towards Interlanguage POS Annotation for Effective Learner Corpora in SLA and FLT. Language Forum. 36: 139–154.

Hana, J., Rosen, A., Škodová, S. and B. Štindlová (2010). "Error-tagged Learner Corpus of Czech." In Proceedings of the Fourth Linguistic Annotation Workshop, Uppsala: Association for Computational Linguistics.

Lüdeling, A. (2008). Mehrdeutigkeiten und Kategorisierung: Probleme bei der Annotation von Lernerkorpora. In Fortgeschrittene Lernervarietäten, Grommes, P. and Walter, M. (eds.), 119-140. Tübingen: Niemeyer.

Meurers, D. (2011). "On Automatically Analyzing Learner Language: Interpreting Form and Meaning in Context." Invited talk at Colloquium of the Research Center for English and Applied Linguistics (RCEAL), 8 February 2011. University of Cambridge. Available at: http://www.sfs.uni–tuebingen.de/~dm/presentations.html

Richter, M. (2010). Pokročilý korektor češtiny [An Advanced Spell Checker of Czech]. Master's Thesis. Charles University, Praha, Faculty of Mathematics and Physics.

Rietveld, T. and R. Van Hout (1993). Statistical Techniques for the Study of Language and Language Behaviour. Mouton de Gruyter.

Rozovskaya, A. and D. Roth (2010). "Annotating ESL Errors: Challenges and Rewards." Proceedings of NAACL'10Workshop on Innovative Use of NLP for Building Educational Applications. University of Illinois at Urbana–Champ.
Available at: http://www.cs.rochester.edu/~tetreaul/naacl–bea5.html

Šebesta, K. (2010). "Korpusy češtiny a osvojování jazyka." [Corpora of Czech and Language Acquisition]. Studie z aplikované lingvistiky/Studies in Applied Linguistics. 2010, 1 (2): 11–34.

Štindlová, B. (2011). Evaluace chybové anotace v žákovském korpusu češtiny [Evaluation of Error Mark-Up in a Learner Corpus of Czech]. Dissertation. Charles University, Praha, Faculty of Arts.

Štindlová, B., Škodová, S., Rosen, A. and J. Hana (in press). "Annotating foreign learners' Czech." In Proceedings of FDSL 8.5, Brno, 2010.

Tetreault, J. and M. Chodorow (2008). "Native Judgements of Non-Native Usage: Experiments in Preposition Error Detection." In COLING Workshop on Human Judgements in Computational Linguistics. Manchester.
Available at: http://portal.acm.org/citation.cfm?id=1611633

Votrubec, J. (2006). „Morphological Tagging Based on Averaged Perceptron." In WDS'06 Proceedings of Contributed Papers, Safrankova, J. and Pavlu, J. (eds.), 191-195. Matfyzpress, Charles University, Praha.

Towards the PELCRA Learner English Corpus

Piotr Pęzik

Abstract

The PELCRA Learner English Corpus (PLEC) is a research project funded by a grant from the Polish Ministry of Science and Higher Education. Launched in December 2010 the project is aimed at compiling an annotated corpus featuring a time-aligned spoken component for quantitative and qualitative analyses of Polish learner English. This paper describes the general design of the corpus including the different layers of linguistic and error annotation. Special emphasis is placed on data exploration and analysis methods for investigating the phraseological competence of Polish learners of English. The paper also introduces some exploratory corpus mining methods such as lexicogrammatical pattern analysis and graph-based visualization of learners' phraseological competence.

Keywords

Learner corpora, English, Polish, data exploration, text mining, error annotation

Introduction

The PELCRA Polish Learner English Corpus (PLEC) is a research project funded by a grant from the Polish Ministry of Science and Higher Education. The project was launched in December 2010 and it aims to compile a linguistically annotated corpus featuring a time-aligned spoken component for quantitative and qualitative analyses of Polish learner English. The present paper describes the design and contents of the corpus as well as the different layers of linguistic and error annotation. The PLEC project has a number of research objectives which can be pursued as the annotated corpus of learner English develops. In addition to using standard techniques of corpus data analysis at the phonetic, lexical and syntactic levels, which rely on explicit error annotation, new methods of exploring corpus data are being developed to identify important aspects of second language acquisition in the areas of phraseology and lexico-grammar. The project revisits the problem of learner error analysis by shifting emphasis from manual annotation of errors to exploratory text data mining techniques.

The data

The total number of word segments in the corpus is expected to reach 3 million by the end of the project (i.e. late 2013). Although most of this data will represent the written register of learner English, spoken language will also be covered in a distinct subcorpus of 200 000 words. In the process of acquiring written learner data, preference is given to spontaneous in-class and in-exam essays, stories and other written assignments. However, since such data is costly to digitize and the average length of such assignments is relatively short, the written part of the corpus will also comprise quite a number of home assignments as well as MA and BA theses written by Polish learners of English whose command of English ranges from the Cambridge pre-intermediate to advanced and proficiency levels. Texts written by beginners and intermediate learners are obviously shorter and thus less represented in the corpus. The source of the texts is documented in the bibliographic annotation headers of the corpus. In addition, each text is scored on a scale from 0 to 2 for the relative level of paraphrasing and quoting, which makes it possible to distinguish spontaneous from heavily influenced writing, e.g. in-exam compositions from research papers. Longer quotes, tables and illustrations are either deleted or explicitly annotated. A significant part of the texts were acquired in paper format and, in many cases, they had to be scanned and oftentimes typed from handwritten source copies. Some 800 000 words of written data have been adapted and converted from archived collections of learner data collected by the PELCRA group at the University of Łódź in the years 1998-2001 (Leńko-Szymańska 2007).

The majority of the spoken data includes transcripts of conversations and mock exams which were either arranged specifically for the PLEC project or acquired from other sources. Small samples of to-be-spoken language are included for the purposes of phonetic analyses of spoken learner data. It needs to be emphasized that the acquisition and transcription of spoken data is a very costly and time-consuming task. In view of the author's previous experiences with compiling spoken corpora and the project's financial and temporal constraints a realistic, if nevertheless ambitious target of a 200 KW spoken subcorpus was set and is being actively pursued at the moment.

Annotation

The PLEC corpus features several layers of corpus annotation. Bibliographic and sociolinguistic metadata descriptors include information about the source, titles and topics of texts and conversations and, whenever available, indications of the authors' and speakers' age, gender, approximate level of proficiency and language learning experiences. At the linguistic level the annotation includes lemmas and parts-of-speech for word segments as well as syntactic dependency labels added using the Stanford Parser (Marneffe et al. 2006) and Tagger (Toutnova et al. 2003) tools.

A subset of the corpus is also being annotated for lexical, phraseological, grammatical and stylistic errors. The different levels of linguistic and error annotation required a non-linear schema, which was implemented both as a relational database.

Table 3.1: Frequency of errors based on a sample of 3302 annotations

Type	Frequency
grammatical	1465
spelling	695
lexical	665
punctuation	301
phraseological	176

An XML version of the corpus is also being developed with stand-off annotation which can be used to handle any number of overlapping descriptors for a single stretch of text. In contrast to some error annotation schemas (i.e. the Cambridge Learner Corpus), we believe that the boundaries of even relatively simple learner errors tend to overlap and thus a stand-off, non-linear schema is required to annotated them in a corpus. Let us for example consider how the following excerpt from the corpus illustrates this problem:

1. <s>It seems to be that teacher's work is so colourful and nice but it isn't.</s>

The first sentence of this passage contains what seems to be a case of a negative transfer of the Polish idiom *nie być/wyglądać kolorowo*, which is used to say that a situation is more difficult than it might seem. The word segments making up this calque happen to coincide with at least two other errors which might be worth annotating, namely the spelling of the adjective *colourful* and the misuse of the Saxon genitive in the word *teacher's* (which could also be interpreted as a lack of the definite or indefinite article if we assume that the learner actually intended to use the noun *teacher* in the singular). A multi-tier annotation schema allows one to properly document such overlapping errors in a stretch of text.

The spoken part of the PLEC corpus is not only transcribed orthographically, but also time-aligned at the level of utterances and annotated for some types of phonetic errors, such as mispronounced words, a term which is taken to mean a situation where at least one sound segment in a word is mispronounced, typically due to the spelling and syllabic stress pattern intricacies of English, although the speaker can generally pronounce this sound correctly, or at least much better in other words and contexts. As an example, the verb *live* may sometimes be mispronounced as */laɪv/* or */laɪf/* and the noun *area* is often mispronounced as /əˈrɪə/ by Polish learners of English. The table below contains an overview of the different layers of annotation used in PLEC:

Table 3.2: Types of annotation in PLEC

Type	Data
Text metadata	author/speaker age, gender, level, spontaneity of writing, resources used, etc.
Structural	paragraphs, sentences, word boundaries, gaps
Linguistic	parts of speech, lemmas, syntactic dependencies
Errors	manually annotated subset of written data, mispronounced words in transcripts of spoken language

ELAN (Wittenburg et al. 2006) is used in the project as the basic tool for transcribing, annotating and aligning the recorded conversations. Additional tiers of annotation can be used independently of the existing markup as illustrated in the screenshot below, which shows discourse-level annotation layers (i.e. *who1_inserts*, *who2_inserts*).

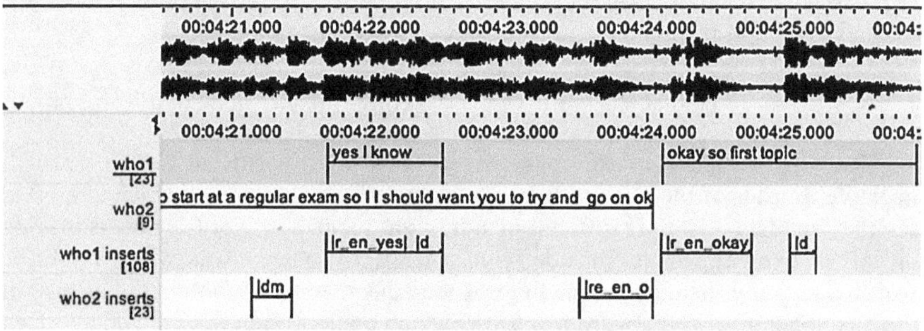

Figure 3.1: Spoken data annotation in the PLEC project

Methodological problems with error annotation

Two main corpus exploration methodologies are used in the analysis of the PLEC data. One the one hand, the explicit, manual annotation of errors marked up in the written and spoken components of the corpus can be easily searched and aggregated thus bringing statistical insights into the quantitative and qualitative characteristics of certain error types. For example, with a single SQL query one can fetch all the contexts annotated as cases of phraseological errors. It turns out that some of such annotations in the data gathered so far reveal an interesting characteristic of the learners' phraseological competence, which can be described as the transfer of polysemy of certain lexemes. The sentence from a learner's essay shown below illustrates this phenomenon:

2. <s>The main disadvantage is that ***work is very ungrateful*** especially in schools where teachers work with teenagers over 18 years old.</s>

The Polish adjective *niewdzięczny* collocates naturally both with nouns denoting humans who are *ungrateful* as in *niewdzięczny syn* (*ungrateful son*) and with inanimate nouns in the sense of *unrewarding*, e.g. *niewdzięczne zadanie* (*unrewarding task*)[1]. *Ungrateful* is probably the psychologically more salient (and hence the primary) sense of the adjective *niewdzięczny*. The learner seems to rely on the polysemy of *niewdzięczny* in contexts where another English word would be more phraseologically valid when expressing the secondary sense of *niewdzięczny* i.e. *unrewarding*. This example shows that explicit mark-up of errors in a corpus can be helpful in identifying some of the less obvious lexical and grammatical problem areas in the acquisition of a foreign language. One advantage of such an approach is that it can be used to identify even relatively rare types of errors, such as the abovementioned transfer of polysemous word distribution.

Despite its advantages when it comes to identifying certain errors of commission, the manual annotation of learner errors poses several methodological problems which may further increase the amount of effort required to make it useful and worthwhile. The first obvious problem to be considered is the development of an error typology to be used in a corpus. Depending on the type of interlanguage found in a learner corpus, a general typology of errors which can be used with a high level of inter-annotator agreement may be difficult if not impossible to develop. Without a clear focus on the types of errors to be annotated, different annotators may tend to mark learner language at different structural levels. This is probably part of the reason why the authors of the Cambridge Learner Corpus admit that they only assigned a single person to the task of error annotation to avoid such problems (Nicholls 2003). However, such a decision certainly did not solve the problem of low inter-annotator agreement.

Secondly, although annotators may, to some extent, rely on the use of reference L1 and L2 corpora to verify their judgments about negative transfer errors for instance, some errors pose genuine problems of interpretation. For instance, in the example sentence (1) above it is possible to classify the use of the phrase "teacher's work" as a grammatical error, but it is impossible to decide whether the learner failed to use a determiner for the singular form of *teacher*, or perhaps she misused the Saxon genitive for the plural form of the noun.

There is yet another methodological problem of semantic nature with error annotation. Oftentimes, when marking up a word, phrase or grammatical structure as erroneous, the annotator has to make assumptions about the intended meaning of a structure the learner used in a given context. This process could be compared to the task of translating the learner's interlanguage into the native form of the target

1 See the National Corpus of Polish: http://nkjp.uni.lodz.pl/?q=6tf2dhu.

language at least in the sense of explaining how the two varieties of L2 would differ from each other in a given context. Evaluating the grammaticality of structures used by learners makes little if any sense in situations where the only way to intelligibly express their intended meaning is by paraphrasing the unit of text which contains such structures. This is similar to the use of a paraphrase as basic translation strategy: structural units of translation are rarely statically fixed. Similarly, annotating errors structure by structure does not provide an exhaustive description of how the learner's interlanguage differs from native-like L2. This problem is less serious when annotating the language of more advanced learners, where erroneous usages are few and far between and a simple linear error annotation schema can do the job of explaining how the learner's language deviates from its idealized native target.

Finally, manual annotation of errors naturally places more emphasis on errors of commission rather than problems of omission. Manual annotation is also quite inefficient in identifying general overuse of certain structures even if they cannot be judged as erroneous in isolated contexts. In the following sections of this paper we explain how some text-mining methods can be used to address this problem.

As already mentioned, there are two main types of explicit error annotation in the PLEC project. The first type covers problematic structures at the orthographic, lexical, phraseological and syntactic levels and it is limited to a relatively small subset of the corpus as it serves more experimental purposes. The spoken part of the corpus is annotated for mispronunciations. The main thrust of the research in the project, however, is concentrated on the development of text data mining and exploration methods which rely on automatic linguistic annotation and quantitative methods and which could complement the analysis of the manual annotation of errors. Two of these methods are briefly described in the remaining sections of this paper.

Text mining and data exploration in PLEC

Individual word segments in the PLEC corpus are marked as either *governors* or *dependents* of syntactic dependencies with the type of dependency found for each annotated pair. For example, the sentence "*I am writing with regard to the position of travel agent's assistant, advertised in a newspaper on the 20th of June*" has the following dependency representation in the PLEC database:

Table 3.3: A dependency-parsed sentence.

Dependency type	Governor	Dependant
nsubj	writing	I
aux	writing	am
det	position	the
prep_with_regard_to	writing	position
nn	agent	travel
poss	assistant	agent
prep_of	position	assistant
partmod	assistant	advertised
det	newspaper	a
prep_in	advertised	newspaper
det	20th	the
prep_on	newspaper	20th
prep_of	20th	June

The availability of syntactic annotation makes it possible to perform a quantitative analysis of the typical lexical realizations of a given syntactic dependency. For example, it is very easy to run a query which generates a frequency list of the typical lexical realizations of all the *direct object* dependencies found in the corpus (a 2 million word subset available at the time of writing):

Table 3.4: Frequency of direct-object dependencies in a subset of the PLEC corpus.

Type	Governor	Dependent	Frequency
dobj	do	it	205
dobj	use	it	159
dobj	have	time	132
dobj	take	part	130
dobj	spend	time	116

(Stefanowitsch and Gries 2003) introduce the notion of *collostructures* to describe a tendency for grammatical structures to attract and repel certain lexical items. It would be interesting to see whether the use of certain lexico-grammatical combinations by learners diverges from native English. One of the exploratory research objectives in the project is thus to compare the frequency distributions of the typical dependencies found in the PLEC with a subset of the BNC (representing similar text genres and registers) to check for statistically significant differences between the two sets of corpus data. This kind of comparison can be expected to reveal some important gaps and possibly cases of interference in the lexico-grammatical patterns used by Polish learners of English. A small pilot study based on a two million word sample of the BNC used as a reference corpus has shown that:

1. There are approximately 20% more distinct lexical realizations of the direct object dependency in the BNC, which is an intuitive finding given that native English is lexically richer than learner English.
2. While some of the top-frequency lexical realizations of direct object dependencies from the PLEC such as *take place* or *spend time* are correct in principle, they seem to be over-used by Polish learners of English. This may be due to the fact that these combinations are overused in language teaching contexts.
3. Some of the top-frequency dependencies found in the BNC, such as *do what* are heavily underrepresented in the PLEC.

The quantitative analysis of syntactic structures certainly complements the manual annotation of errors in that it shows "errors" of omission and overuse which often go unnoticed in the process of manual annotation.

Another data exploration method used in the project relies on the generation of the so-called colosaurus graphs, which are basically graph-based visualizations of collocational patterns for a set of roughly synonymous words. The term colosaurus is a blend of *colo-* (for collocational) and *–saurus* (for thesaurus). Let us suppose we want to know how learners of Polish use the different synonyms of the word *frightening*, such as *scary*, *alarming* and *spooky*. Of course, synonymy is a lexicographically useful concept, but textually interchangeable words are a rare phenomenon in naturally occurring language. Nevertheless, it is interesting to note that some dictionaries of English for learners of this language rely on and reaffirm the notion of synonymy when defining the above-mentioned words. *Frightening* is the most common of the four adjectives and it is used, and probably rightly so, in the definitions of the other three in the Longman Dictionary of Contemporary English for example. In order to identify and visualize the typical textual company of the four words in question, we have extracted a table of their significant nominal collocates from the BNC, such as *alarming rate*, *alarming frequency*, *frightening experience*, *scary moment* and *spooky atmosphere*. If we represent each unique word in the table as a vertex in a graph and each identified collocation as an edge between a given pair of word vertices, whose width is proportionate to the strength of a given collocation, then we get the planar graph available at *http://pezik.pl/?attachment_id=325*. Interestingly, the vertex representing the word *frightening* is a bridge in the graph theory sense (if removed it disconnects the graph) and it shares the largest number of edges with the other three adjectival vertices. This seems to confirm the intuition that *frightening* is the most general of the four synonyms; hence it shares the highest number of collocations with the other three adjectives. A graph for the same set of lexemes has been generated from the learner data collected so far and it is revealing at least in one respect (see *http://pezik.pl/?attachment_id=326*). Apart from the fact that the graph obtained is obviously much sparser, which is partly due to the fact that the BNC graph was generated from a much larger corpus, what is striking is the fact that the bridge node representing the adjective *frightening* is missing from the learner corpus graph altogether. In other words, Polish learners of English seem to be reluctant to use the most frequent synonym from the set as an adjectival premodifier in simple noun phrases. One possible explanation is that they prefer to use it in predicative structures which may seem to be a more natural context for adjectives which resemble adjectival participles ending in –ing. Another possibility is that –ing adjectives may be perceived to be relatively simple lexical items (obtained through derivation from know verbs) and advanced learners are expected to use more sophisticated vocabulary. Yet another obvious explanation could be the fact that the word *frightening* is relatively difficult to spell. In any case, the data exploration method used to visualize the phraseological profiles of words in native and learner English allowed us to discover the surprising lack of the adjective *frightening* in Polish learners' vocabulary.

Summary

The PELCRA English Learner Corpus project is still in the phase of data acquisition and tool development. However, the preliminary results of the research conducted in the project so far look promising. Apart from the collection of data, the PLEC project has more ambitious goals of developing new text mining methods which may advance our understanding of learners' interlanguage and result in very practical knowledge of some types of problems of omission and overuse which are difficult to identify with the more traditional methods of corpus data analysis. Current information on the project can be found at http://pelcra.pl/plec.

Acknowledgements

This research has been funded in the years 2010-2012 by a grant from the Polish Ministry of Science and Higher Education (N N104 205039).

References

Leńko-Szymańska, A. (2007). "The Role of L1 Influence and L2 Instruction in the Choice of Rhetorical Strategies by EFL Learners." In Corpora and ICT in Language Studies, Waliński, J., Kredens, K. and Góźdź-Roszkowski, S. (eds.). Frankfurt am Main: Peter Lang.

Marneffe M-C., MacCartney B. and C. Manning (2006). "Generating Typed Dependency Parses from Phrase Structure Parses," LREC 2006.

Nicholls, D. (2003). "The Cambridge Learner Corpus – Error Coding and Analysis for Lexicography and ELT." Proceedings of the Corpus Linguistics 2003.

Stefanowitsch, A., and S. Th. Gries. (2003). "Collostructions: Investigating the Interaction of Words and Constructions." International Journal of Corpus Linguistics 8 (2): 209-243.

Toutanova K., Klein D., Manning C., and Y. Singer (2003). "Feature-Rich Part-of-Speech Tagging with a Cyclic Dependency Network," Proceedings of HLT-NAACL 2003, pp. 252-259.

Wittenburg, P., Brugman, H., Russel, A., Klassmann, A. and H. Sloetjes (2006). "ELAN: a Professional Framework for Multimodality Research." Proceedings of LREC 2006, Fifth International Conference on Language Resources and Evaluation.

A New Look at Materials Evaluation: Using Corpus to Count Collocations in EFL Textbooks Used in Venezuela

Jersus Colmenares

Abstract

The present paper argues for the addition of a corpus assessment of language teaching materials as part of an overall process of evaluation for selection purposes. Vocabulary analysis via corpus can be used to predict success or to analyze performance retrospectively in materials. However, while the literature offers a variety of proposals for materials examination, it seems that more empirical methods to evaluate the role of vocabulary remain absent from consideration in the whole appraisal. Accordingly, I will describe and discuss selected aspects from a larger study on collocations in English as a foreign language (EFL) textbooks used in Venezuela, which can serve as guidelines for similar procedures elsewhere.

Keywords

Materials evaluation, corpus methods, predictive evaluation, retrospective evaluation, collocations

Introduction

With the rise of corpus linguistics as an approach to answering a wide range of challenging questions about language, the present paper explores its applications to materials evaluation within the context of secondary education. Despite the growing number of studies that attempt to compare textbook descriptions of vocabulary with actual language use in real life (Barbieri and Eckdhart 2007; Biber and Reppen 2002; Jiménez Catalán 2008; Juffs 1998), it seems that reported uses in materials evaluation for selection and adaptation purposes are hardly common in the literature. Traditional methods for materials evaluation have consisted of confirming the existence of target elements through the use of surveys or checklists. However, more often than not these methods do not in fact provide an in-depth understanding of critical aspects pertaining to vocabulary, in particular regarding its potential to promote fluency development in learners. Therefore, I shall describe some experiences from a larger, ongoing research project on evaluating materials using the corpus approach in Venezuela. It is hoped that the elements from the study highlighted here can serve as guidelines for a more accurate, principled selection and/or adaptation of educational materials that best meet specific needs in light of current vocabulary acquisition research.

Materials evaluation in language teaching: A brief overview and criticism

A number of articles and books have been written about methods for materials evaluation. For convenience such methods can be referred to as the checklist or scheme method (Sheldon 1988; Williams 1983), and the impressionistic method (Breen and Candlin 1987; McDonough and Shaw 2003). Evaluating materials through the use of schemes or checklists has long been a common practice among language teaching professionals world wide. The scheme method as the name suggests, consists of designing or adapting a set of criteria in the form of questions or rating tables in order to make possible verifications for the existence of features in materials under examination. Brown (1995), Cunningsworth (1995), Sheldon (1988), and Williams (1983) agree that, based on predefined criteria, evaluation checklists should aim at confirming physical characteristics of educational materials such as layout, organizational, and logistical characteristics. Other important goals in using schemes are to identify methodology, goals, and approaches and the degree to which a set of materials fits the needs of the teacher and students. Alternatively, the main goal of the impressionistic method is to obtain a general impression of the materials for the purpose of making comparisons and ultimate selection decisions. For Breen and Candlin (1987) and McDonough and Shaw (2003) there is relevant information in general or external aspects such as the blurb, table of contents and design features. If these elements are considered as appropriate to the overall need of educational materials within a specified context, then a second assessment phase, an internal analysis will be implemented. Such analysis would seek to answer questions that are more related to the reality of the classroom, as well as other considerations regarding content grading and sequencing, tasks for skills development, and authenticity for which potential materials under evaluation may be adopted.

The checklist and the impressionistic methods have been quite popular among language teachers and researchers because of their systematic way of evaluating materials, covering a wide range of aspects stemming from their contextualized criteria. However, as a consequence, assessment results in a very general view of the materials, and thus important aspects such as vocabulary in its various dimensions are rendered equally general in scope. It has been known for over three decades that vocabulary functions as central to language and is crucially important to success in language learning (Nation 2001; Zimmerman 1997). This indeed is acknowledged even in the literature on materials evaluation in the form some of the questions or categories take in popular checklists: "this textbook...selects vocabulary on the basis of frequency, functional load, etc." (Williams 1983: 255); and "does the introduction, practice and recycling of new linguistic items seem to be shallow/steep enough for your students? ...is there a discernable system at work in the selection and grading of these items (e.g. on the basis of frequency counts, or on the basis of useful comparisons between the learner's mother tongue and

English?)" (Sheldon 1988: 243). Similarly, McDonough and Shaw (2003) suggest that evaluators take into account grading and sequencing as part of their analysis. The treatment of vocabulary under these approaches suggests that authors do not seem to go beyond limited operational requirements, leaving criteria for scrutinizing the role of vocabulary in educational materials at the discretion of evaluators. This seems to be even more paradoxical considering authors' claims that materials evaluation methods should not be perceived as static (Sheldon 1988) but rather as frameworks (Cunningsworth 1995; McDonough and Shaw 2003) that need to be customized according to the particular educational contexts for which materials assessment are to take place. For this reason, in the seeming absence of a comprehensive assessment of the role of vocabulary within a given process of materials evaluation, I propose the use of corpus methods as a suitable response.

How can corpus complement an overall process of materials examination?

A corpus is a principled collection of texts in electronic form designed for linguistic research. It is normally investigated through specialized software generating output that is expected to respond to previously formulated questions (Biber, Conrad and Reppen 1998). Over the last twenty years or so, a number of innovative uses of corpora have been proposed and implemented successfully in the field of language teaching. One important area strongly influenced is that of materials development, where a great deal of information on language characteristics and use from different kinds of corpora now shape curricula. However, materials are yet to receive more attention from corpus in terms of assessment for selection purposes, given that the status of vocabulary is a crucially determining factor in successful language learning and use. It is for this reason that I propose the use of corpus assessment of vocabulary as an important element within any given process of materials evaluation.

There is a consensus that a preliminary evaluation of materials needs to be done for the purpose of narrowing down those whose unsuitability for adoption is readily apparent (Cunningsworth 1995; McDonough and Shaw 2003; McGrath 2002). Once some potential choices have been identified, a second phase is usually entered during which the existence of diverse elements is expected to be identified.

Corpus analysis of vocabulary can be done parallel to most traditional frameworks or checklist-based assessments of materials for language teaching and learning. It is right at the beginning of the second phase where a corpus analysis of vocabulary should be made. Its implementation, as explained below, should be carried out systematically to assure practicality and to help those involved spend no more time than needed. The combination of traditional and corpus methods assures a more comprehensive view of materials upon the end of the examination process.

Better choices and more appropriate adaptations can be made when organizational, methodological, and learner-related aspects of importance and linguistic content can be examined more thoroughly. In conducting a corpus investigation within a larger materials assessment process, a corpus needs to be built using information from those materials. But before this can be done, particular needs are to be identified and requirements acknowledged. From these, guidelines will be derived for corpus design and construction. Additionally, appropriate corpus tools must be adopted to make possible an effective analysis and discussion of the results in terms of the potential implications. In the remainder, I will describe these procedures making reference to some important outcomes from the ongoing study of multiword units in popular EFL textbooks used in Venezuela mentioned earlier.

Identifying particular needs for corpus analysis

Most corpus investigations seek to answer questions that fill gaps in existing research, to answer problems related to language views and use within diverse contexts and in combination with different subfields in applied linguistics and other disciplines (Biber, Conrad and Reppen 1998). In terms of materials evaluation, corpus methods can answer questions related to particular needs, preferences or demands in a given language program or educational institution. A corpus can also be used to establish comparisons among selected materials with respect to theories of vocabulary acquisition. Once the reasons for corpus research are identified, clearly defined questions can be posed. An instance of this process involves the study on how materials promote vocabulary growth in students in Venezuela's secondary education system (Colmenares, in preparation). I examined the occurrence of verb and noun (V+N) lexical collocations in the reading sections of popular EFL textbook series used Venezuelan high-schools. Learning collocations bring about important benefits such as fluency development and naturalness in communication (Pawley and Syder 1983). Collocations are ubiquitous in language (Hill 2000) and could comprise as much as 80% of a written text (Hill 2003). However, V+N lexical collocations have been reported as the most difficult to learn by EFL learners with diverse linguistic backgrounds (Bahns and Eldaw 1993; Barfield 2001; Biskup 1992), including Spanish (Zinkgräf 2008). Focus on surveying V+N lexical collocation frequency in the reading components of these textbooks stems from research findings in the Venezuelan context reporting that EFL teachers emphasize developing reading skills and comprehending grammar (Chacon 2005) in secondary education. Today, reading is still one of the most important sources of input for students the world over (Grabe 2009), and decades of research have confirmed that for a word to be learned it needs to be encountered multiple times and in multiple contexts (Grabe 2009; Nation 2001). Through reading, learners can gain knowledge of many aspects that are said to be involved in knowing a word (Grabe 2009; Nation 2001; Schmitt 2000), including its collocations. Therefore, it was only logical to ask: How many different V+N lexical collocations are present in reading sections of three EFL textbook series used in Venezuelan high schools? And what is the frequency of occurrence of V+N lexical collocations in each of the three series? These questions were also used as a starting point in planning the corpus where suitable answers were likely to be found.

Corpus design and compilation

All corpora need to have a clear orientation and be designed according to principled criteria (Sinclair 2005). If the purpose of the corpus is to ascertain the occurrence of particular vocabulary items in different prospective materials for ultimate adoption in a given context, then its orientation should be for comparisons of educational curricula in terms of the role of lexis. Moreover, there is important information that needs to be specified in order to state sound rationale or criteria for corpus compilation. Among Sinclair's key specifications, those relevant to a process of materials evaluation through corpus are: text mode (e.g. written, spoken); text type (e.g. magazine, newspaper or atlas excerpts, extracts from service encounters, etc.); text domain (e.g. for general or special purposes); text location (e.g. Taiwan, Venezuela); and language variety (e.g. American or Australian English, etc.). Obviously, the resulting criteria should make the corpus representative of the needs, interests and demands particular to the contexts for which the given materials are being selected. For the study of V+N lexical collocations in Venezuela, I chose three textbook series. Regarded as the most popular, they are widely used across the nation. Their contents seem to meet most government's curriculum requirements. As explained earlier, reading is one of the skills which Venezuelan teachers are more inclined to emphasize, and thus the reading sections of each textbook from all the series were chosen. Given that the selected textbooks were written specifically for EFL for general purposes programs, it was expected that the readings would come from diverse sources, and therefore would be of different types. These sections in fact were based on excerpts from magazines, biographies, newspapers, textbooks and websites. Although two of the textbooks were published in Venezuela, and one in the United States, all their contents are in American English.

In order to make comparisons among textbooks series, a mini-corpus of each series was built. This involved a few and yet very specific tasks. First, the reading sections were scanned using optic character recognition (OCR) software (so that actual words were captured from the texts) or transcribed manually when needed.

Every extract and accompanying tasks and instructions were stored as standard text documents (Microsoft Notepad®, also TXT document) which were coded following a predetermined system (Table 1).

Table 4.1: Coding scheme for corpus text files

Series	Volumes	Page	Example	Name of textbook
SP	1	Corresponding number of page transcribed/scanned for the corpus	SP1p12	Super Goal
SP	2			
SP	3			
ENG	1		ENG7 p12	English
ENG	2			
ENG	3			
T	1		T7p12	Teens
T	2			
T	3			

The first document from Super Goal, for example, was coded as SP1p12, where SP identified the series, 1 the volume, and indicating that it was taken from page 12 (i.e. p12). As a result, there were three separate digital files or sub-corpora, each containing the coded TXT documents from a different series. This made possible the analysis of each series and further comparisons. Finally, in order to enhance accuracy in the search of V+N lexical collocations, each word in the sub-corpora was assigned a part of speech (POS) tag[1].

Corpus analysis of predefined language items

Corpus linguistics has a wide variety of techniques and tools that can serve in the process of materials evaluation. Those which are most appropriate are chosen, according to the objectives or research questions, since they specify the unit or units of analysis and the way in which it should best be researched. Common techniques and tools were also used to survey collocations in the Venezuela-based study referred to thus far in this paper.

As was mentioned before, the unit of analysis was any collocation consisting of a verb and a noun. Benson, Benson and Ilson (1997) classify this kind of collocation as lexical, because it usually is found in speech and writing as having these two lexical words combined to express a specific idea. In each sub–corpus, these collocations were searched using Collocate 1.0, a software program that can identify these combinations, terms, and other formulas[2]. Because the corpus was POS tagged in its entirety, the software was able to identify those combinations of verb and noun upon selecting specific commands from the several options

1 POS tagging makes information extraction more efficient, because it helps researchers identify those units of analysis they are interested in more quickly and accurately. The corpus for this study was tagged at no cost at the University Centre for Computer Corpus Research on Language (UCREL) website: http://ucrel.lancs.ac.uk/.

2 <http://www.athel.com/colloc.html>

available[3]. The collocations identified by the software were manually matched against two specialized collocations dictionaries[4], to verify they were indeed the target V+N lexical collocations for this study. Those items excluded were either free combinations (e.g. clean a house, etc.), very infrequent collocations (e.g. oppose Hitler), and of course, all other lexical and grammatical collocations. During the selection process, every lemma of the potential combination that would possibly meet Benson et al.'s V+N lexical collocations description was studied carefully. Those which matched the criteria were later lemmatized, in order to calculate the total number of collocations present in the reading passages throughout the series. Finally, the collocations from each sub-corpus found in one or both dictionaries were recorded in separate Microsoft Excel® files. This was done in order to count each group of collocations separately and to compare the results. To answer the first question—how many collocations are present in the reading sections in each series—a simple addition was performed using the respective commands in Excel. On the other hand, cross tabulation using Stat Graphics® was required in order to answer the second question[5].

Results interpretation and implications: How can they inform a larger process of materials evaluation?

Answers to corpus research questions help evaluators make empirically informed decisions. Upon comparing two or more textbooks in terms of corpus findings regarding vocabulary, different decisions can be made. However, these decisions may not only include the simple dichotomy of whether or not to choose or to continue using a set of materials, but also if one finally is chosen, what adjustments need to be made, and here is where corpus information can orient the process.

I compared the three series of EFL textbooks in light of two premises from the current literature on vocabulary acquisition. One was Hill's (2000) recommendation that around ten new collocations be taught in every lesson. Another element of the construct was the researchers' (Timkhan 1993; Kachroo; 1962) suggestion that for a word to be learned it should occur between 7 and 19 times. The totals found do not seem to agree with the first premise (Table 2). Even though each series consisted of three textbooks, the total amount of collocations combined was 147 (English=42, Super Goal=60, Teens=45). This obviously indicates that there are by far fewer collocations than are recommended. More

3 The statistical tests in the software were not taken into account, since the size of the sub-corpora was small and therefore the scores would not be accurate. Hence the use of specialized dictionaries, which are based on institutionalized corpora.

4 The BBI Dictionary of English Word Combinations and the LTP dictionary of selected collocations.

5 Another way to calculate frequency of occurrence of vocabulary is through percentages, tables and graphs using Microsoft Excel.

specifically, the means in Table 2 indicate that, despite having the highest number of collocations, Super Goal apparently has around 20 collocations per book. The means in English indicates that there are close to 14 collocations per textbook in that series, and Teens seem to have 15. Next, when their repetitions in the three series were studied, it was found that despite the suggestions from previous research findings as summarized in the second premise, of the 147 collocations found, only 19 occur two times, seven collocations occur three times, and two more occur eight times (Table 3).

Table 4.2: V+N lexical collocations found in the textbook series

	Series		
	English	Super Goal	Teens
Series totals	42	60	45
Volume means	14	20	15

Whether the evaluation has been carried out to predict usefulness in materials for potential adoption or to review performance of those which have already been used, the corpus findings referred to here provide interesting insights that suggest several actions to take. First, under the assumption that any one of these series is adopted or used again in the future, the totals found (Tables 2 and 3) call for a principled supplementation of at least the reading sections in them. An obvious initial decision is to increase the number of collocations, although this can be problematic considering the vast number of them, in this case, in the English language. Koprowski (2005) recommends assessing their usefulness, in terms of frequency and range, since these allow learners to be in contact with those collocations that are more common and that are present in varied types of texts. There are pedagogical considerations critical to the success in supplementing language teaching materials with fewer collocations than desirable. In Section 3.1 I

Table 4.3: Selected frequency ranges of V+N lexical collocations

Frequency ranges	English	Super Goal	Teens	Total by range
2	8	5	6	19
3	3	1	3	7
7	0	1	0	1
8	0	1	1	2
Total collocations combined	11	8	10	29

mentioned that collocations play an important role in the development of language fluency and naturalness in learners. At the same time, they have been reported as the most difficult to learn, and are pervasive in speech and writing. The low number of collocations and their frequency of occurrence used as examples here suggest two approaches need to be considered: to provide opportunities for incidental learning and a selected configuration of form-focused instruction.

Concluding remarks

I hope to have shown a systematic, principled way of operationalizing so far broad suggestions for assessing important aspects of vocabulary by way of corpus methods, and how this can be placed within a traditional materials evaluation framework for selection or adaptation purposes. It is interesting to see that to this date, conventional methods and corpus have not been proposed as elements that can complement each other in the quest for more suitable educational resources. Conventional methods tend to be subjective and do not offer empirical evidence for the presence of current theory and research of vocabulary in materials. The growing body of research shows striking inconsistencies between information in textbooks for both general and specific purpose language learning and actual language use (Barbieri and Eckdhart; 2007; Biber and Reppen; 2002; Jiménez Catalán; 2008; Juffs; 1998), which therefore calls for a more critical stance towards textbook selection, adaptation and use. To conclude this paper, I will briefly discuss some implications related to the implementation of corpus in the context of materials evaluation.

First, corpus analysis of linguistic features such as collocations should be included as an essential part of the final outcomes in any overall predictive evaluation process. There are no educational resources in the market that can perfectly fit in a particular language classroom. By implementing corpus techniques as suggested in this paper, however, most materials can be supplemented based on a detailed understanding of a given educational context, and the linguistic contents that need to be provided for a suitable adaptation. On the other hand, assessing currently adopted materials under the light of corpus as a stand-alone process can render useful findings for after-use reflection. Such findings may include linguistic content that needs to be supplemented as well as opportunities for introducing more suitable pedagogical techniques.

Second, corpus assessment of materials can also be carried out in attention to other reasons such as a) to verify official mandates from ministries of education as to specific contents, b) how best to supplement materials to meet additional requirements from employers in educational institutions, and c) to inform potential adaptations that best satisfy teachers' and students' needs and interests.

Third, the role of vocabulary can also be examined in other parts or sections such as transcripts of conversations and oral communication tasks though corpus. Evaluators can compare their findings with insights from spoken corpora or any aspect of interest in the literature on language fluency development in order to make decisions about how best to enhance teaching and learning of oral and aural skills.

I feel that the steps described and illustrated here represent a useful interface to a practical implementation of corpus assessment in the world of materials evaluation that can help teachers and learners meet their educational goals.

References

Bahns, J. and M. Eldaw (1993). "Should We Teach EFL Students Collocations?" System, 21(1): 101-114.

Barbieri, F. and S. E. B. Eckhardt (2007). "Applying Corpus-Based Findings to Form-Focused Instruction: The Case of Reported Speech." Language Teaching Research 11(3): 319–346.

Barfield, A. W. (2001). "Collocation Design and Development." Paper presented at the 11th Vocabulary Acquisition Research Group Network Conference, Swansea University, UK.

Benson, M., Benson, E. and R. Ilson (1997). The BBI Dictionary of English Word Combinations. John Benjamin's Publishing Company.

Biber, D., Conrad, S. and R. Reppen (2008). Corpus Linguistics: Investigating Language Structureand Use. Cambridge University Press.

Biber, D. and R. Reppen (2002). "What Does Frequency Have to Do With Grammar Teaching?" Studies in Second Language Acquisition, 24: 199-208.

Biskup, D. (1992). "L1 Influence on Learners' Renderings of English Collocations: A Polish/German Empirical Study." In Vocabulary and Applied Linguistics, Arnaud, P. and Bejoint, H. (eds.), 85-93. MacMillan.

Breen, M. P. and C. N. Candlin (1987). "Which Materials? A Consumer's and Designer's Guide." In ELT Textbooks and Materials: Problems in Evaluation and Development, Sheldon, L. E. (ed.), 13-28. ELT Document. Modern English Publications.

Brown, J. D. (1995). Elements of Language Curriculum: A Systematic Approach to Program Development. Heinle and Heinle.

Chacón, C. (2005). "Teachers' Perceived Efficacy among English as a Foreign Language Teachers in Middle Schools in Venezuela." Teaching and Teacher Education, 21: 257-272

Colmenares, J. (in preparation). "Repetition of Collocations in the Reading Component of EFL Textbooks Used in Venezuela: A Corpus-Based Study."

Cunningsworth, A. (1995). Choosing Your Course Book. Heinemann.

Grabe, W. (2009). Reading in a Second Language. Cambridge University Press.

Hill, J. (2000). "Revising Priorities: From Grammatical Failure to Collocational success." In Teaching Collocation: Further Developments in the Lexical Approach, Lewis, M. (ed.), 47-69. Language Teaching Publications.

Jiménez Catalán, R. (2008). "Vocabulary Input in EFL Textbooks." RESLA, 21: 147-165.

Juffs, A. (1998). "The Acquisition of Semantics–Syntax Correspondences and Verb Frequencies in ESL Materials." Language Teaching Research, 2(2): 93–123.

Kachroo, J. N. (1962). "Report On an Investigation into the Teaching of Vocabulary in the First Year of English." Bulletin of the Central Institute of English 2: 67-72.

McDonough, J. and C. Shaw (2003). Materials and Methods in ELT. Blackwell.

Nation, I. S. P. (2001). Learning Vocabulary in Another Language. Cambridge University Press.

Pawley, A. and F. H. Syder (1983). "Two Puzzles for Linguistic Theory: Nativelike Selection and Nativelike Fluency." In Language and Communication, Richards, J. C. and Schmidt, R.W. (eds.), 191-226. Longman.

Sheldon, L. E. (1988). "Evaluating ELT Textbooks Standard Textbooks Used in Romanian Primary and Materials." ELT Journal 42(4): 237-46.
Schmitt, N. (2000). Vocabulary in Language Teaching. Cambridge University Press.
Sinclair, J. (2005). "Corpus and Text – Basic Principles." In Developing Linguistic Corpora: a Guide to Good Practice, Wynne, M. (ed.), 1-16. Oxbow Books. Available at: http://ahds.ac.uk/linguistic-corpora.
Williams, D. (1983). "Developing Criteria for Textbook Evaluation." ELT Journal, 37(3): 251-255.
Zimmerman, C. B. (1997). "Historical Trends in Second Language Vocabulary Instruction." In Second Language Vocabulary Acquisition: A Rationale for Pedagogy, Coady, J. and Huckin, T. (eds.), 5-19. Cambridge University Press.
Zinkgräf, M. (2008). "V+N Miscollocations in the Written Production of University Level Students." ELIA, 8: 91-116.

Enhancing Intercultural Communicative Competence in an Online Collaborative Assessment Environment: CEFcult project

Jacek Waliński

Abstract

The CEFcult Project provides an online environment that enables self-, peer- and expert evaluation of spoken language proficiency and intercultural communicative competence in professional communication. By combining the CEFR scales for language proficiency with the INCA rating scales for intercultural competence the project has translated the concepts of linguistic competence and intercultural competence into a single assessment framework (based on Byram's model of Intercultural Communicative Competence) that is applicable in practice through the use of operationalized scales. The project has developed a flexible collaborative assessment platform to measure and raise intercultural communicative competence through implementation of real-life scenarios based on spoken interaction typical of the modern international enterprise. Educators and professionals in intercultural communication and collaboration can contribute to the CEFcult environment with new custom scenarios and further expansion of the assessment framework.

Keywords

CEFcult, intercultural competence, intercultural communicative competence, assessment, oral proficiency, learning platform, CEFR, INCA, WebCEF

Introduction

Facing a financial crisis, baby bust, and increasing global competition, the European Union needs to implement profound changes in education, economy and society in order to cope with challenges of the present times. There is an urgent need to equip Europeans, both young and old, with increased mobility skills, initially focused on learning, but ultimately for jobs, competitiveness, cultural exchange and European citizenship. As outlined in the European Report of the High Level Expert Forum on Mobility (RHLEFM 2008) the Union needs to forge a new generation of citizens with openness and multicultural cooperation skills for intercultural dialogue in the globalizing world.

Another document (CEDEFOP 2009) focusing on Europe's future occupational skill needs recognizes challenges for the European economy in globalization, ageing population, and productivity gap that require a more flexible labor force capable of adaptation to changing demands of the present economy. Taking into consideration the increasing contact between people from different linguistic and cultural backgrounds through international migration and collaborations, workers need to develop adequate linguistic and intercultural skills to act successfully in the global market.

Moreover, it has already been established (CILT 2006) that European business is losing ground due to insufficient language skills. Thus, a central element of this new mobility and flexibility strategy is to expand the opportunities to learn a second and third European language, especially in professional settings. To develop the required flexible labor force, graduate, post-graduate, and vocational education needs to advance pedagogical efforts to support learners in understanding and building their international communication skills.

The above mentioned studies clearly point out that being successful in international communication requires not only foreign language skills, but also the ability to deal with the cultural diversity of a foreign country environment. To address this problem CEFcult project was established to provide a platform for integrated training of intercultural and oral language skills, thereby addressing increased needs for this type of training in commercial and educational institutions.

CEFcult system development

The CEFcult has been in existence since November 2009. It is funded by the EU Lifelong Learning Programme of the Education, Audiovisual and Culture Executive Agency (project no. 505246-LLP-1-2009-1-BE-KA2-KA2MP). The project consortium brings together 12 partners from 8 different counties including: KU Leuven (coordinator); Open Universiteit Nederland; Technische Universität Dresden; Groep T - Internationale Hogeschool Leuven; Université de Savoie; Università di Bologna; University of Lodz, University of Helsinki; University of Jyväskylä; The Open University (UK); Fontys Hogescholen; Euneos Oy (commercial partner). The project is advised by an Advisory Board composed of academics, e-learning professionals, global employers and international language training and assessment organizations. To learn more about project objectives and structure visit the project website at: www.cefcult.eu

The CEFcult project focuses on the increasing demand for foreign language competence for intercultural communication which, for the reasons mentioned above, can currently be observed in institutions and enterprises acting at the trans-European and global level. To satisfy this need the project has developed an online learning platform to train and assess intercultural communication competence in spoken interaction. The CEFcult system provides a flexible environment for integrated assessment of oral language skills together with intercultural communication skills in a self-directed, socially embedded way.

The platform has been built on CEFcult's predecessor, the WebCEF project (www.webcef.eu), which created a platform for collaborative online assessment of oral proficiency using the CEFR scales (Council of Europe 2001) for oral production. The assessment of spoken language is particularly complex due to the multiplicity of components in this macro-skill and to the variety of language teaching and assessment traditions. Thus, to achieve this goal the WebCEF platform (Walinski 2011) included a showcase with representative samples of spoken production at different CEFR levels in selected European languages, annotated by experienced teachers and assessors with the CEFR descriptors presented in an online grid. It was used for comparison of oral skill assessment among language teachers and teacher trainees as well as for providing their students with a safe environment for online self- and peer-assessment.

However, the CEFcult online learning platform is gauged towards the assessment of oral proficiency for intercultural communication purposes in the realm of enterprise. Among its target users are employees about to (re)enter the workplace in another country, business language teachers, and in-house trainers working in a commercial setting. The project assumes that learners entering the platform engage in oral activities for intercultural communication purposes in scenarios typical for entrepreneurial activities. Therefore, the project's ultimate output is an e-learning platform that allows for self-, peer- and expert assessment of intercultural communicative competence in a commercial context.

Assessment of Intercultural Communicative Competence

Assessment of intercultural competence is a profoundly complex task since, as summarized by Deardorff (2006: 242), in the past 30 years even a definition of intercultural competence has not been fully agreed among scholars. However, her earlier study (Deardorff 2004: 194) points out that a generic definition commonly accepted by intercultural scholars defines it as "the ability to communicate effectively and appropriately in intercultural situations based on one's intercultural knowledge, skills, and attitudes". Deardorff research (2006: 255-257) resulted in two innovative, static and dynamic, models of intercultural competence illustrating a cyclic and complex nature of its acquisition. However, she also noticed that among educators Byram's definition is regarded as highly suitable for pedagogical purposes. Byram defines intercultural competence as "Knowledge of others; knowledge of self; skills to interpret and relate; skills to discover and/or to interact; valuing others' values, beliefs, and behaviors; and relativizing one's self. Linguistic competence plays a key role (...)" (Byram in Deardorff 2006: 248).

In Byram's model (Byram 2009: 323) presented in Figure 1 below, Intercultural Communicative Competence is composed of two closely related areas including communicative competence, and intercultural competence. The communicative competence consists of linguistic competence, sociolinguistic competence, and discourse competence. Intercultural competence consists of three components (knowledge, skills and attitudes) and is supplemented by five values:

(1) intercultural attitudes, (2) knowledge, (3) skills of interpreting and relating, (4) skills of discovery and interaction, (5) critical cultural awareness (Byram et al. 2002: 11-13). These five major intercultural competences are strongly interrelated. Byram argues that "the basis of intercultural competence is in the attitudes of the person interacting with people of another culture." Without this basic competence, the other four cannot truly develop.

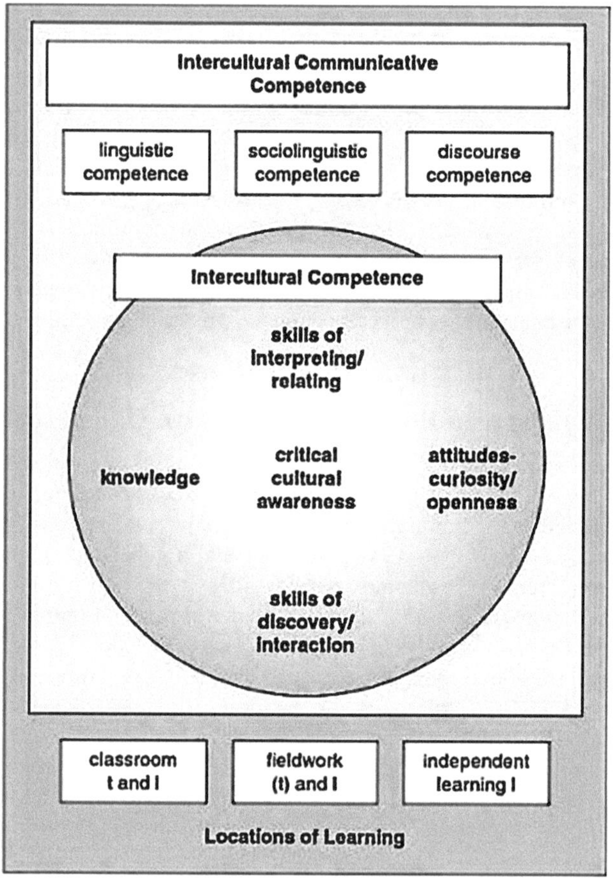

Figure 5.1: Byram's model of Intercultural Communicative Competence

The Byram's model of intercultural communicative competence has been adopted for the execution of the CEFcult project due to a number of reasons. First of all, it sees the development of intercultural communicative competence, as a combination of communicative competence and intercultural competence, both of which are fully supported in the CEFcult learning platform. Moreover, it fits well within recent Deardorff's models mentioned above, but is less complex and therefore easier to implement in practical assessment conditions. Finally, it is widespread in the European context and has formed the basis for the majority of work currently published by the Council of Europe on intercultural competence, including the assessment scales of intercultural competence defined in the INCA scales that have been implemented in the CEFcult assessment system.

INCA scales

The Byram's model presented above provides vital insight into the assessment criteria for intercultural communicative competence, however it is not specific enough to be applied for objective assessment in practice. Therefore, the project looked for available assessment frameworks that could be applied for practical evaluation on the CEFcult platform. Unfortunately, the sociolinguistic competence is not very thoroughly covered in creation of the CEFR scales. As put by Byram (2003: 5) "For although the CEF included a discussion of intercultural competence and intercultural awareness, the question of assessment and the defining of levels of intercultural competence, had to be left aside as the CEF went to press. Furthermore, rapid change in contemporary Europe means that the ways in which the CEF can be read and used are also changing." This has been confirmed by North (2008: 30, 40-41) who states that the sociolinguistic dimension in the CEFR scales is not fully backed by empirical data.

Therefore, the system employs an additional framework, namely the INCA scales, for assessment of intercultural competence. The INCA project (www.incaproject.org) developed a framework, a suite of assessment tools, and a portfolio for the assessment of intercultural competence linked to language and subject knowledge competence. Although still tentative, the INCA scales measure a learner's proficiency on six intercultural competence dimensions referred to as six *elements* of competence: "It has been observed how people in groups of mixed cultural background recognize and deal with the differences that emerge as the group works together. From such observations, it has been possible to identify a number of 'elements' of competence that people bring to bear on the situation. These elements are not definitive. Intercultural competence can include other 'elements' of competence, but the INCA project 'elements' provide a snapshot, useful as an assessment tool, to provide a baseline to inform training programmes." (INCA Project 2004: 5-7). These six elements include: 1. Tolerance of ambiguity; 2. Behavioral flexibility; 3. Communicative awareness; 4. Knowledge discovery; 5. Respect for otherness; 6. Empathy.

Level ⇨ Competence ⇩	1 'Basic'	2 'Intermediate'
General profile	The candidate at this level is on the ladder of progression. They will be disposed to deal positively with the situation. Their responses to it will be piecemeal and improvised rather than principled, even though mostly successful in avoiding short term difficulties. These will be based on fragmentary information.	The candidate at this level has begun to induce simple principles to apply to the situation, rather than improvise reactively in response to isolated features of it. There will be evidence of a basic strategy and some coherent knowledge for dealing with situations.
i) Tolerance of ambiguity	1T Deals with ambiguity on a one-off basis, responding to items as they arise. May be overwhelmed by ambiguous situations which imply high involvement.	2T Has begun to acquire a repertoire of approaches to cope with ambiguities in low-involvement situations. Begins to accept ambiguity as a challenge.
ii) Behavioural flexibility	1B Adopts a reactive/defensive approach to situations. Learns from isolated experiences in a rather unsystematic way.	2B Previous experience of required behaviour begins to influence behaviour in everyday parallel situations. Sometimes takes the initiative in adopting/conforming to other cultures' behaviour patterns.
iii) Communicative awareness	1C Attempts to relate problems of intercultural interaction to different communicative conventions, but lacks the necessary knowledge for identifying differences; tends to hold on to his own conventions and expects adaptation from others; is aware of difficulties in interaction with non-native-speakers, but has not yet evolved principles to guide the choice of strategies (metacommunication, clarification or simplification).	2C Begins to relate problems of intercultural interaction to conflicting communicative conventions and attempts to clarify his own or to adapt to the conventions of others. Uses a limited repertoire of strategies (metacommunication, clarification, simplification) to solve and prevent problems when interacting with a non-native-speaker.

Figure 5.2: A fragment of the assessor version of the INCA framework

The assessment according to each of these scales is performed by evaluating learner behavior or responses and relating those responses to descriptors that represent a level of proficiency in a competence. As shown in Figure 2 above, each of the elements is described at three (*Basic, Intermediate, Full*) levels of competence, corresponding to the abilities achieved by a learner. As the descriptors are rather abstract, in the CEFcult system they are operationalized for each specific assessment scenario, which relates the abstract descriptors to the specific situation that the learner enacts.

Scenarios

The CEFcult platform includes scenarios and tasks that require activation of both language and intercultural competencies. Learners are asked to perform specific tasks that have been devised to stimulate certain intercultural behavior through spoken language. They sometimes make use of trigger texts or videos to create an intercultural context first. Those tasks are usually a part of a larger scenario, which is a description of a real-life situation accompanied by a series of assignments for the learner designed to prompt spoken interaction. In the CEFcult platform, the scenarios are intended to provoke, apart from spoken conversation, a certain type of intercultural behavior, which is assessed at a later stage together with oral proficiency. A task usually provides a single assignment to be accomplished by the learner. For example, one scenario covers a job interview for a multinational company, which includes such tasks as presenting yourself, describing suitability for the job, talking about extra-curricular activities, and closing the interview.

In CEFcult these scenarios can have several formats, including monologue, dialogue and group role-play situations and the resulting behavior is captured using audio/video recording equipment. Thus, in result three major types of scenarios are used, depending on how the learner is asked to interact.

1. The learner individually sits in front of a computer to perform tasks: intended behavior, actual behavior, and observations in reaction to trigger texts or videos are captured in a video recording. Live interaction is also possible (e.g. online job interview).
2. The learner performs a task in dialogue situation with others (e.g. teacher, other learner, or the assessor). The resulting dialogue is captured as a video recording and made available on the platform.
3. The learner performs a task as part of a group role play with others (other learners and/or assessors). The role play is captured in a video recording and made available on the platform for assessment.

As intercultural communicative competence development is an ongoing process, new scenarios can be added to sustain its headway (e.g. through increasing level of intercultural subtlety in tasks). Educators and professionals in intercultural communication and collaboration can contribute to the CEFcult environment with new made-to-measure scenarios and further expansion of the assessment framework. In the development of scenarios, it should be taken into consideration that a scenario should be clearly defined by multiple dimensions, like task type, language used, scales used to assess the results, format, production and observation/reflection, etc. Since in the CEFcult system learners invite both peers and experts to assess their recordings, it may also be also necessary to provide clear guidelines for assessors of the scenarios, including self-assessment, peer assessment and expert assessment.

Project outcomes and summary

The project has contributed to the ongoing development and validation of both CEFR (language proficiency) and INCA (intercultural competence) frameworks. Moreover, by linking the CEFR scales with the INCA scales, the CEFcult project has translated the concepts of both linguistic competence and intercultural competence into a single assessment framework, based on Byram's model, that is applicable in practice through the use of operationalized scales.

The major outcome of the project is an innovative and user friendly online learning platform based on modern principles of a Web 2.0 websites, for language learners to assess and raise their foreign language speaking performance combined with intercultural communicative competence in a multilingual professional environment. However, the platform itself is not limited to implementation in professional training and can be as well used for general education, simulations and trainings in the broad area of intercultural competences through implementation of different scenarios that can be easily added to the system.

Apart from the platform the project intends to develop other substantial outputs, including:

1. a set of scenarios (authentic communication tasks) through which learners can assess their speaking skills for intercultural professional purposes in different European languages;
2. research-supported guidelines for foreign language teaching and educational policy based on observed international inter-rater differences;
3. viable and tested models for collaborative assessment among higher education institutes, enterprises, and other cooperation initiatives;
4. training materials for self-, peer- and expert assessment in education and enterprises.

The project promotes the new e-learning culture bringing together self-learning in the realms of business and education. As shown in Figure 3 above the platform puts the learner in the center of attention. By encouraging self-awareness, and the self- and peer-assessment, it enables learners to become more autonomous. The environment is designed to support informal learning initiatives – initiated by learners themselves, but can also be used in formal learning settings (e.g. in schools or universities).

As shown in the diagram on the next page (Baten et al. 2010), the learner is in charge, but experts can be called in to feed the assessment from a professional perspective. Learners are able to record themselves and make annotations, and to submit their assessments for peer review in social networks, e.g. LinkedIn, etc. They are also provided with an opportunity to employ the e-Portfolio based assessment in line with European Language Portfolio (Council of Europe 2010) guidelines for internal learning and monitoring processes in educational institutions and other organizations.

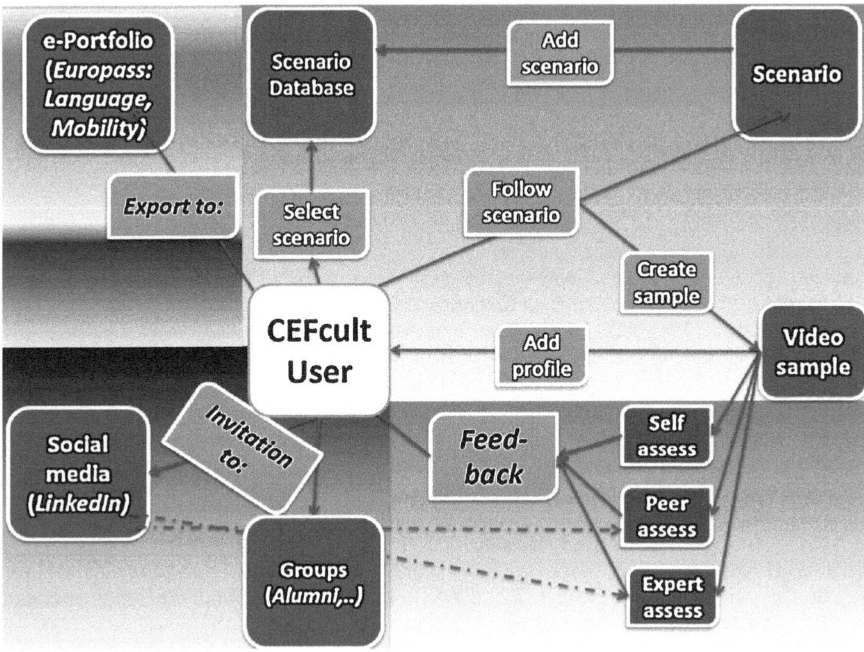

Figure 5.3: Actions available to a CEFcult platform user

Therefore, the platform should be viewed as a vehicle in which learners and assessors apply their interests, critical thinking, and creative ideas to self-selected areas of interest. It provides a secure environment that assists language learners in refining and improving their performance and intercultural communication skills in situations where spoken language is related to intercultural professional communication. As employees increasingly work in multi-cultural settings, such system offers an invaluable tools to build not only language skills, but also the ability to deal with cultural and linguistic diversity.

References

Sinclair, J. (1991). Corpus, Concordance, Collocation. Oxford University Press.

Baten, L. Dusar, L. and J. Van Maele (2010). Online CEF-Based Assessment of Oral Proficiency for Intercultural Professional Communication. Presentation for ONLINE EDUCA Conference in Berlin.

Byram, M., Gribkova, B. and H. Starkey, H. (2002). Developing the Intercultural Dimension in Language Teaching: a Practical Introduction for Teachers. Available at: http://www.lrc.cornell.edu/director/intercultural.pdf

Byram, M. (ed.). (2003). Intercultural Competence. Strasbourg: Council of Europe.

Byram, M. (2009). "The Intercultural Speaker and the Pedagogy of Foreign Language Education." In The SAGE Handbook of Intercultural Competence, Deardorff, D. K. (ed.), 321-332. Thousand Oaks, CA: Sage.

CEDEFOP (2009). European Centre for the Development of Vocational Training. Skills for Europe's Future: Anticipating Occupational Skills Needs.
Available at: http://www.cedefop.europa.eu/EN/Files/5194_en.pdf

CILT (2006). ELAN: Effects on the European Economy of Shortages of Foreign Language Skills in Enterprise. London: CILT, the UK National Centre for Languages.

Council of Europe. (2010). European Language Portfolio.
Available at: http://www.coe.int/portfolio

Council of Europe. (2001). Common European Framework of Reference for Languages: Learning, Teaching, Assessment. Cambridge: Cambridge University Press.

Deardorff D. K. (2004). The Identification and Assessment of Intercultural Competence as a Student Outcome of International Education at Institutions of Higher Education in the United States. North Carolina State University, Raleigh.

Deardorff, D. K. (2006). "Identification and Assessment of Intercultural Competence as a Student Outcome of Internationalization." Journal of Studies in International Education, 10(3): 241-266.

INCA Project. (2004). "Intercultural Competence Assessment." INCA Assessor Manual.
Available at:
http://www.incaproject.org/en_downloads/21_INCA_Assessor_Manual_eng_final.pdf

North, B. (2008) "The CEFR Levels and Descriptor Scales." In Multilingualism and Assessment, Studies in Language Testing 27, Taylor, L. and Weir, C. J. (eds.). Cambridge: UCLES/Cambridge University Press.

RHLEFM (2008) Report of the High Level Expert Forum on Mobility. Making learning mobility an opportunity for all.
Available at:
http://ec.europa.eu/education/doc/2008/mobilityreport_en.pdf

Verjans, S. and Rajagopal, K. (2011). "D4.1. CEFcult Framework and Methodology." CEFcult project deliverables: CEFcult project.

Waliński, J. (2011). The WebCEF e-Platform in Testing Learners' Oral Proficiency Across Europe. In Interdisciplinary Approaches to Communication Studies, Bednarek A. and Witczak-Plisiecka I. (eds.). Łódź: Wydawnictwo WSSM.

A Parallel Latin – Old English Corpus of Biblical Translations as a Tool for Word Order Studies

Anna Cichosz

Abstract

The present paper aims to examine the advantages and limitations of biblical translations as a study material for scholars interested in Old English word order. This attempt may seem unjustified since translations are usually neglected by historical linguists as a text type unsuitable for the purposes of syntactic analyses, the assumption being that such texts reflect the word order of the source language rather than the natural syntax of the target language. Nonetheless, I would like to claim that before excluding such a huge body of texts from analysis, we should first check to what extent they are copied, and not assume, *a priori*, that they always strictly follow the syntax of the original. The tool which will be used to present the degree of (in)dependence of the analysed translations will be a parallel Latin-Old English corpus, which enables the researcher to identify clauses with copied word order. Surprisingly enough, the frequency of such clauses in the sample analysed for the purpose of the present study (the Old English translation of the first 16 chapters from the Book of Genesis) is in fact quite low.

Keywords

Old English word order, parallel corpora, Old English Bible.

Introduction – why translations?

Translations are traditionally considered to be a risky choice for a syntactic study, which is naturally related to the possible influence of the source language on the translated text. However, in the case of certain Old Germanic languages (such as e.g. Old High German or Gothic), scholars are left without a choice and need to analyse word order on the basis of translations because these texts are the only examples of prose writing in a given language (for an informative discussion, see Fleischer at al. 2008). Theoretically, Old English is in a better situation because in the case of this language there are some prose works which can be a "safe" subject of such an analysis. As a result, though, Old English word order is studied virtually only on the basis of a limited number of texts; the most popular sources which are usually selected for analysis are homilies by Aelfric (e.g. Barret 1953, Reszkiewicz 1966, Kohonen 1978, Davis and Bernhardt 2002) or the Anglo-Saxon Chronicle (e.g. Smith 1971, Bean 1983). Even more recent studies which make use of Old English electronic corpora illustrate the rules of Old English word order mostly (though not only) with examples from Aelfric's homilies (cf. Fischer et al. 2000: 37-67). As a result, our knowledge of Old English word order is, to a certain extent, limited because the best part of the Old English corpus of texts, that is poetry and translations, is almost completely ignored. The main question which needs to be answered is whether we can afford to exclude so many sources from analysis only because we suspect their syntax of being 'unnatural' or copied. It is not plausible that all translations are so strongly dependent on the original that their study can give us absolutely no new information about the syntax of Old English. In addition, most translations created in Anglo-Saxon England come from the Late Old English period (i.e. the end of the 10th century or the beginning of the 11th century), which means that the language had already had quite a long literary tradition (first Old English texts come from the 8th century); translators could base their work on original Old English texts, and that may have increased their confidence and freedom of expression, thus making such translations relatively independent. If we can use original works written by Aelfric to study the rules and principles Old English syntax, then moving on to his translations of Latin texts does not seem to be such a risky path.

The last argument for the study of Old English word order on the basis of translations is comparative work – right now all comparative studies of Old English and Old High German word order take as their subject texts from different domains; Davis and Bernhardt (2002) compare homilies of Aelfric (Old English original prose) and Tatian (Old High German translation); Smith (1971) compares a mixture of Old High German texts (poetry, original and translated prose) and the Anglo Saxon Chronicle. The text type variable is controlled in Cichosz (2010), though to have a full picture of the situation it is necessary to analyse the problem of word order in translations in more detail, with reference to the Latin original. With the help of proper methodology, the study of word order on the basis of translated texts may be, if not the best choice, then at least a source of some interesting additional observations concerning Old Germanic languages, including Old English.

The research project

The present study is a part of a bigger research project which has three main objectives: to investigate the syntactic dependence of selected Old English and Old High German translations on the Latin original; to see whether the degree of syntactic copying is related to the time of composition and the character of the text (secular vs. religious translations) and; to determine whether (selected) translations can be used to study the word order of Old English and/or Old High German.

The project is supposed to examine a selection of translations created at different times, both religious (including biblical) and secular, thus making it possible to draw conclusions regarding the influence of these factors on the (in)dependence of the translated texts.

The tool which is being created for the purpose of the project is a parallel corpus of Latin original texts, linked on the clause level with the translations. All clauses are annotated syntactically (clause types and clauses elements, i.e. subject, finite and non-finite verb, object, conjunction, adverbial, etc.). As a result, it is possible to determine whether the word order pattern identified in a given Old English/Old High German clause is a direct copy of the Latin original or whether the translator modified the original order of elements in any way.

Old English Bible and the design of the present study

The aim of the present study is to investigate the interrelations between the Latin Vulgate and the Old English translation of the Book of Genesis, thus determining whether the Old English text can be treated as idiomatic Old English. As Marsden (1991) claims, no full study of Aelfric's Genesis in relation to its Latin source has ever been made and there are very different opinions regarding the quality of the translation.

> Greenfield and Calder claim that (…) Aelfric was so conservative on this point that he was willing to translate an occasionally incomprehensible passage from Jerome's Latin (itself based on an impenetrable Hebrew) into a "nonsense" Old English in order to keep the deep spiritual meaning intact, something he had avoided in his looser homiletic paraphrases. The Genesis remains, in fact, Aelfric's only literal translation, although even here he omitted "catalogs" and abstruse passages. The curious idea that a dedicated pedagogue and champion of plain English should have produced a vernacular Genesis so deliberately literal as to be sometimes incomprehensible has not yet, so far as I know, been challenged.
>
> (Marsden 1991: 320)

Marsden himself does not agree with these accusations and in his article he proves that Aelfric very often paraphrased the Latin and did not closely follow the source text. In fact, Aelfric himself commented on the proper way of translating the Bible in his preface to the translation:

> [...] we ne durron na mare awritan on Englisc þonne þæt Leden hæfþ, ne þa endebirdnisse awendan, butan þam anum þæt þæt Leden and þæt Englisc nabbað na ane wisan on þære spræce fadunge._Æfre se ðe awent oþþe se þe tæcþ of Ledene on Englisc, æfre he sceal gefadian hit swa þæt þæt Englisc hæbbe his agene wisan, elles hit biþ swiþe gedwolsum to rædenne þam þe þæs Ledenes wisan ne can
>
> (Marsden 2004: 128).

> [we dare not write in English anything that is not in the Latin, nor change the order, except in one case: when Latin and English do not have a single way in the arrangement of the language. Always, he who translates or interprets from Latin to English should order elements so that English keeps its own manner, or it will be very confusing to read for those who do not know Latin.]

Aelfric's reflections are very commonsense: the translator cannot add things that are not mentioned in the original, but at the same time he cannot translate the text word by word, because this would make no sense in English. Where "Latin and English do not have a single way in the arrangement of the language", i.e. in their syntax, he has to change the structure for the reader to be able to understand the sense of the passage. This is also the interpretation made by Stanton (2002), who claims that in Aelfric's text "order ('endebyrdnysse') must be changed, not occasionally, but consistently". Thus, we can assume that, if Aelfric's translation practice went hand in hand with his declarations, the Old English text may contain numerous departures from the Latin original, also on the level of word order.

For the purpose of the present study, the first 16 chapters from the Book of Genesis have been analysed. They were all translated by Aelfric, who is responsible for the translation of the first 24 chapters. There are 1195 clauses identified in the source text (a clause being defined as a syntactic unit centred around a verb), which is equivalent to 1006 clauses in the target text.

Results

After the syntactic analysis, Old English and Latin equivalent clauses were linked and it turned out that the text is definitely not a "clause by clause" translation since only 73% of Latin clauses were translated by a single Old English clause, as shown in Table 1.

Table 6.1: Copying on the level of clause

1 to 1	omitted	added	paraphrased	total
876 (73%)	231 (19%)	43 (4%)	45 (4%)	1195

Quite a substantial number of clauses was omitted in the translation and this was mainly related to the fact that certain fragments were significantly shortened in the translation (e.g. 'catalogs' mentioned by Marsden in the abovementioned quotation) , as shown by examples 1 and 2, which are equivalent fragments:

1. soror vero Thubalcain Noemma. dixitque Lamech uxoribus suis Adae et Sellae, audite vocem meam uxores Lamech, auscultate sermonem meum, quoniam occidi virum in vulnus meum et adulescentulum in livorem meum septuplum ultio dabitur de Cain de Lamech vero septuagies septies, cognovit quoque adhuc Adam uxorem suam et peperit filium, vocavitque nomen eius Seth, dicens (...)
2. seo hatte Noema. Eft Adam gestrynde sunu ðone he nemde Seth, & ðus cwæð: (...)

In the present study, the main focus of attention will be main declarative clauses; they are most numerous and thus the results can be treated as representative for the whole text. Only clauses in 1-to-1 correspondence will be analysed, because this is the context in which a possible influence of the Latin original can be objectively checked and assessed. After applying the abovementioned criteria, the research corpus is narrowed down to 551 Old English clauses, corresponding to 551 Latin clauses.

Position of the finite verb in the target text

Table 2 shows the frequency of 5 possible finite verb positions in the translation.

Table 6.2: Position of the finite verb in the target text

V-1	%	V-2	%	V-3	%	V-F	%	ambiguous	%	Σ
92	17	305	55	79	14	23	4	52	9	551

The word order patterns are V-1 (the verb takes the first position in the clause), V-2 (the verb takes the second position), V-F (the verb is the last element of the clause), V-3 (the verb is pushed towards the end of the clause, but it is not the last element) and ambiguous (very short clauses where the verb is at the same time the first and last or second and last element). The patters are illustrated with the examples given below (the finite verb is shown in italics):

a. V-1: *Wæron* ða Noes suna Sem & Cham & Iaphet; (cl. 635)[1]
[were then Noe's sons Sem and Cham and Iaphet][2]
b. V-2: Heo *com* ða on æfnunge eft to Noe (cl. 561)
[she came then in the evening again to Noe]
c. V-3: Agar þa *clypode* Godes naman (cl. 994)
[Agar then called God's name]
d. V-F: & hine nan man syððan ne *geseah* (cl. 408)
[and him no man afterwards not saw]
e. ambiguous: & Enos *forðferde* (cl. 386)
[and Enos died]

1 Numbers assigned to clauses in the database (a separate numbering for Latin and Old English).
2 Translations of clauses from the database have been provided by the author and they are meant to be word by word renderings of the syntactic phenomena they illustrate.

First of all, it should be noted that conjunctions are not counted as parts of the clause.[3] Secondly, in the following calculations ambiguous clauses, which are very difficult to classify because of their shortness, have been counted together with V-1 and V-2 clauses unless indicated otherwise, not to obscure the results with additional categories.

As shown in Table 2, the dominant word order pattern in the translation is V-2 (55%), which comes as no surprise as this is the unmarked word order used in main declarative clauses in all Old Germanic languages. However, the relatively high frequency of V-1 clauses (17%) seems quite surprising, given that this order is traditionally regarded as marked:

> After 600 A.D. the verb-second order seems to have attained the status of non-marked order in the Germanic dialects generally.
>
> (Smith 1971: 138)

> Sometimes the V-1 construction also occurs in OE, but it denotes an exceptionally marked, or even formulaic style.
>
> (Onesti 1993: 90)

What needs to be checked before any definite conclusions are drawn, however, is if the V-1 clauses enumerated in Table 2 contain an expressed subject (and thus they can be considered as 'real V-1 clauses'), as illustrated by examples 3 and 4:

3. *Bið* ðonne **se min renboga** on ðam wolcnum (cl. 628)
   [will be then this rainbow of mine in the sky]
4. & *het* ðæt leoht dæg (cl. 11)
   [and called the light day]

It may seem that both clauses are V-1 and these are the results rendered from the database. Nonetheless, only clauses like (3) can be treated as authentic V-1 because this clause contains an expressed subject (shown in bold type). Clauses like (4) in fact represent a "hidden V-2" pattern; the subject is elided, but there is 'an empty subject slot' at the beginning of the clause. Such clauses are very often conjoined, as in:

3 In this paper, conjoined clauses are counted together with non-conjoined ones so as not to obscure the results with too many subdivisions though conjoining is taken into consideration when the results are analysed.

5. **God** *geseah* ða (cl. 8)
   [God saw then]
   ðæt hit god *wæs*, (cl. 9)
   [that it good was]
   & **he** *todælde* leoht fram ðam ðystrum. (cl. 10)
   [and he divided light from darkness]
   & *het* ðæt leoht dæg (cl. 11)
   [and called the light day]
   & þa ðystru niht: (cl. 12)
   [and the darkness – night]

There are 92 V-1 clauses in the translation and only 17 of them contain an expressed subject. Thus, we may modify the results shown in Table 2 in the following way:

Table 6.3: Position of the finite verb in the target text (hidden V-2 counted together with V-2)

V-1	**%**	**V-2**	**%**	**V-3**	**%**	**V-F**	**%**	**ambiguous**	**%**	**Σ**
17	3%	380	69%	79	14	23	4	52	9	551

Now, the V-2 order becomes clearly dominant and V-1 has a low frequency, natural for a marked pattern, represented by the following clauses:

6. & *wæs* ða geworden **æfen & mergen oðer dæg**. (cl. 23)
   et factum *est* **vespere et mane dies secundus** (cl. 23)
7. & *wæs* geworden **æfen & mergen se ðridda dæg**. (cl. 40)
   factumque *est* **vespere et mane dies tertius** (cl. 40)
8. & *wæs* geworden **æfen & mergen se feorða dæg**. (cl. 58)
   et factum *est* **vespere et mane dies quartus** (cl. 60)
9. *Wæs* ða geworden **æfen & merien se sixta dæg**. (cl. 104)
   et factum *est* **vespere et mane dies sextus** (cl. 107)
10. *Nis* na god ðisum men **ana to wunigenne**; (cl. 160)
    non *est* bonum esse **hominem solum** (cl. 162)
11. *is* **seo eorðe** awyrged on ðinum weorce: (cl. 265)
    maledicta **terra** in opera tuo (cl. 261)
12. *Wæs* ða geworden **micel flod** (cl. 516)
    factumque *est* **diluvium** quadraginta diebus super terram (cl. 554)
13. *wurdon* ða behelede **ealle ða heahstan duna** under ealre heofenan. (cl. 523)
    opertique *sunt* **omnes montes excelsi** sub universo caelo (cl. 561
14. *Wearð* ða fornumen **eal flæsc manna & fugela, nytena & creopendra**. (cl. 525)
    consumptaque *est* **omnis caro** (cl. 564)

15. *Nelle* **ic** nateshwon awyrgean ða eorðan heononforð for mannum; (cl. 586)
    nequaquam ultra *maledicam* terrae propter homines (cl. 635)
16. *Bið* ðonne se **min renboga** on ðam wolcnum (cl. 628)
    eritque **arcus** in nubibus (cl. 682)
17. *Wæron* ða Noes **suna** Sem & Cham & Iaphet; (cl. 635)
    erant igitur **filii** Noe Sem Ham et Iafeth porro Ham (cl. 690)
18. *beo* **Chanaan** his ðeowa. (cl. 659)
    sit **Chanaan** servus eius (cl. 716)
19. *Gemænifylde* **God** Iapheð, (cl. 660)
    dilatet **Deus** Iafeth (cl. 717)
20. & *wæron* ða gefyllede **ealle his dagas** nygonhund geara & fiftig geara, (cl. 664)
    et impleti *sunt* **omnes dies eius** nongentorum quinquaginta annorum (cl. 721)
21. *næfde* **heo** nan bearn. (cl. 705)
    nec *habebat* liberos (cl. 848)
22. *Wearð* eac ðurh þone intingan **sacu betwux Abrames hyrdemannum & Lothes**; (cl. 798)
    unde et facta *est* **rixa inter pastores gregum Abram et Loth** (cl. 950)

Of course, one of the main issues under scrutiny is the influence of Latin on the identified structures. Therefore, it needs to be determined how many of the V-1 clauses are modelled on the Latin original and which are used in the sample independently. Out of the 17 clauses presented above, only 4 (ex. 16, 17, 18, 19) reflect the word order of the original Latin clauses. In the case of the remaining 13 clauses, the Latin word order is different, though it must be noted that there is a striking similarity between most of the examples: the clauses contain a complex verb phrase and the superficial difference between Old English and Latin clauses boils down to the regular change of Latin non-finite + finite sequence ('factum est') into the Old English finite + non-finite pattern ('wæs geworden'); this regularity is visible in 9 cases out of 13 (ex. 6, 7, 8, 9, 12, 13, 14, 20, 22). In the case of the remaining 4 clauses, if the negative adverbs are counted as parts of the verb phrase, then the OE clauses 160 and 705 can be treated as close copies of the Latin clauses 162 and 848 respectively (ex. 10 and 21), whereas in Old English clauses 586 and 265 we can observe a clear intervention by the translator: a non-finite clause is rendered as finite (ex. 11) and a negative adverb 'nequaquam' (by no means) is reflected by a different part of speech, the verb 'nellan' (be unwilling to, refuse) (ex. 15).

To sum up, when the V-1 pattern appears in the Old English translation, it is usually a subjectless conjoined main declarative like:

23. & *geworhte* ðæt rib to anum wifmen (cl. 175)
24. & *cwæð* to hyre were: (cl. 951)

Such structures can be identified in all Old English text types and thus, even though such clauses are mostly copies (the issue of copying is discussed in detail in the following sections), they cannot be treated as examples of 'bad syntax'. When a subject is used in a V-1 main declarative clause, in most cases (9 out of 13) the clause contains a complex verb phrase and the order of non-finite and finite part is fixed.

Latin V-1 clauses and their Old English equivalents

Bearing in mind the discussion presented above, let us consider the problem from the perspective of the other language, i.e. Latin. What happens when the original text uses a V-1 declarative main clause, which in Old English is a marked structure that would typically be avoided? Table 4 illustrates the techniques used in the translation with numbers:

Table 6.4: Strategies for translating Latin V-1 clauses

V-1 to V-1	%	V-1 to V-2	%	V-1 to V-3	%	V-1 to V-F	%	Σ
70	28%	132	53 %	40	16%	9	4%	251[4]

One of the first observations that should be made on the basis of Table 4 is that the V-1 pattern is very frequent in the original Latin text (251 out of 506 clauses, so almost 50% of all main declarative clauses represent this pattern). It is clearly visible that the main strategy of the translator was to change the original V-1 pattern into V-2, so to avoid using the order which in Old English is clearly marked (in 53% of cases), whereas he stuck to the original order in 28% of clauses and in 20% pushed the verb towards the end of the clause (V-3 or V-F). Nonetheless, numbers alone do not make it possible to draw any final conclusion. The results presented in Table 4 are based on V-1 clauses both with and without an expressed subject. In the first category, V-1 to V-1, out of 70 clauses only 7 Latin and 5 Old English clauses contain a subject:

25. *eritque* **arcus** in nubibus (cl. 682)
    Bið ðonne **se min renboga** on ðam wolcnum (cl. 628)

4 Calculated for the sample of 506 main declarative clauses in 1-to-1 correspondence with an expressed finite verb in the source and target text (the corpus of 551 clauses is narrowed down to 506 when Latin clauses without a finite verb are eliminated).

26. *erant* igitur **filii Noe** Sem Ham et Iafeth porro Ham (cl. 690)
    Wæron ða **Noes suna** Sem & Cham & Iaphet; (cl. 635)
27. *sit* **Chanaan** servus eius (cl. 716)
    beo **Chanaan** his ðeowa. (cl. 659)
28. *dilatet* **Deus** Iafeth (cl. 717)
    Gemænifylde **God** Iapheð, (cl. 660)
29. et *aedificavit* **Dominus Deus** costam in mulierem (cl. 176)
    & *geworhte* ðæt rib to anum wifmen (cl. 175)
30. *sitque* **Chanaan** servus eius (cl. 719)
    & *beo* **Chanaan** his ðeowa. (cl. 662)
31. *dixit* autem **rex Sodomorum** ad Abram (cl. 1055)
    & *bæd* (cl. 864)

It is visible that all Old English V-1 clauses with an expressed subject are copies of a similar Latin structure, whereas two such Latin clauses lost their subject in the process of translation (ex. 29 and 31). The remaining 63 clause pairs are all subjectless as e.g.

32. et *adduxit* eam ad Adam (cl. 178)
    & *gelædde* hi to Adame. (cl. 177)
33. *benedixit* ei (cl. 1048)
    & *bletsode* Abram, (cl. 881)

It should also be noted that 65 out of 70 OE clauses are conjoined; lack of an expressed subject and conjoining increase the frequency of 'hidden V-2' structures. In short, it can be concluded that the high number of V-1 clauses in the translated text is caused by copying but for the copying to take place, the clause had to fulfil a certain set of conditions: a) it had to be subjectless and, preferably, conjoined (which results in a 'hidden V-2' order), or b) the subject had to be a heavy lexical phrase (which creates a 'real V-1' pattern; see examples 6-22 and 25-31, exceptions: ex. 15 and 21). All exceptions to the rule can be explained by emphatic use (ex. 15) or negation (which increases the frequency of V-1, see ex. 21).

Even though in the case of the V-1 pattern copying is an important strategy, the one employed much more often is modification, in most cases into the neutral V-2 pattern, as e.g. in:

34. *dixit* quoque **Deus** (cl. 74)
    God *cwæð* eac swilce: (cl. 72)
35. *scit* enim **Deus** (cl. 203)
    Ac **God** *wat* soðlice (cl. 203)

36. *dixitque* **Cain** ad Abel fratrem suum (cl. 309)
    Đa *cwæð* **Cain** to Abele his breðer: (cl. 309)
37. *intellexit* ergo **Noe** (cl. 606)
    Đa *undergeat* **Noe** (cl. 563)
38. *dixit* enim (cl. 1188)
    Heo *cwæð*: (cl. 998)
39. *multiplicabo* aerumnas tuas et conceptus tuos (cl. 252)
    Ic *gemænifylde* ðine yrmða & ðine geeacnunga; (cl. 256)
40. *eduxitque* eum foras (cl. 1085)
    God *lædde* hyne þa ut, (cl. 904)

There are three main phenomena visible here:

a. the order of verb and subject is reverted as in ex. 34 and 35, the word order of the clause is completely changed;
b. the V-S order is retained by providing an initial adverbial, usually 'ða', which commonly triggers verb-subject inversion in Old English, as in ex. 36 and 37;
c. the missing personal pronoun is provided in the translation, so we can observe a change from 'hidden' to real V-2 order, as in ex. 38 and 39; sometimes a full lexical phrase is provided as in ex. 40.

It seems that for the translator the modification was quite natural since he used the three aforementioned strategies interchangeably and copied the V-1 order only in a selected environment.

Modifications of the original V-1 order into V-3 and V-F are less frequent, but their number is also quite high:

42. *dixitque* **Cain** ad Dominum (cl. 328)
    Witodlice **Cain** *cwæð* to Drihtne: (cl. 331)
43. et *peperit* filium (cl. 371)
    Eft **Adam** *gestrynde* sunu (cl. 367)
44. *fecit* ergo **Noe** omnia (cl. 522)
    Noe soðlice *dyde* ealle ða ðing, (cl. 491)
45. *dixit* ergo **Abram** ad Loth (cl. 952)
    Abram þa *cwæð* to Lothe: (cl. 800)
46. et *genuit* filios et filias (cl. 419)
    & syððan **he** *gestrynde* suna & dohtra. (cl. 395)
47. et *videbo* illum (cl. 683)
    & **ic** hine *geseo* (cl. 629)

Examples 41-46 clearly show that there are some patterns common to the modifications:

a. an adverbial is provided at the beginning though it does not cause a subject-verb inversion, as in ex. 41 and 42;
b. an adverbial takes the second position while the verb and subject exchange positions as in ex. 43 and 44;
c. a missing personal pronoun is provided, as in ex. 45 and 46;
d. there is a change in the position of the object: in Old English the light (pronominal) object is moved to the position preceding the verb, as in ex. 46.

It is evident that the phenomena which take place here are similar to the ones involved in the V-1 into V-2 modifications, though the provision of objects and adverbials at the beginning of the clause makes them longer and results in a V-3 or a V-F pattern.

Latin V-2 clauses and their Old English equivalents

Moving on to the next pattern in the source text, that is V-2, it must be noted that it is also relatively frequent (172 out of 506 clauses, which constitutes 34% of all Latin clauses in the sample). Table 5 shows how often the order is copied and modified in the translation.

Table 6.5: Strategies for translating Latin V-2 clauses

V-2 to V-1	%	V-2 to V-2	%	V-2 to V-3	%	V-2 to V-F	%	Σ
19	11%	112	65%	35	20%	6	3%	172[5]

As could be expected, in most cases the pattern is copied because there is no need for modification when the syntax of the target language licenses a structure found in the source text. Thus, the most common situations would be the ones illustrated by examples 48 and 49:

47. in principio *creavit* **Deus** caelum et terram (cl. 1)
    On angynne *gesceop* **God** heofonan & eorðan. (cl. 1)
48. **hic** *erit* ferus homo (cl. 1180)
    Đes *byð* reðe mann, (cl. 990)
49. et factum *est* ita (cl. 103)
    Hit *wæs* ða swa gedon. (cl. 100)

5 Calculated for the sample of 506 main declarative clauses in 1-to-1 correspondence.

50. egressus *est* autem **rex Sodomorum** in occursum eius (cl. 1042)
    Þa *eode* **Sodomitiscra cyning** sona him togeanes. (cl. 863)

In ex. 47 and 48, the original word order is retained literally without any change, but the resulting Old English clause fulfils all the rules set for Old English syntax on the basis of original texts. Sometimes, however, the strategy "V-2 to V-2" does not involve word for word repetition. In example 49 we can see that even though the finite verb takes the second position in both clauses, in Old English the finite form precedes the participle and the two verbal forms are separated by adverbials, unlike in the Latin original. The first position in the clause, which in Latin is occupied by the non-finite form of the verb, is taken by a subject (ex. 49), an adverbial (ex. 51) or an object. In most cases these clauses contain a complex verb phrase (though in ex. 50 the Latin complex verb phrase is rendered by a single verbal element in Old English). Sometimes the V-2 to V-2 modifications can involve other structures:

51. servus servorum *erit* fratribus suis (cl. 713)
    & **he** *byð* ðeowena ðeowa his gebroðrum. (cl. 656)

When a constituent (mostly a complement) is fronted in Latin, its place in the Old English translation is taken by the subject, which results in a V-2 clause which cannot be treated as a calque. All in all, from the 112 Latin V-2 clauses which are rendered as Old English V-2 clauses only 58 are calques; in 54 cases the order of other constituents (non-finite verbs, subjects, objects, complements, adverbials) is changed to make the clause more natural.

Nonetheless, if the translator strived to avoid the unnatural V-1 order, as was shown in the previous sections, it has to be determined why cases of "V-2 into V-1 strategy" can be detected in the examined sample. This phenomenon is, once again, related to clauses with a complex verb phrase:

52. factumque *est* **diluvium** quadraginta diebus super terram (cl. 554)
    Wæs ða geworden **micel flod** (cl. 516)
53. et mortuus *est* in Haran (cl. 855)
    & *forðferde* on Aran. (cl. 713)

The order of the finite and non-finite elements is reversed (like in ex. 52) or a complex verb phrase is substituted with a single verbal constituent (ex. 53). The modification of V-2 order into V-3 or V-F can mostly be explained by providing a personal pronoun in the translation (ex. 54); the resulting clause is longer and thus the verb is no longer the second constituent:

54. de fructu lignorum *vescemur* (cl. 194)
    Of ðæra treowa wæstme **we** *etað*. (cl. 193)
55. ecce *eicis* me hodie a facie terrae (cl. 330)
    Nu todæg **ðu** me *aflymst* (cl. 334)

In many cases we can also observe a complete modification in the order of clause constituents (ex. 55).

Latin V-F clauses and their Old English equivalents

The last word order pattern to be considered in the analysis will be V-F.[6] Table 6 indicates that the main direction of change is the same as in the previous cases – into V-2.

Table 6.6: Strategies for translating Latin V-F clauses

V-F to V-1	%	V-F to V-2	%	V-F to V-3	%	V-F to V-F	%	Σ
1	2%	25	54%	16	35%	4	9%	46[7]

The V-F order, which in Germanic languages is characteristic of subordinate clauses, is very rarely copied (4 cases), the order is clearly avoided though the data are less reliable compared to Table 4 and 5 because the V-F order is relatively infrequent in the Latin original. On the whole, the unnatural (from the Old English perspective) Latin word order is completely changed in the translation and sometimes more than one constituent needs to be moved (like in ex. 56), in other cases one change was enough (ex. 57).

56. fenestram in arca *facies* (cl. 503)
    Ðu *wyrcst* ðæron egðyrl (cl. 473)
57. **ego** protector tuus *sum* (cl. 1071)
    ic *eom* ðin wergend, (cl. 892)
58. aves autem non *divisit* (cl. 1108)
    buton þa fugelas **he** ne *todælde*. (cl. 923)

6 There are only 37 V-3 clauses in the original and their modifications are in almost all cases related to changes in the complex verb phrase; since this phenomenon has already been discussed in detail in the preceding sections, these clauses will not be presented separately.

7 Calculated for the sample of 506 main declarative clauses in 1-to-1 correspondence.

Summary

The results presented in section 4 indicate without any doubt that the mostly intuitive assumption made by scholars such as Marsden or Stanton had been confirmed by the analysis:

> His (Aelfric's) translation practice leads one to the same conclusion: his version of Genesis is flexible, idiomatic, and far from slavishly literal.
>
> (Stanton 2002: 137)

The Old English translation is by no means literal: we can observe numerous modifications in main declarative clauses which can be formulated as "rules" or very strong tendencies, violated occasionally for stylistic reasons:

a. by default, the finite verb takes the second position in the clause;
b. the finite verb takes the first position in the clause when the subject is unexpressed and the clause is conjoined;
c. the finite verb takes the third or final position in the clause when an adverbial or object is added towards the beginning of the clause (before or after the subject);
d. in clauses with a complex verb phrase the finite verb always precedes the non-finite form;
e. fronting of complements and objects is avoided, they are moved towards the end of the clause and the first place in the clause is usually taken by the subject.

All these tendencies are consistent with the rules of Old English syntax worked out on the basis of non-translated texts. There may be frequency differences related to stylistics, but the general picture of Old English word order that we get from the analysis of the Book of Genesis is very close to the standard created on the basis of other Old English texts.

Conclusions

Considering all the findings of the present study, it can safely be stated that the Old English found in the translation of the Book of Genesis can and should be treated as idiomatic form of the language, where Latin influences are very limited. The word order of most main declarative clauses examined during the study turned out to be different from the word order of corresponding Latin clauses. If the word order was copied, the clauses had to fulfil certain conditions and thus such copying should not be treated as a translation weakness. As Marsden admits:

> [...] we must then note also that 'literalism' does not necessarily involve the writing of bad, let alone incomprehensible, OE prose.
>
> (Marsden 1991: 322)

The results show, beyond any doubt, that a translation can be a good source of information about a language, provided that proper methodology is applied and strictly followed. Consistent avoidance of certain structures by a translator shows that they were unacceptable in the target language, whereas consistent copying of other patterns indicates that they must have sounded natural in the target language and they should not be treated as thoughtless calques. Naturally, basing our knowledge of Old English syntax on translations only would be unreasonable, but as additional sources of information they can still shed some light on the Anglo-Saxon past of the language and help to develop an effective methodology for the study of other Old Germanic languages, where translations are the only available option.

Acknowledgements

This research has been supported by a grant from the National Science Centre (Research project N N104 379140, "A corpus-based study of the influence of Latin syntax on the word order of selected Old English and Old High German translations" – Anna Cichosz, Jerzy Gaszewski, Piotr Pęzik).

References

Barret, C. R. (1953). Studies in the Word-order of Ælfric's Catholic Homilies and Lives of the Saints. Cambridge: W. Heffer.

Bean, M. C. (1983). The Development of Word Order Patterns in Old English. London: Croom Helm.

Cichosz, A. (2010). The Influence of Text Type on Word Order of Old Germanic Languages. Frankfurt: Peter Lang.

Davis, G. and K. A. Bernhardt (2002). Syntax of West Germanic: The Syntax of Old English and Old High German. Göppingen: Kümmerle Verlag.

Fischer, O., van Kemenade, A., Koopman, W. and W. van der Wurff (2000). The Syntax of Early English. Cambridge: Cambridge University Press.

Fleischer, J., Hinterhölzl, R. and M. Solf (2008). "Zum Quellenwert des althochdeutschen Tatian für die Syntaxforschung: Überlegungen auf der Basis von Wortstellungsphänomenen", Zeitschrift für germanistische Linguistik: 210-239.

Kohonen, V. (1978). On the Development of English Word Order in Religious Prose around 1000 and 1200 A.D. Abo: Abo Akedemi.

Marsden, R. (1991). "Ælfric as Translator: The Old English Prose Genesis", Anglia, 109: 319–358.

Marsden, Richard (2004). The Cambridge Old English Reader. Cambridge: Cambridge University Press.

Onesti, Nicoletta Francovich. 1993. "Verb Syntax in the Peterborough Chronicle (1132–54)". In English Diachronic Syntax, Gotti, M. (ed.), 89-110. Milano: Guerini Studio.
Reszkiewicz, A. (1966). Ordering of Elements in Late Old English Prose in Terms of Their Size and Structural Complexity. Wrocław/Warszawa/Kraków: Wydawnictwo PAN.
Smith, J. (1971). Word Order in the Older Germanic Dialects. Ph.D. Dissertation, University of Illinois.
Stanton, R. (2002). The Culture of Translation in Anglo-Saxon England. Cambridge: D.S. Brewer.

Applications of the Lexical Bundles Method in Historical Corpus Research[1]

Joanna Kopaczyk

Abstract

In this paper I review and explore potential applications of the lexical bundles method in studies based on historical corpora. The paper starts with the discussion of lexical bundle methodology and its range of applications in Present-Day English studies. Then I move on to the challenges posed by the special character of historical corpora for the implementation of this method in historical and diachronic studies, and continue with examples of research questions which have been addressed so far by means of lexical bundles. Special attention is paid to the investigation of repetitive patterns in early Scots legal and administrative texts. The paper closes with suggestions for further applications of lexical bundles in historical corpus linguistics.

Keywords

Lexical bundles, historical corpora, Scots

Introduction

Lexical bundles, a relatively recent tool in corpus linguistics, have been discussed from a present-day English perspective at PALC conferences and have inspired several publications in the post-conference volumes (Biber 2004, Partington and Morley 2004, Jendryczka-Wierszycka 2008, Maia *et al.* 2008). This paper aims at summarising the trends in using lexical bundles so far, with a special focus on diachronic and historical studies where this method is new. Because of this novelty factor, the range of research questions answerable by means of this methodology has not been given a comprehensive consideration yet. Therefore, my second aim is to address the research potential of this method in historical inquiries. The paper will also pay attention to the technical implementation of the lexical bundles method in historical research as it still poses obstacles and creates unresolved issues.

Defining lexical bundles

Lexical bundles as a corpus tool have been in use for just over 10 years. Altenberg (1998) is the first study where the author discusses recurrent elements of spoken English on the basis of repetitive strings automatically extracted from a corpus.

---

1 This project is funded by the individual post-doctoral Ministry of Science and Higher Education grant (2009-2012, nr N N104 014337).

This method was adopted by Biber *et al.* (1999) in their monumental *Longman Grammar of Spoken and Written English*, a major endeavour in which the label *lexical bundle* was coined and which established a firm ground for the use of this method in corpus linguistics. The extraction of lexical bundles consists in running the corpus through software which automatically identifies repetitive strings of words of a given length, *n*-grams. The material gathered in this manner is not biased towards any particular research question but provides raw data for further interpretation. Thus, the method is *corpus-driven*, rather than corpus-based (Tognini-Bonelli 2001, Lewandowska-Tomaszczyk 2005: 133), and allows the researcher to make inductive analyses.

Biber's definition of lexical bundles stressed their recurrent quality and high frequency. Automatically extracted bundles would simply repeat enough times in a corpus in exactly the same form, regardless of semantic and/or structural completeness. This is the approach adopted in the present overview, with major focus placed on:

1. actual word-forms, not lemmas,
2. sequences of word-forms, disregarding their grammatical status,
3. "frequent, recurrent combinations of word forms" (Biber 2009: 281).

Lexical bundles are thus retrieved solely on the basis of frequency,[2] which lies at the heart of "a radical corpus-driven approach to formulaic language" (Biber 2009: 281).

Lexical bundles in Present-Day English research: An overview

Linguistic bundles enjoy widening popularity in present-day corpus research, which is best visible in the large numbers of studies employing this methodology (cf. the Corpus Linguistic conferences Liverpool in 2009 – fourteen papers, and in Birmingham in 2011 – ten papers). The most rampant fields where lexical bundles have been employed are the following:

---

2 Some scholars have claimed that frequency should not be the only criterion in bundle retrieval. They argue that frequency-based inquiry ignores the fact that all lexical strings appear in more typical and in less typical contexts and in the vicinity of specific words. Therefore the methodology has been expanded with Mutual Information [MI] scores, keyness-based counts (based on likelihood scores), concgrams (Cheng et al. 2009) and psycholinguistic salience parameters (Simpson-Vlach and Ellis 2010). Nevertheless, Biber (2009) shows that MI scores, keyness and other such additions render multi-word collocations rather than lexical bundles "proper", which are simply frequency-based multi-word formulaic sequences, regardless of contextual parameters. Both are valid research goals but they stem from different research questions.

1. corpus-based grammars of contemporary English (Biber et al. 1999, 2007; Carter and McCarthy 2006),
2. academic discourse: identifying typical features of academic discourse, functional units in classroom discourse, comparing students' writing to professional writing; e.g. Cortes 2004),
3. identification and extraction of multi-word sequences for pedagogic purposes, creating teaching materials (Biber et al. 1999), machine translation, and language processing;
4. comparative genre analysis (Stubbs and Barth 2003), comparative analysis of disciplines in English for Academic Purposes (Hyland 2008),
5. specialised discourse features (structural and functional): political discourse (Partington and Morley 2004), legal discourse (Goźdź-Roszkowski 2006);

Inquiries using the lexical bundles method go beyond the study of English and have also addressed Spanish (Butler 2003, Cortes 2008) and German as a foreign language (Krummes *et al.* 2011) as well as metaphors in Portuguese (Berber Sardinha 2011). In general, studies based on lexical bundles most often have pedagogical motivations. They frequently concern differences between spoken and written registers (e.g. Biber 1997; Biber 2004; Biber, Conrad and Cortes 2004; Biber and Barbieri 2007). They also aim to discover units of meaning larger than a single lexical item in specific discourse situations, and explore the mental processing of such units.

Lexical bundles in historical and diachronic studies

Problems for historical research

Corpus size

Applying the same methodology to historical corpora poses at least three major problems. The first one is linked to the relatively small size of historical corpora. Due to external causes which influence the availability of historical texts in a more or less random fashion, a historical linguist is always facing the "bad data" problem. In their research into lexical bundles in speech-based registers, Culpeper and Kytö (2010) used c.300,000-word samples from plays and trial proceedings respectively. One may ponder on how such corpus size relates to modern corpus-driven queries on millions of words of text (e.g. c.5mln words each for spoken and written registers in Biber *et al.* 1999), and whether the findings from both areas may be taken to illuminate respective results. In other words, one should be careful in constructing teleological interpretations. It is tempting to move from a state of affairs established for a historical period towards another state of affairs at a later stage, disregarding the fact that much more material becomes available and searchable as the time progresses.

The size of the corpus also has influence on the cut-off points for lexical bundles which "count". Every researcher sets his or her own, largely intuitive parameters for how many instances of a given string will count as a lexical bundle. In a corpus of 0.5mln words the cut-off point will be different than in a 40mln words corpus, or, conversely, the same cut-off point would render significantly different pools of data depending on the corpus size. Table 1 presents a useful summary of how the thresholds have been set in several selected studies based on lexical bundles.

Table 7.1: Lexical bundle cut-off points in selected studies (1998-2011) (Kopaczyk forthcoming)

Author(s) and date	Type of texts in the corpus	(sub)Corpus length (words)	Length of the selected bundle	Nr of instances at cut-off point
Altenberg (1998)	PDE: spoken	0.5mln	1- to 8-grams	10
Biber *et al.* (1999)	PDE: conversation, fiction, press, academic discourse	40mln	3- to 6-grams	10/5per 1mln in ≥5 texts
Biber *et al.* (2003)	PDE: conversation, academic discourse	7mln+5.3mln	4-5-grams	20 per 1mln
Biber *et al.* (2004)	T2K-SWAL; spoken and written academic language	2mln	4-grams	40 per 1mln
Cortes (2004)	PDE: academic vs student writing	2mln vs 0.9mln	4-grams	20 per mln in ≥5 texts
Goźdź-Roszkowski (2006)	PDE: legal discourse	0.3mln	4-grams	15
Biber and Barbieri (2007)	PDE: T2K-SWAL + LSWE subsection: spoken and written academic language	c.7.9mln	4-grams	40 per 1mln
Hyland (2008)	English for Academic Purposes	3.5mln	4-grams	20 per 1mln in ≥10% of texts
Culpeper and Kytö (2010)	EModE plays EModE trials[3]	0.22mln 0.25mln	3-grams	10
Kopaczyk (2011)	Middle Scots legal texts	0.6mln	3- to 8-grams	≥10 in ≥10texts

3 Two genres from the CED: EModE trials (252,607 words) and EModE plays (221,196 words) plus comparative PDE corpora of British trial proceedings and drama, not easily accessible, but through the BNC – 126,271 words of trials and 38,190 words of direct speech from plays (2010: 111-112).

Clearly, historical inquiries are conducted on the basis of smaller corpora than the majority of their PDE counterparts. If one wants to achieve a more comprehensive coverage of historical material and conflate several relevant corpora, as was the case in the study on recurrent elements of Scots legal discourse (see 4.3. below), one should bear in mind the compilation methodologies of respective corpora.

Editorial intervention

Historical corpora are built out of digitised versions of texts whose original composition may have relied on various channels and modes. The input for digitisation may have been handwritten (as is the case with the Edinburgh Corpus of Older Scots [ECOS], see 4.3. below), printed (e.g. Early English Books Online), or printed in modern times on the basis of an earlier manuscript or early print (e.g. the Helsinki Corpus material [HC]). In each case, corpus creation methodology has specific repercussions. The corpora which are transcribed directly from manuscripts exhibit a variety of conventions to represent the complex reality of a handwritten text. The corpora which are based on, for example, nineteenth-century editions of early prints or manuscripts may or may not have been checked against the original texts by the corpus compilers. Not all historical corpora are tagged for parts of speech or other structural units, which makes it impossible at this stage to extract PoS-grams or congrams. The extraction of lexical bundles proper is possible, although not free of methodological problems.

This varied character of original input carries potential for different degrees of editorial intervention and a whole range of editorial conventions. The consequences for the lexical bundles method are two-fold: on the one hand, one should consider the problem of editorial procedures while extracting bundles from a historical electronic corpus, and on the other – exercise caution in drawing comparisons between different corpora on the basis of automatically extracted repetitive strings.

Spelling variants

Historical corpora abound in spelling variants. The study of early graphemic systems and their relationship with the phonological systems lies at the centre of many historical inquiries. The corpora are usually compiled with a view to study language *change* on different levels, often on the basis of spelling variants, which may be interpreted as, for instance, indicating the spread or dialectal presence of a particular phonological trait, or pointing towards various stages of grammaticalization (as in *pray thee* vs *prithee*). The study of syntactic or pragmatic features on the basis of historical corpora is usually less sensitive to the preservation of original spelling conventions of the input text, which is why even a large degree of editorial intervention does not impede a systematic inquiry.

In order for the lexical bundles method to work and render reliable results, spelling variation must be reduced to the minimum. This is a crucial issue in extracting repetitive sequences from historical texts because we want to make sure that the software picks out every instance of a sequence of the same word-forms not on a graphemic level, but on a lexico-syntactic level. As in historical linguistics the major interest focusses on texts from before spelling standardisation, and the editorial conventions may have already blurred some original spelling distinctions to various degrees, spelling in the corpus should be standardised artificially before the bundle extraction.

Manual spelling unification would be a truly benedictine job. This problem was first recognised by the Lancaster team who have developed a tool for artificial spelling regularisation – Variant Detector (VARD) (Rayson, Archer, Baron and Smith 2007, Baron and Rayson 2008). The program is currently available as VARD2.3 (http://www.comp.lancs.ac.uk/~barona/vard2/). The software uses a modern English dictionary as an underlying pool of target spellings against which spelling divergence is decided. This is problematic if one wants to apply VARD to a language different than (early) modern English. Indeed, the newest version of the program can be manually taught to recognize and replace variants, but to work properly it still requires a dictionary of target forms, and the default target dictionary is based on modern English. So far, no better solution has been proposed (see, however, 4.3. below).

Historical and diachronic studies so far

Regardless of the limitations described above, the lexical bundles method clearly has research potential for historical linguistics. First of all, the extracted strings can be analysed from a purely structural point of view, in order to show which types of phrases tend to be most fixed and repetitive. Moreover, due to the corpus-driven nature of the bundles, we can also observe to what extent fixed sequences do or do not form full phrasal or clausal patterns. Secondly, lexical bundles have been used to investigate functional characteristics of particular historical discourse situations on the basis of the most recurrent patterns. The best framework to apply in the functional interpretation is a continuation of Halliday's work on register and discourse functions (1978). Individual adjustments are usually necessary depending on the kind of texts one works with, as is the case in present-day functional interpretations using the same Hallidayan framework (e.g. Biber, Conrad and Cortes 2003).

Spoken discourse

The earliest application of lexical bundles in historical corpus research was the investigation of Early Modern English dialogues by Culpeper and Kytö (2002), a pilot study for a chapter in their recent monograph on spoken interaction as dialogue (Culpeper and Kytö 2010). The lexical bundles have been employed to highlight orality features observable in written, or rather, printed texts. The study has addressed the problems posed by the special character of historical data outlined above. For spelling unification, the authors decided to employ VARD and its dictionary of modern target forms. Their cut-off thresholds are presented in Table 1 (above).

The discussion of findings should be read in the context of the exhaustive methodological background presented in their book, concerning the retrieval of the features of spoken discourse from written genres. The lexical bundles are only one among the corpus tools used for this investigation. Perhaps this is why the ultimate discussion centres on the relatively small number of extracted constructions – top-twenty bundle types in the whole Corpus of English Dialogues (Culpeper and Kytö 2010: 114). The bundles are given a structural as well as functional interpretation, and are compared against PDE data from Biber *et al.* (1999), with some degree of caution as to the differences between modern and historical lexical bundle searches, outlined above.

Genre-specific features and specialised discourse

Lexical bundles have been employed in the study of textual standardisation, i.e. in establishing when and how specific structural and functional elements of a given text type or genre emerged or stabilised. This kind of inquiry links to the research by Culpeper and Kytö outlined above. This methodology is also employed in a diachronic comparison of religious discourse by Shrefler (2011), who compares the readability of Reformation Bible versus the 21st c. Bible, designed to meet the needs of the modern reader. Other genres, also literary, may be explored by means of lexical bundles, as suggested by Scott, whose project on characterisation and plot construction in the Shakespeare corpus is in progress, "not expected to conclude for many years" (2009).

Linguistic standardisation

The inquiries into genre characteristics lead to the assessment of linguistic stability in different genres. This line of investigation was followed by Kytö and Smitterberg (2006) on the basis of nineteenth-century speech-related and written genres. Similarly, Bürki (2011) is working on identifying stable lexico-syntactic patterns in a diachronic corpus of 20th-century Swiss-German texts. Also the project on textual standardisation in medieval and early modern legal discourse in Scotland (see below) stems from the recognition of the link between frequency of repeated strings and the expected, or even standard, genre characteristics.

Working with Scots corpora and lexical bundles (Kopaczyk 2011)

In my project, lexical bundles are employed to explore textual standardisation,[4] whereby specific lexico-syntactic patterns recur and thus create a recognisable text type in a given discourse setting. The texts in the corpus are written in Scots and come from the legal domain; these are burgh records, notarial protocols, statutes and other official and administrative texts. The corpus is a compilation of three available resources, comprising legal and administrative texts in early Scots: the Edinburgh Corpus of Older Scots [ECOS], the relevant parts of the Helsinki Corpus of Older Scots [HCOS], and an unpublished transcript of a burgh court book from the south-west of Scotland [WgtCtBk] (see References and Table 1 for word counts and thresholds).

As signalled above, there is no freely available tool for spelling unification when dealing with a language different than (early) modern English. For the Scots project, a list of variants for each spelling in the lexicon of the whole corpus had to be prepared manually,[5] and then this list was uploaded into VARD to serve as the base for automatised spelling unification. The problem of editorial intervention in corpus design was also encountered: ECOS had a very idiosyncratic tagging for part of speech and some semantic features, while HCOS and WgtCtBk had none. Therefore, working with all three required stripping all the texts of tagging. This procedure was necessary before the lexical bundles could be extracted from clean text files.

One of the outcomes of this investigation is the pool of long lexical bundles (8-grams), which recur in the corpus with substantial frequency (Table 2). Repetition of such long strings with exactly the same content in exactly the same order can hardly be attributed to chance, and has been taken to indicate textual standardisation. In general, the longer the bundle, the more formulaic it becomes.

4 On the distinction between extra-linguistically determined language standardisation and the internal linguistic standardisation, see Kopaczyk (2011a) and (forthcoming).

5 An automatic conversion check-list could be designed but due to the large degree of editorial idiosyncracies of the three corpora, as well as the Scots graphemic system of the time (Kopaczyk 2011c and forthcoming), it was decided that a manual compilation should be more reliable.

Table 7.2: Top-20 8-grams in the Scots corpus (Kopaczyk forthcoming).

Rank	8-gram[6]	tokens[7]	files[8]	FF[9]
1	*chalans for ye wrangus haldin fra him of*	297	146	100
2	*ye yhere of oure lord a thousande four*	120	104	76
3	*kend til all men be thir present letteris*	131	129	68
4	*ye yhere of god a thousande four hundereth*	117	114	66
5	*be it kend til all men be thir*	126	126	66
6	*it kend til all men be thir present*	116	114	65
7	*yhere of oure lord a thousande four hundereth*	94	89	61
8	*til all men be thir present letteris me*	91	91	55
9	*chalans for ye wrangus haldin fra hir of*	45	34	50
10	*that tyme and than incontenent ye said balze*	38	28	46
11	*in that tyme and than incontenent ye said*	37	28	44
12	*of ye monath of juli ye yhere of*	37	29	42
13	*balze in that tyme and than incontenent ye*	28	15	42
14	*day of ye monath of juli ye yhere*	36	28	42
15	*of ye monath of may ye yhere of*	39	32	41
16	*day of ye monath of may ye yhere*	38	31	41
17	*ye yhere of god a thousande v hundereth*	52	49	41
18	*yhere yhere of god a thousande v hundereth and*	52	49	41
19	*sutis callit ye curt effermit and absentis demyt*	60	60	40
20	*ye quhilk day ye sutis callit ye curt*	57	56	40

Difficult to classify structurally as they are, the 8-grams collected from the corpus point towards most recurrent functional elements of legal texts in medieval and early modern Scotland. The most formulaic fragment extracted by means of the lexical bundle method is the accusation of theft or wrongful seizure (1), clearly a frequent crime brought to court at that time (cf. (9), where the goods were stolen from a woman). Also the date of the document comes across as formulaic, be it in

6 All 8-gram types above the threshold (see Table 1) = 321.

7 All 8-gram tokens above the threshold (see Table 1) = 7,098.

8 Nr of files in the combined corpus = 1818.

9 FF stands for Formulaicity Factor, a measure of formulaicity based on the normalised frequency of occurrences, the number of texts in which a given bundle occurs, and the relative weighting of these two parameters, where the first acoounts for 75% of the overall score (Kopaczyk forthcoming). The FFs for individual bundles stand in relation to the most formulaic bundle of a given length.

reference to the year (2, 4, 7, 17, 18; notice the two competing options of formulaic reference to divine authority) or month (12, 14, 15, 16). Another functional element is the directive speech act composed of overlapping bundles in (3, 5, 6, 8), announcing a legal act and binding the audience to comply with it. The focal element of the overlapping fragments in (10, 11, 13) is the sequence of events, signalled by the adverb *incontenent* 'immediately after', which serves as a textual organisational device. Finally, the list closes in another formulaic speech act, a declaration of the opened court and calling the suits (19, 20). This short overview of findings from a much larger project reveals the functional preferences for lexico-syntactic fixing. It points towards genre and specialised discourse characteristics and, what should be borne in mind, draws attention to the extralinguistic conditions in which the texts were produced. These circumstances should always be given a thorough investigation prior to any functional interpretation of recurrent elements in texts.

Further research potential

Lexical bundles as a subcorpus

Because of the corpus-driven character of lexical bundles, they may constitute a systematically extracted subcorpus, from which further structures can be derived. In PDE studies, the researchers who applied further criteria for bundle extraction, e.g. psychological salience, were in fact drawing further subcorpora of multi-word collocations from a general pool of lexical bundles (see fn.2 above). For my purpose, bundles were especially useful in extracting formulaic bi- and multinomials from historical Scottish legal texts in a thorough manner (Kopaczyk forthcoming). If the goal is to identify all potential bi- and multinomials, the researcher may not (and usually does not) know in advance which specific lexemes make up such coordinated structures. It is impossible to build specific lexeme-based, or word-form-based queries for every type of construction. With lexical bundles this problem is solved because already at the outset there is a pool of formulaic constructions, on the basis of which further extraction can be carried out, e.g. by looking at the coordinating device (most frequently *and* or *or*).

Authorship investigations

Socially-oriented historical linguistics pays attention to the authors of historical texts. It appreciates the fact that these authors select specific variants from a range of possibilities, thus infoming us about their own provenance, social status, style, education level, etc. Lexical bundles may bear testimony to the individual linguistic profiles of specific authors (which is useful in modern forensic investigations), or to the shared linguistic practices by specific groups of people. As I have shown in a recent paper (Kopaczyk 2011b), the community of burgh clerks and notaries in medieval and early Renaissance Scotland may be identified as a discourse community not only on the basis of extralinguistic criteria (Swales 1990), but also on the basis of commonly employed textual patterns. These patterns, extracted with the lexical bundle methodology, point to textual and discourse standardisation and derive from several interrelated sources: Latin legal formulas, copying the predecessors' wording and using their protocol books as blueprints, and the oral formulaic residue in legal discourse. The stable fragments of texts serve as memory aids and point towards growing uniformity in drawing legal documents across the country.

Stylistic investigations

Similarly to Scott's long-term project on the basis of the Shakespeare corpus (see 4.2.2. above), lexical bundles may be employed to reveal stylistic patterns in literary and utilitarian texts from various periods. This kind of research has not yet been attempted on a larger scale.

Concluding remarks

This overview has summarised trends in the application of lexical bundles in corpus linguistics, in an attempt to highlight the research potential of the automatic, corpus-driven extraction of lexico-syntactic repetitive strings for historical linguistics. The lexical bundles may render new findings in this subdiscipline as they have done in PDE studies. Even though PDE applications are mainly centered around language pedagogy, in historical inquiries the same tool may help to establish genre characteristics, standardisation patterns and forensic profiles, as well as become a subcorpus for other searches. There are certain technical problems to be borne in mind and to be overcome, which is worth trying in view of the advantages to be gained.

Corpora used in the project

Williamson, K. (comp.) (2008). The Edinburgh Corpus of Older Scots. University of Edinburgh. [ECOS]

Meurman-Solin, A. (comp.) (1993). The Helsinki Corpus of Older Scots. University of Helsinki. [HCOS]

Wigton Burgh Court Book; 1512-1534. Unpublished transcript by A. Truckell, digitised by J. Kopaczyk. Dumfries Archive Centre. [WgtCtBk]

References

Baron, A. (2010). VARD 2 Homepage.
Available at: http://www.comp.lancs.ac.uk/~barona/home/

Baron, A. and P. Rayson. (2008). VARD2: "A Tool for Dealing with Spelling Variation in Historical Corpora." Proceedings of the Postgraduate Conference in Corpus Linguistics, Aston University, Birmingham, 22 May 2008.

Berber Sardinha, T. (2011). "A Tool for Finding Metaphors in Corpora Using Lexical Patterns", paper presented at Corpus Linguistics 2011, Birmingham, UK.

Biber, D. (1997). "Lexical Bundles in Spoken and Written Discourse: What the Grammar Books Don't Tell You". In An Update on Grammar: How It Is Learnt – How It Is Taught, Gerome, S. B. (ed.), 4-8. Paris: TESOL France.

Biber, D. (2004). "Lexical Bundles in Academic Speech and Writing". Practical Applications in Language Corpora (PALC 2003), Lewandowska-Tomaszczyk, B. (ed.), 165-178. Hamburg: Peter Lang.

Biber, D. and F. Barbieri (2007). "Lexical Bundles in University Spoken and Written Registers", English for Specific Purposes 26: 263-286.

Biber, D., Conrad, S. and V. Cortes (2003). "Lexical Bundles in Speech and Writing: An Initial Taxonomy". In Corpus Linguistics by the Lune. A Festschrift for Geoffrey Leech, Wilson, P., Rayson, P. and McEnery, T. (eds.), 71-92. Frankfurt am Main / New York: Peter Lang.

Biber, D., Conrad, S. and V. Cortes (2004). "If You Look At... Lexical Bundles in University Teaching and Textbooks", Applied Linguistics 25(3): 371-405.

Biber, D. et al. (1999). Longman Grammar of Spoken and Written English. London: Longman.

Bürki, A. (2009). "Multi-Word Sequences in Motion: on the Extent and Speed of Diachronic Change in Patterns of German (Work in Progress Report)". In Proceedings of the Corpus Linguistics Conference CL2009, Mahlberg, M., Gonzáles-Diaz, V., and Smith, C. (eds.), pages?. University of Liverpool, UK

Cheng, W. et al. (2009). "Uncovering the Extent of the Phraseological Tendency: Towards a Systematic Analysis of Concgrams", Applied Linguistics 30(2): 236-252.

Conrad, S. and D. Biber (2004). "The Frequency and Use of Lexical Bundles in Conversation and Academic Prose." Lexicographica: International Annual for Lexicography 20: 56-71.

Cortes, V. (2002). "Lexical Bundles in Freshman Compositions". In Using Corpora to Explore Linguistic Variation, Reppen, R., Fitzmaurice, S. M. and Biber, D. (eds.), 131-146. Amsterdam: John Benjamins.

Cortes, V. (2004). "Lexical Bundles in Published and Student Writing in History and Biology", English for Specific Purposes 23(4): 397-423.

Cortes, V. (2008). "A Comparative Analysis of Lexical Bundles in Academic History Writing in English and Spanish", Corpora 3(1): 43-57.

Culpeper, J. and M. Kytö. (2002). "Lexical Bundles in Early Modern English Dialogues. A Window into the Speech-Related Language of the Past". In Sounds, Words, Texts and Change. Selected Papers from 11 ICEHL, Santiago de Compostela 7-11 September 2000, Fanego, T. et al. (eds.), 45-63. Amsterdam / Philadelphia: John Benjamins.

Culpeper, J. and M. Kytö. (2010). Early Modern English Dialogues: Spoken Interaction as Writing. Cambridge: Cambridge University Press.

Ellis, N. C. and R. Simpson-Vlach (2009). "Formulaic Language in Native Speakers: Triangulating Psycholinguistics, Corpus Linguistics, and Education", Corpus Linguistics and Linguistic Theory 5(1): 61-78.

Halliday, M. A. K. (1978). Language as a Social Semiotic. The Social Interpretation of Language and Meaning. London: Edward Arnold.

Hyland, K. (2008). "As Can Be Seen: Lexical Bundles and Disciplinary Variation", English for Specific Purposes 27: 4-21.

Jendryczka-Wierszycka, J. (2008). "Vagueness in Polglish Speech". In Corpus Linguistics, Computer Tools, and Applications – State of the Art. PALC 2007, Lewandowska-Tomaszczyk, B. (ed.), 599-615. Frankfurt a/Main: Peter Lang.

Kopaczyk, J. (2011a). "Standaryzacja tekstów w perspektywie historycznej. Analiza zbitek leksykalnych" [Text-type standardisation in a historical perspective: Lexical bundles]. In Metodologie językoznawstwa. Od genów języka do tekstów [Linguistic methodologies: From language genes to texts], Stalmaszczyk, P. (ed.). Łódź: Wydawnictwo Uniwersytetu Łódzkiego.

Kopaczyk, J. (2011b). "Pisarze miejscy i notariusze a standaryzacja tekstów administracyjnych i prawnych w Szkocji" [Burgh clerks and notaries – working towards text-type standardisation in administrative and legal Scots], paper presented at Communicative communities: the Memorial Conference for prof. Ludwik Zabrocki, Poznań 2011.

Kopaczyk, J. (2011c). "Scots Historical Corpora and the Lexical Bundles Method", paper presented at New Methods in Historical Corpora, Manchester, UK, 2011.

Kopaczyk, J. (Forthcoming). Standardising legal discourse. The language of Scottish burghs 1380-1560. publisher?

Krummes, C., Jaworska, S. and A. Ensslin (2011). "The Use of Discourse-Structuring Sequences by Advanced Learners of German: Corpus-driven Investigations", paper presented at Corpus Linguistics 2011, Birmingham, UK.

Kytö, M. and E. Smitterberg (2006). "19th-century English: An Age of Stability of a Period of Change?" In Corpus-based Studies of Diachronic English, Facchinetti, R. and Rissanen, M. (eds.), 199-230. Bern: Peter Lang.

Lewandowska-Tomaszczyk, B. (2005). "Analiza języka z zastosowaniem korpusu". In Podstawy językoznawstwa korpusowego, Lewandowska-Tomaszczyk, B. (ed.), 133-173. Łódź: Wydawnictwo Uniwersytetu Łódzkiego.

Maia, B., Silva, R., Barreiro, A. and C. Frois (2008). "N-grams in Search of Theories". In Corpus Linguistics, Computer Tools, and Applications – State of the Art. PALC 2007, Lewandowska-Tomaszczyk, B. (ed.), 71-84. Frankfurt a/Main: Peter Lang.

Partington, A. and J. Morley (2004). "At the Heart of Ideology: Word and Cluster / Bundle Frequency in Political Debate". In Practical Applications in Language and Computers (PALC 2003), Lewandowska-Tomaszczyk, B. (ed.), 179-192. Bern: Lang.

Rayson, P., Archer, D., Baron, A. and N. Smith (2007). "Tagging Historical Corpora – the Problem of Spelling Variation", Proceedings of Digital Historical Corpora, Dagstuhl-Seminar 06491, International Conference and Research Center for Computer Science, Schloss Dagstuhl, Wadern, Germany, December 3rd-8th 2006.

Shrefler, N. (2011). "Lexical Bundles and German Bibles", Literary and Linguistic Computing 26(1): 89-106.

Simpson-Vlach, R. and N. C. Ellis (2010). "An Academic Formulas List: New Methods in Phraseology Research", Applied Linguistics 31(4): 487-512.

Swales, J. 1990. Genre Analysis. Cambridge: Cambridge University Press,

Tognini-Bonelli, E. (2001). Corpus Linguistics at Work. Amsterdam: John Benjamins.

Tracy-Ventura, N., Biber, D. and V. Cortes (2007). "Lexical Bundles in Spanish Speech and Writing". In Working with Spanish Corpora. London: Continuum Parodi, G. (ed.), 217-231.

Talking about Europe in British, Italian and Polish TV News Programmes

Silvia de Candia, Mikołaj Deckert and Marco Venuti

Abstract

The present study investigates the role of "accessed voices" in British, Italian and Polish TV news reports through the analysis of a comparable multilingual corpus consisting of transcripts of TV news programmes (both public and commercial channels). All news stories included in the corpus have been divided into items related to 'Europe' on the one hand, and 'other' (both domestic news and international non-European stories) on the other. We will focus on the role of attribution, mainly drawing on the Appraisal System (Martin and White 2005), in utterances by "accessed voices", and the rhetorical effects deriving from such positioning. In order to carry out the comparison, the corpus will be queried exploiting the XML annotation which allows for detailed comparisons between countries and voices.

A quantitative analysis will make it possible to compare different uses of sources in TV news programmes when news items deal with Europe vis-à-vis other topics. The comparison of TV news programmes in the three countries will show the way different forms of attribution are used when Europe related topics are dealt with. The quantitative analysis will be complemented with a more qualitative approach to a set of news items on climate change which will help shed light on the differences in attitude towards Europe across the three countries.

Keywords

IntUne TV corpus, accessed voice, keywords.

Introduction

News programmes present a very specific structure with specific participants' roles (Hartley 1982). These include "accessed voices" such as legitimated persons (LPs) – experts and public figures – and ordinary people (VOXs). These voices play different roles in the reports (Montgomery 2007) mutually affecting the news reception by the audience.

The study of "accessed voices" in TV news reports can shed light on the perception of EU institutions by citizens, since they still regard TV as the most important source of information on European matters (Eurobarometer 74, 2001). Our analysis is based on a set of quantitative and comparative observations across Italian, Polish and UK data, with special regard to the voices of LPs and VOXs in order to investigate the overall effect that they can play in the representation of EU institutions and European countries. Our analysis is thus concerned with their language in the context of European news.

Data and Methodology

The present study is based on the analysis of the IntUne corpus, a collection of media texts compiled over two months in 2007, as part of a Sixth Framework European project, "Integrated and United: a Quest for Citizenship in an ever closer Europe"[1]

Corpus description

The linguistic observations made in this paper are concerned with the Italian, Polish and UK television sub-corpora only. News programmes were collected and orthographically transcribed from the evening RAI Tg1 and Canale 5 Tg5 in Italy, the evening TVP1 and Polsat in Poland and the evening BBC News and ITV1 News in the UK, from 12 February to 6 April 2007. These subcorpora include both public service broadcasters, RAI, TVP1 and BBC, and commercial ones, Canale 5, Polsat and ITV, as they cover the popular sources of television news information in the three countries. Data collection was not based on a prearranged selection of news topics, therefore anything that was reported over the two months of data collection was included and a detailed catalogue of the news items included was drawn up afterwards; the catalogue was used in the annotation process to make important contextual information available during the analysis, as the following section will make clear.

Table 8.1: Partition size in terms of running words and news items

Country	Running words	Total news items	European news items	
Italy	290,469	1,456	135	(9.27%)
Poland	250,352	764	57	(7.46%)
UK	322,745	962	63	(6.55%)

The Italian, Polish and UK TV sub-corpora of the IntUne data consist of 290,469, 250,352, and 322,745 words respectively. Table 1 also shows the number of news items and the percentage of news items concerning Europe. Even if it is not directly within the scope of the present analysis, it is worth noting that the Italian sub-corpus displays the highest number of news items relating to Europe, and also the highest number of news items, hinting at a possibly specific organisation of the news programme compared to the other two countries.

As described earlier in this section, our linguistic observations are based on a set of comparisions across TV news participants aimed at highlighting differences between journalists and accessed voices. Table 2 shows word distribution in the different topics for speaker roles. In Italian news items about Europe, journalists

1 For detailed information about the research project visit http://www.intune.it (last accessed 31 August 2011).

speak 82.53 per cent of the total number of words in the Italian corpus while accessed voices talk represents 17.47 per cent of European news talk, the lowest percentage in the corpus. In Polish news programmes journalists speak 73.55 per cent compared to the 26.45 per cent of words by accessed voices, the highest rate in the three sub-corpora. In the British sub-corpus journalists were found to speak 77.84 per cent in European news items compared to 22.16 per cent of accessed voices news talk. As with previous statistics, it seems that the Italian sub-corpus is the one with the most clearly marked difference in the organisation of media talk.

Table 8.2: Word distribution in European news and "other" topics according to speaker roles

Country	role and topic	number of words	% according to total	% according to European news
Italy	Accessed voices, "Europe"	4,417	1.52	17.47
	Accessed voices "other"	60,399	20.79	
	Journalists, "Europe"	20,851	7.18	82.53
	Journalists, 'other'	204,802	70.51	
Poland	Accessed voices, "Europe"	4,225	1.69	26.45
	Accessed voices "other"	74,731	29.85	
	Journalists, "Europe"	11,761	4.70	73.55
	Journalists, 'other'	159,635	63.76	
UK	Accessed voices, "Europe"	5,966	1.85	22.16
	Accessed voices "other"	67,074	20.78	
	Journalists, "Europe"	20,983	6.50	77.84
	Journalists, 'other'	228,722	70.87	

Keywords identification

In order to highlight differences between speaker roles we relied on keyword analysis as our starting point. Keywords analysis is a debated issue in corpus linguistics literature. According to Stubbs (2010) there are three main loosely related uses of the term 'keyword'. The first one sees keywords as pivotal elements in the organisation of cultural domains. The second use is statistical: "keywords are words which are significantly more frequent in a sample of text than would be expected, given their frequency in a large general reference corpus" (Stubbs 2010: 25). The third use is corpus driven, focusing on phraseological patterns in relation with extended units of meaning.

In our study we adopted a statistical approach which differs from the one presented by Scott. At a recent conference, Kilgarriff (2009) presented a simple yet flexible way of identifying keywords, which enables the researcher to easily focus on higher or lower frequency words, depending on the research being carried out. It is this approach that we followed. Due to the relatively small size of the sub-corpora, we opted for a procedure which highlighted also low frequency words.

Quantitative data analysis

Italian news programmes

The keywords generated for this comparisions, included in Table 3, illustrate an interesting usage of self-refence in the Italian LP and VOX talk via a number of personal pronouns such as *io, noi, mi, ci* ('I', 'we', 'me', 'us').

Table 8.3: Italian accessed voice keywords vs. JOURNALISTS in European news

n	word	key	freq.	n	word	key	freq.	n	word	key	freq.
1	credo	3.33	2.49	19	tutti	2.00	4.07	37	pace	1.59	1.81
2	quindi	3.29	3.39	20	essere	1.98	3.17	38	sono	1.56	8.83
3	molto	3.01	5.20	21	che	1.93	32.36	39	stata	1.55	2.94
4	ho	3.01	3.17	22	quella	1.89	2.26	40	cui	1.55	2.26
5	perché	2.85	5.43	23	questo	1.87	4.75	41	altro	1.54	1.58
6	noi	2.81	3.17	24	fare	1.86	1.58	42	questa	1.52	3.17
7	io	2.62	3.39	25	stessa	1.86	1.58	43	ci	1.50	3.62
8	occorre	2.58	1.58	26	politica	1.85	3.62	44	un	1.50	17.65
9	mi	2.53	2.26	27	capo	1.80	1.58	45	europea	1.49	2.94
10	siamo	2.28	2.26	28	politico	1.80	1.58	46	avere	1.46	1.58
11	verità	2.26	1.58	29	paese	1.78	1.81	47	uniti	1.46	1.58
12	grande	2.07	2.26	30	sia	1.78	1.81	48	vita	1.46	1.58
13	italiani	2.07	2.26	31	c	1.73	2.49	49	quello	1.43	1.81
14	non	2.02	17.88	32	paesi	1.73	1.81	50	fatto	1.42	1.58
15	abbiamo	2.01	2.26	33	europa	1.72	4.30	51	italiana	1.38	1.58
16	può	2.01	2.26	34	era	1.67	3.39	52	qui	1.38	1.58
17	vuole	2.00	1.58	35	nell	1.63	1.81	53	nel	1.35	4.98
18	se	2.00	4.07	36	dire	1.59	1.58	54	unione	1.35	2.04

In terms of lexical items, the keywords list a number of nouns and adjectives mainly relating to 'Europe' (*Europa, Europea, Unione Europea*) and to the broad Italian political background, *italiano/italiana, Capo (di Stato), Politica* ('Italian', 'Head of State', 'Politics'). As far as the markers of evaluations are concerned, keywords highlight an interesting usage of graduation words (Martin and White 2005) such as *molto, grande, tutti* ('much', 'big', 'everybody') and an outstanding occurrence of the verb form *credo* ('I believe'). In particular, the outstanding frequency of the verb *credo* suggests that accessed voices use more explicit expressions of personal opinion compared to jounalists.

Although the contrastive analysis between journalist and non-journalist talk highlighted a number of interesting aspects about the European news discourse, a closer analysis was needed to identify differences across LP and VOX talk. Tables 4 and 5 illustrate the keywords in LPs and VOXs respectively.

Table 4 shows a frequent usage of lexical items *italiana, politico, maggioranza, politiche, conferenza* ('Italian', 'politician', 'majority', 'policies', 'conference') which give insights into the aboutness of this sub-corpus (Scott and

Tribble 2006: 55-72), mainly referring to the political scenario in Italy. Explicit markers of evaluation do not seem to be an outstanding feature of the LPs' talk apart from a limited number of graduation words *solo, nessuno* ('only', 'nobody') and the use of the adjective *importante* ('important'). An interesting usage of the modal verb forms *dovrebbe, dovremmo* ('it/we should') was also identified as particularly frequent in LP discourse.

Table 8.4: Italian LP keywords vs. VOX in European news

N	word	key	freq.	N	word	key	freq.	N	word	key	freq.
1	nella	14.02	13.02	19	conferenza	4.49	3.49	37	mia	3.32	2.32
2	italiana	10.07	9.07	20	soprattutto	4.49	3.49	38	nessuno	3.32	2.32
3	o	9.83	8.83	21	sul	4.49	3.49	39	politiche	3.32	2.32
4	politico	9.60	8.60	22	continuare	4.25	3.25	40	principi	3.32	2.32
5	cioè	9.37	8.37	23	così	4.25	3.25	41	abarth	3.09	2.09
6	d	9.37	8.37	24	croato	4.25	3.25	42	alema	3.09	2.09
7	stessa	7.28	6.28	25	verso	4.25	3.25	43	all	3.09	2.09
8	uniti	6.81	5.81	26	dello	4.02	3.02	44	questi	3.09	2.09
9	due	6.58	5.58	27	dobbiamo	4.02	3.02	45	allora	2.86	1.86
10	loro	5.88	4.88	28	È	3.79	2.79	46	altra	2.86	1.86
11	possono	5.88	4.88	29	ed	3.79	2.79	47	andare	2.86	1.86
12	vita	5.88	4.88	30	mi	3.56	33.01	48	area	2.86	1.86
13	dovrebbe	5.42	4.42	31	importante	3.56	2.56	49	avevo	2.86	1.86
14	prima	5.18	4.18	32	incontro	3.56	2.56	50	cambia	2.86	1.86
15	questioni	5.18	4.18	33	liberazione	3.32	2.32	51	carta	2.86	1.86
16	sbocco	4.72	3.72	34	libertà	3.32	2.32	52	certo	2.86	1.86
17	solo	4.72	3.72	35	luogo	3.32	2.32	53			
18	altri	4.49	3.49	36	maggioranza	3.32	2.32	54			

Table 5, which includes keywords used by VOXs, shows several lexical items which give us information on the aboutness of this subset of data *stadio, vincere, amicizia, assordante, chiasso, contenti/felice* ('stadium', 'to win', 'friendship', 'deafening', 'noise', 'happy'), mainly consisting of news about sports events in Europe. Self-reference appears to be a feature of accessed voices as the keyword list reports an outstanding presence of personal pronouns like *ci, noi* ('us', 'we') and conjucated verbs *siamo, abbiamo, andiamo, eravamo, guardo* ('we are', 'we have', 'we go', 'we were', 'I look'). Interestingly, lexical items and verb forms providing reference to future events are also found in accessed voices, i.e. *domani, futuro, faremo* ('tomorrow', 'future', 'we will do').

As far as linguistic markers of evaluation are concerned, the analysis of keywords reveals a number of features: a set of graduation words like *molto* and *tutto* (much, all) – expressing the speakers' assessment about entities and processes – are found, as well as the conjunction *ma* (but) which is generally used to replace opinions stated elsewhere in the text and to close down the space for dialogic alternatives in discourse (Martin and White 2005: 120-121).

Table 8.5: Italian VOX keywords vs. LP in European news

n	word	key	freq.	n	word	key	freq.	n	word	key	freq.
1	e	1.18	34.19	19	vostra	18.09	17.09	37	da	1.69	8.55
2	domani	15.70	25.64	20	a	0.76	8.55	38	dati	9.55	8.55
3	la	1.22	25.64	21	abbiamo	3.09	8.55	39	degli	3.63	8.55
4	siamo	10.14	25.64	22	allo	4.42	8.55	40	dorato	9.55	8.55
5	al	5.85	17.09	23	amicizia	7.75	8.55	41	è	0.51	8.55
6	bene	9.38	17.09	24	anche	1.56	8.55	42	entrambi	9.55	8.55
7	ci	4.25	17.09	25	andiamo	7.75	8.55	43	eravamo	9.55	8.55
8	di	0.47	17.09	26	appuntamento	9.55	8.55	44	esiste	9.55	8.55
9	gli	3.49	17.09	27	assordante	9.55	8.55	45	essere	2.37	8.55
10	il	1.11	17.09	28	bevi	9.55	8.55	46	faremo	9.55	8.55
11	ma	3.08	17.09	29	bianco	9.55	8.55	47	fatto	3.99	8.55
12	molto	3.08	17.09	30	c	2.87	8.55	48	felice	9.55	8.55
13	noi	4.77	17.09	31	che	0.28	8.55	49	fieri	9.55	8.55
14	non	0.96	17.09	32	chi	6.52	8.55	50	fisica	9.55	8.55
15	qui	8.37	17.09	33	chiasso	9.55	8.55	51	forza	5.62	8.55
16	stadio	18.09	17.09	34	come	1.69	8.55	52	futuro	4.95	8.55
17	tutto	8.37	17.09	35	con	0.89	8.55	53	guardo	9.55	8.55
18	vincere	18.09	17.09	36	contenti	9.55	8.55	54	in	0.61	8.55

Polish news programmes

From the comparison between the language of accessed voices and journalists, illustrated in Table 6, a salient keyword emerges, *żeby* ('in order to/so that'). It foregrounds purposefulness, motivation and the cause and effect relation. Another keyword – *no* ('yep', yeah', 'well') – operates in Polish both as a particle and an interjection. In the latter case it serves as an informal way to express agreement. It might also signal uncertainty of a speaker or function as a filler which gives the speaker more time to word a thought. As for self-reference, the pronoun *nas* ('us') has high keyness and it shows that non-journalists view themselves more as group members than journalists do. This point is supported by *my* ('we') whose usage is particularly relevant: inserting the personal pronoun in Polish is often optional because the verb suffix carries information about the person – the pronoun could be used to reinforce messages. As for verbs, noteworthy ones are *chcemy* ('we want') and *mamy* ('we have') whereby issues are again addressed by group members and proxies rather than unaffiliated individuals. Moreover, the evaluative intensifier *bardzo* ('very') in accessed voices contrasts with a more clearly distant social role of journalists. It is to be noted that the intensifier reappears in the comparison of LPs and VOXs in European news below.

Table 8.6: Polish accessed voice keywords vs. JOURNALISTS *in European news*

n	word	key	freq.	n	word	key	freq.	n	word	key	freq.
1	żeby	4.99	5.68	15	mamy	2.12	1.66	29	prostu	1.76	1.66
2	no	3.17	3.79	16	wszystkim	2.12	1.66	30	tak	1.71	5.21
3	nas	3.15	4.02	17	da	2.07	1.42	31	tylko	1.67	4.50
4	bardzo	2.91	6.86	18	to	2.04	29.35	32	tego	1.64	4.26
5	mieć	2.45	1.66	19	jest	2.04	17.51	33	nie	1.63	28.17
6	powiedzieć	2.45	1.66	20	mi	2.03	1.89	34	są	1.63	4.50
7	tutaj	2.41	2.84	21	czy	1.90	5.92	35	że	1.63	20.12
8	coś	2.36	2.37	22	tej	1.90	3.31	36	taka	1.60	1.42
9	chcemy	2.34	2.13	23	prawo	1.86	2.13	37	wszystko	1.49	1.89
10	ludzi	2.31	1.89	24	ten	1.86	3.08	38	tam	1.44	1.42
11	my	2.31	1.89	25	kraju	1.81	1.89	39	był	1.44	1.66
12	oczywiście	2.23	1.42	26	jako	1.81	1.42	40	była	1.43	2.13
13	było	2.15	4.26	27	siebie	1.81	1.42	41	by	1.42	3.08
14	ludzie	2.14	2.60	28	będzie	1.79	6.86	42	ale	1.40	10.18

Coming to the discourse of VOXs (Table 7), the "collective speaker" is present with *my* ('we') whose keyness is higher than in the case of the non-journalist *vs.* journalists list. That VOX utterances display a less visible tendency to objectify evaluations is supported by the verb *lubię* ('I like'). In turn, items such as *coś* ('something') could confirm the postulate that there is a lower degree of precision in VOX language. Likewise, *wszyscy* ('everybody') and *wszystko* ('everything') show that VOXs more than VOXs or journalists make generalisations in news items on Europe.

The imprecision in the talk of VOXs contrasts content words such as *Polska* and *polski* (denoting Poland or referring to Poland) present in LP discourse (Table 8). What is more, there are some interesting pronominal choices like *nas* ('us'), or *nasze* ('our'), *wam* ('to/for you', second person plural), *ich* (a variant of 'them') – constructing a joint identity and a sense of belonging – displayed either by directly referring to oneself as a member of a group or using pronouns that presuppose such a relation. In line with that, a relevant verb form is *mamy* ('we have') with which LPs talk on behalf of an ensemble rather that for themselves. With high keyness of the graduation marker *bardzo* ('very') evaluation is manifest in the language of LPs as they talk in European news.

Table 8.7: Polish vox keywords vs. LP *in European news*

n	word	key	freq.	n	word	key	freq.	n	word	key	freq.
1	wszyscy	4,73	3,73	19	mojej	2,87	1,87	37	bez	2,18	1,87
2	dni	3,80	2,80	20	momencie	2,87	1,87	38	choć	2,18	1,87
3	lubię	3,80	2,80	21	mówię	2,87	1,87	39	człowiek	2,18	1,87
4	pracować	3,80	2,80	22	połowa	2,87	1,87	40	dać	2,18	1,87
5	spa	3,80	2,80	23	pracę	2,87	1,87	41	decyzji	2,18	1,87
6	taką	3,80	2,80	24	uczciwie	2,87	1,87	42	dlaczego	2,18	1,87
7	więc	3,59	3,73	25	wolne	2,87	1,87	43	nam	2,18	1,87
8	tu	3,38	5,60	26	wrażenia	2,87	1,87	44	ona	2,18	1,87
9	po	2,92	7,46	27	zmieni	2,87	1,87	45	parę	2,18	1,87
10	my	2,90	4,66	28	vero	2,87	1,87	46	polak	2,18	1,87
11	wszystko	2,90	4,66	29	mieć	2,42	3,73	47	właśnie	2,18	1,87
12	jesteśmy	2,88	2,80	30	polsce	2,42	3,73	48	wreszcie	2,18	1,87
13	czekają	2,87	1,87	31	u	2,42	3,73	49	żadnego	2,18	1,87
14	czekamy	2,87	1,87	32	no	2,39	7,46	50	co	2,09	8,40
15	głodny	2,87	1,87	33	czas	2,32	2,80	51	jednak	2,09	3,73
16	kolegę	2,87	1,87	34	taki	2,32	2,80	52	ten	2,05	5,60
17	kupi	2,87	1,87	35	coś	2,19	4,66	53	ludzie	1,95	4,66
18	małym	2,87	1,87	36	ani	2,18	1,87	54	jako	1,95	2,80

Table 8.8: Polish LP *keywords vs.* VOX *in European news*

n	word	key	freq.	n	word	key	freq.	n	word	key	freq.
1	ich	3,54	3,54	14	sprawie	2,59	2,59	27	ma	1,46	4,17
2	którzy	3,54	3,54	15	które	2,16	4,17	28	który	1,34	2,59
3	polska	3,22	3,22	16	prawo	1,83	3,54	29	mogą	1,34	2,59
4	tych	3,22	3,22	17	do	1,73	14,64	30	można	1,34	2,59
5	jeśli	2,90	2,90	18	dla	1,68	6,39	31	oczywiście	1,34	2,59
6	polski	2,90	2,90	19	go	1,67	3,22	32	sobie	1,34	2,59
7	z	2,70	15,27	20	kraju	1,67	3,22	33	te	1,34	2,59
8	będą	2,59	2,59	21	ludzi	1,67	3,22	34	ze	1,34	2,59
9	będziemy	2,59	2,59	22	by	1,57	4,49	35	bardzo	1,26	8,29
10	chodzi	2,59	2,59	23	był	1,50	2,90	36	się	1,22	25,10
11	jego	2,59	2,59	24	mamy	1,50	2,90	38	była	1,12	3,22
12	która	2,59	2,59	25	powiedzieć	1,50	2,90	39	może	1,12	3,22
13	których	2,59	2,59	26	przez	1,50	2,90				

UK news programmes

The comparison between journalists and accessed voices (Table 9) shows a frequent usage of personal pronouns and adjectives in non-journalist talk: the outstanding frequency of *my, I me, you, we, us, them* confirms the usage of more personal stance-taking, as in the Italian data. Another recurrent feature, also identified in Italian non-journalists, is the occurrence of the verbs *think* and *know* which introduces an assessment with regards to the level of certainty of knowledge in a proposition (Martin and White 2005: 105-110). A set of frequent lexical items (*child, benefits, money, work, parents, children, poverty*) gives us information on the main topics accessed voices talk, i.e. family policies. Keywords analysis also underlines a frequent presence of adverbs (*very, just, completely, really, quite, actually, many*) in non-journalists discouse. The use of these items indicates that accessed voices take a more personal stance.

Table 8.9: UK accessed voice keywords vs. JOURNALISTS in European news

n	word	key	freq.	n	word	key	freq.	n	word	key	freq.
1	my	4.82	4.28	19	benefits	2.16	1.26	37	money	1.82	1.51
2	I	4.63	22.17	20	completely	2.16	1.26	38	like	1.82	4.28
3	know	4.23	5.04	21	expect	2.16	1.26	39	really	1.81	2.27
4	am	3.52	3.53	22	fast	2.11	1.51	40	help	1.76	2.02
5	need	3.21	3.28	23	poverty	2.11	1.51	41	work	1.71	2.02
6	do	2.94	11.34	24	good	2.07	1.76	42	put	1.70	1.51
7	drink	2.76	1.76	25	you	2.04	12.35	43	quite	1.70	1.51
8	going	2.75	5.54	26	over	2.02	3.53	44	things	1.69	1.26
9	child	2.74	2.27	27	or	1.98	3.53	45	working	1.69	1.26
10	think	2.64	5.79	28	make	1.98	2.77	46	go	1.67	2.02
11	we	2.46	15.87	29	single	1.98	1.26	47	me	1.67	2.02
12	sure	2.35	2.02	30	can	1.93	5.79	48	day	1.65	1.51
13	because	2.33	3.78	31	get	1.90	3.53	49	every	1.64	1.26
14	lot	2.33	2.77	32	give	1.90	1.26	50	actually	1.60	1.51
15	not	2.25	15.62	33	parents	1.90	1.26	51	see	1.58	2.02
16	together	2.23	1.76	34	children	1.89	2.52	52	again	1.58	1.26
17	very	2.22	6.30	35	got	1.85	2.27	53	happy	1.58	1.26
18	just	2.21	6.05	36	until	1.82	1.26	54	them	1.56	3.02

The contrastive analysis between LPs and VOXs (Table 10) mainly highlights a number of lexical items related to the aboutness of this sub-corpus (*school, police, cannabis, fans*) as well as a number of graduation words such as *quite, bit, just, some* which are generally used to estimate evaluative meaning in discourse. The keywords analysis does not present other linguistic features bringing attitudinal meaning as such apart from an interestingly frequent occurrence of the verb *know* which expresses general subjectivity in discourse.

Table 8.10: UK LP keywords vs. VOX in European news

n	word	key	freq.	n	word	key	freq.	n	word	key	freq.
1	give	3.88	1.88	19	help	2.16	0.92	37	just	1.65	23.98
2	hit	3.56	1.56	20	been	2.16	0.92	38	police	1.64	2.52
3	work	3.24	1.24	21	school	2.15	3.16	39	here	1.64	2.52
4	why	3.24	1.24	22	there	2.13	21.10	40	could	1.64	2.52
5	know	3.03	3.16	23	bit	1.94	5.41	41	fast	1.63	13.41
6	free	2.94	5.09	24	late	1.92	0.60	42	others	1.53	0.60
7	out	2.92	0.92	25	high	1.92	0.60	43	longer	1.53	0.60
8	back	2.92	0.92	26	fans	1.92	0.60	44	further	1.53	0.60
9	into	2.84	2.84	27	them	1.90	1.24	45	find	1.53	0.60
10	living	2.60	0.60	28	home	1.77	4.12	46	cannabis	1.48	1.56
11	one	2.40	1.24	29	over	1.73	1.56	47	any	1.48	5.73
12	use	2.28	0.28	30	not	1.73	1.56	48	him	1.43	4.45
13	trouble	2.28	0.28	31	five	1.73	1.56	49	child	1.42	9.89
14	too	2.28	0.28	32	together	1.69	0.28	50	some	1.35	2.20
15	started	2.28	0.28	33	ten	1.69	0.28	51	twenty	1.35	1.24
16	quite	2.28	0.28	34	side	1.69	0.28	52	I	1.34	10.21
17	next	2.28	0.28	35	now	1.69	0.28	53	years	1.34	0.28
18	is	2.28	0.28	36	days	1.69	0.28	54	third	1.34	0.28

Table 8.11: UK VOX keywords vs. LP in European news

n	word	key	freq.	n	word	key	freq.	n	word	key	freq.
1	my	6,08	7,03	19	son	2,41	1,41	37	thought	2,05	1,05
2	he	4,68	6,68	20	person	2,41	1,41	38	stabbed	2,05	1,05
3	was	3,97	14,42	21	parent	2,41	1,41	39	sixteen	2,05	1,05
4	just	3,95	10,55	22	okay	2,41	1,41	40	nice	2,05	1,05
5	had	3,69	3,87	23	occasion	2,41	1,41	41	moment	2,05	1,05
6	drink	3,46	2,46	24	how	2,36	2,11	42	missing	2,05	1,05
7	again	3,46	2,46	25	fast	2,36	2,11	43	maybe	2,05	1,05
8	got	3,15	3,16	26	family	2,36	2,11	44	lone	2,05	1,05
9	there	3,13	9,14	27	me	2,32	2,81	45	later	2,05	1,05
10	thing	2,76	1,76	28	children	2,32	2,81	46	head	2,05	1,05
11	single	2,76	1,76	29	I	2,19	31,29	47	fence	2,05	1,05
12	look	2,76	1,76	30	his	2,11	2,46	48	feeling	2,05	1,05
13	everybody	2,76	1,76	31	child	2,11	2,46	49	easter	2,05	1,05
14	when	2,62	2,46	32	working	2,09	1,76	50	drive	2,05	1,05
15	lot	2,48	3,87	33	happy	2,09	1,76	51	both	2,05	1,05
16	young	2,41	1,41	34	country	2,09	1,76	52	am	2,03	4,92
17	waters	2,41	1,41	35	week	2,05	1,05	53	were	1,94	2,81
18	trying	2,41	1,41	36	told	2,05	1,05	54	she	1,94	2,81

Table 11 outlines outstanding frequent linguistic features in VOX news talk. Keywords present various lexical items (*children, child, stabbed, parent, family,*

Eastern, waters) referring to news topics covered during the two-month data collection. The usage of personal pronouns and adjectives (*my, I, me*) reveals a more personal attitude in VOX discourse.

Qualitative data analysis

The quantitative observations explored in the previous sections helped us identify trends in accessed voices' discouse with respect to European news across the three languages/cultures. The following sub-sections will include more in-deph, qualitative observations based on a set of news items aired on 8-9 March 2007. These focused on the approval of a European plan on climate change, reached after months of negotiations between member countries. The plan consisted of strict measures adopted by EU countries to tackle climate change, mainly focusing on emissions cuts and renewables.[2]

Italian news programmes

The topic was covered in both Italian public and private broadcasters' (RAI and Mediaset) main news bulletins (TG1 and TG5 respectively). Since TG5 report included only journalists' talk, we focused on TG1 report as it also referenced LPs. VOXs were included in none of the Italian reports.

Correspondent Mariolina Sattanino introduces the TG1 report by summarising the EU directives on emissions cut and renewables and political reactions across Europe. Interestingly, non-journalist voices referenced in the Italian news item are mostly experts in the field. Carlo Rubbia (Italian particle physicist and inventor) states that "Italy must be ready for this challenge [...]. Research must be applied as much as possible to develop innovative resources. In particular, both direct and indirect solar energy must be taken into account like helical and biomass sources". Chicco Testa (expert on Sustainable Development and Investment in Italy) emphasises that "this is a landmark decision which requires that all EU member countries make a huge economic, financial, industrial and technological effort". Both contributions bring strong expertise to Italian TV viewers; this is highlighted by the usage of very specialised language.

The report closes with Pier Luigi Bersani's (Minister of Economic Development at the time of the report) words commenting with great emphasis on the EU directive, the Italian contribution and commitments to the agreement: "This is clearly a big achievement which I believe shows Italy's contribution in many aspects. In particular, we can affirm we have started ahead of time, having

2 Examples in the following paragraphs will be provided in English translations only due to space constraints.

presented a plan on energy efficiency a month ago. The plan, concerned with citizens and renewables, reveals our commitment toward the EU decisions".

Polish news programmes

In the Polish part of the news corpus there are altogether four news items related the EU summit, distributed over two subsequent days. We will here focus on the ones broadcasted on March 8 2007 to see how the topic is first introduced and which facets are designated as well as because there are some visible differences to be addressed between the two Polish newscasters.

On Polsat, the topic of the summit is mentioned by the news presenter to proceed with the issue of European constitution and the president's position on this. The only non-journalist speakers in that material are Lech Kaczyński (Polish President) and Hans-Gert Pöttering (President of the European Parliament). They are authoritative LPs directly involved in the matter they comment on.

Kaczyński's comment is: "This is an important issue and every country stands for the solutions that are beneficial for that country – for us the Nice solutions are beneficial but obviously Europe is the world of compromise – I agree with this." Straightaway Pöttering's utterance from the same press conference is given in which he argues that "if a country wants to have its postulates realised in one hundred per cent and cannot compromise, there will be no agreement important for the people of Europe but I hope that the agreement will be reached". Then the correspondent's live commentary is given again and the item is concluded by the news presenter.

Wiadomości – the news programme of TVP1, Poland's major state channel – offers a more comprehensive account. It gives an overview of what the summit is devoted to and discusses Poland's position with respect to it while Polsat focused on a more particular topic of the European constitution. The topic of the new European constitution is mentioned on TVP1 as one potentially to be discussed but the correspondent explicitly states that the number one topic will be energy policy.

Significantly, on TVP1 more sources are employed. The item begins similarly to its counterpart on Polsat – with a live commentary from a correspondent on location – but interestingly the correspondent quotes Kaczyński's comment which is presented directly on Polsat. That section is followed by a pre-produced material on renewable energy featuring a number of sources. First, there is a VOX from Brussels commenting on the use of wind for energy generation, and then several LPs talk: Jose Manuel Barroso (President of the European Commission) highlights the global importance of the EU's decision; Danuta Hübner (European Commissioner for Regional Policy) expresses her hopes that "the summit will adopt a plan and European energy policy will be gradually built"; Lech Małecki (representing the Ministry of Economy) argues that meeting some of the energy requirements proposed by the European Commission would require considerable financial outlays, thus hindering Poland's economic development; and Jadwiga Emilewcz (Tischner European University) claims that Germans want to "make the [Berlin] Declaration a preamble to the Constitutional Treaty".

While the two items rely on accessed voiced to a different extent and place emphasis on different aspects of the topic (which is then partly levelled out but items broadcast the following day), both tend to intertwine factual elements related to the EU's policy with a discussion of the Polish perspective. That predominantly centres on Poland's inferior position with respect to some of the other members states in terms of infrastructure and financial capability. Stemming from that premise is the argument that allowances should be made for Poland until it comes abreast of the rest of the EU.

UK news programmes

The example explored in this section includes a news report aired on BBC news at 18:00 which includes both LP and VOX news talk. The report is introduced by Correspondent Rory Cellan-Jones providing background on climate change damages, weather and agriculture and the need for immediate political actions. The first voice introduced in the report is a Spanish VOX (Angel Oliveros Zafrarole) who comments on the industry: "production is down ninety percent. We have suffered huge losses and we are not making any profit. The year may come when we have to give up the fight and abandon the land". The farmer here acts as a witness (Montgomery 2007: 168) of the tough situation of agriculture production in Spain, and at the same time as 'spokesperson' for Spanish farmers, fighting hard for a business no longer profitable and risking of giving up the land.

Moving to the carbon emissions cut as part of the EU measures, LP (Natasha Kazmer) talks about the growing travel industry in Poland, as one of the most blamed sectors for environmental impact: "I think that the travel industry, the aviation, contributes significantly to the economic development. I do not think that this factor can be just put aside by environmental issues". This short extract shows the direct expression of beliefs by using *I think* twice in the text and the adverb *significantly* as graduation words, which confirms what was also found out in the quantitative analysis. Compared with the utterance by the VOX, the LP does not provide additional information supporting the viewpoints stated in the text, overall looking more like a statement that could be perceived by viewers as a more distant message.

The last part of the report references Mr Tony Blair, Prime Minister at the time of the EU summit on climate change, stating that: "If we can agree an ambitious set of targets for Europe, that gives us a far greater position of strength and leverage than to say to the other countries, notably America and China and India, let us try and agree the principles of a new deal for all of us to play our part in reducing these damaging emissions". Interestingly, Tony Blair here describes EU measures in a positive way, by using the adjective *ambitious* as an opportunity of growth and strength for the country. The authoritative and professional status of the British Prime Minister, especially at the time of the report, together with the usage of personal pronouns (*we, us, us all*) – which creates a more personal stance-taking in discourse – is surely meant to be perceived as a positive and strong message by UK TV audience.

Concluding remarks

The analyses have shown that both similarities and differences emerge from the comparisons. The most marked difference in the structure of the news programmes concerns the Italian subcorpus. Italian news programmes have the highest number of European news stories (9.3% of the total) and the lowest number of words uttered by accessed voices (17.5%) in news items about Europe. Even if the Polish and the UK news programmes share a similar amount of European news coverage (7.5% and 6.6% respectively) they vary in the usage of accessed voices. Polish non-journalists speak for the 26.5% of the news items, the highest percentage in the corpus, while British ones are used in 22.2% of the coverage of European news stories.

The most remarkable similarity is the use of a more personal stance in the language of non-journalists in all three subcorpra. Accessed voices, compared to journalists, use more personal pronouns, possessive adjectives and graduation devices, showing a greater involvement in what they are talking about.

The analysis of LP talk has shown both similarities and differences. Compared to VOXs, in all three countries legitimated people are used in the news programme to focus on politics. This feature is particularly relevant in Italian and Polish news where LPs talk about both national and European politics. In the UK LPs also tend to focus either on more everyday topics or on the outcomes of policies, as both analyses have highlighted. In the three sub-corpora LPs display features of authoritative sources, confirmimg assumptions of their role in the news making process (Montgomery 2007). In UK news they also tend to take a more personal stance.

Another difference is the very limited use of VOXs in Italian news programmes. The quantitative analysis has shown that they are used only in reference with Sports news items, and the qualitative analysis has confirmed that they are not used in the Italian news items on Climate change. On the other hand VOXs are equally employed in Polish and UK sub-corpora to convey subjectivity and a more personal perspective on news items about Europe as both the quantitative and qualitative analyses have highlighted.

To conclude, we have observed that the Italian news programmes give the greates prominence to European issues both in terms of time devoted to Europe and in terms of the number of authoritative sources and the topics they cover. UK news programmes, on the other hand, seem less interested in European issues and display a different use of accessed voices who tend to approach the topics with more ordinary, everyday concerns, in addition to the more official voice of politicians. Polish news programmes seem in between these two attitudes. The relatively high reliance on accessed voices shows that LPs talk about more official topics, often focusing on the relationship between European and Polish politics, while VOXs are used to introduce a more personal approach to the topic, a feature that they share with British programmes and that is completely absent from the Italian ones.

References

Bondi, M. and M. Scott (eds.) (2010). Keyness in Texts. Amsterdam: John Benjamins Publishing Company.

Eurobarometer (2010). Report 74.
Available at:
http://ec.europa.eu/public_opinion/archives/eb/eb74/eb74_infor_en.pdf Accessed on 29 July 2011

Galtung, J. and K. Ruge (1965). "The Structure of Foreign News," Journal of Peace Research, 2 (64): 64-91.

Groothues, F. (2004). "Television News and the European Public Sphere: A Preliminary Investigation," European Political Communication Working Paper Series, Issue 6/04

Haarman, L. (1999). Television Talk. In Massed Medias: Linguistic Tools for Interpreting Media Discourse, Lombardo L., Haarman, L., Morley, J. and Taylor, C. (eds), 157-245. Torino: LED.

Haarman L. and L. Lombardo (2009). Introduction. In Evaluation and stance in war news, Haarman, L. and Lombardo, L. (eds), 1-26. London: Continuum.

Hartley, J. (1982). Understanding News. London: Methuen.

Kilgarriff, A. (2009). "Simple Maths for Keywords," Proceedings of fifth Corpus Linguistics Conference. Liverpool, UK. 20-23 July 2009. Available at:
http://www.kilgarriff.co.uk/Publications/2009-K-CLLiverpool-SimpleMaths.doc
Accessed on 30 September 2009

Marchi, A. and M. Venuti (2009). Mark-up and the Narrative Structure of TV News. In Evaluation and stance in war news, Haarman, L. and Lombardo, L. (eds), 27-47. London: Continuum.

Martin, J. R. and P. R. R. White (2005). The Language of Evaluation. Appraisal in English. London and New York: Palgrave Macmillan.

Montgomery, M. (2007). The Discourse of Broadcast News: A Linguistic Approach. London: Routledge.

Scott, M. and C. Tribble (2006). Key Words and Corpus Analysis in Language Education. Amsterdam: John Benjamins.

Stubbs, M. (2010). Three Concepts of Keywords. In Keyness in Texts, Bondi, M. and Scott, M. (eds), 21-42. Amsterdam: John Benjamins Publishing Company.

Keywords and the Discourse of Presidential Election Campaign in the USA, 2007-2008 – a Case Study in McCain's and Obama's Speeches

Katarzyna Fronczak-Bartnikowska

Abstract

The main aim of this paper is to conduct a textual analysis of a language used in Obama's and McCain's speeches which come from the period of presidential election campaign in the USA, specifically from June 2007 to November 2008. The author pays attention to the rhetoric used by both candidates in their political oratories, especially to ways and techniques of manipulation, encouragement and persuasion employed on potential voters in order to gain their support. A detailed analysis of keywords obtained after comparison of both politicians' speeches (a web-based application 'Wmatrix2' (Rayson, 2009) is used to carry out this comparison) makes it possible to reveal differences and similarities between Obama and McCain who come from different ideological backgrounds, and who also differ in other dimensions such as age, origin, education, social and economical status, etc.

However, consideration of space and time limits in this paper prevent us from a detailed analysis of all significant keywords, therefore I decided to concentrate on two words *government* and *Washington* which I believe are worth analyzing. Investigating context, patterns and collocations of selected keywords allow us to identify each candidate's attitude towards certain political issues, sometimes the controversial ones, like for example war in Iraq or international politics.

Keywords

Government, keyword, McCain, Obama, political discourse, presidential election campaign in the USA, Washington

Introduction

A presidential election campaign in the USA is a huge enterprise, not only a marketing, but also a linguistic one. Speeches delivered during this campaign are carefully and strategically planned and prepared by specialists trained to accomplish such a demanding task. The prize in this competition is very high – presidency – hence, candidates outdo each other in techniques and strategies employed in their rhetoric in order to manipulate, encourage and persuade potential voters to support. Also J. S. Tuman (2008: 4-5) argues that elections can be compared to contests such as "a popularity contest, a contest based on personal appearance, a contest based on the stated or perceived stance of candidate on specific issues, a contest of imagery".

The most powerful weapon which candidates possess is language and the way they communicate their ideas, plans, motives and attitudes, highly affects voters' final decision. In addition to this, J. S. Tuman (2008: 6-7) highlights that a lot of people in the USA recognize political communication in different ways. According to him, one group of people argues that "political communication refers to the tools employed by different groups and individuals to express their differences and celebrate their unity which means that political communication is a key to participation in democracy". The second one views "political communication as a way of describing the interaction of different groups that influence political decisions making in this country, in other words, they see it as discussion between political elites, the media and the public". Finally the third group of people defines "political communication as a misnomer – suggesting no information is being shared; rather, it is argued that distortion, propaganda, exaggeration, and half-truths make up the nature of American political communication, in an attempt to unethically manipulate and influence voters in election". Taking into consideration all the above mentioned ways of viewing political communication, J. S. Tuman (2008: 8) defines it as "the discursive process by which political communication is shared and promotes awareness, ignorance, manipulation, consent, dissent, action, or passivity".

In presidential election campaign in the USA, 2007-2008, leaders of two main American parties – McCain from the Republican Party and Obama from the Democratic Party were striving and contending for victory. Candidates use various strategies and rhetorical figures: strategy of positive self presentation and negative other presentation (van Dijk 2006), post hoc reasoning, anaphora, personification, exemplum, prolepsis, and metonymy.

Data and Methodology

The data consisted of Obama's and McCain's speeches, delivered during the presidential election campaign in the USA, 2007-2008, which were downloaded from their official websites on 26th of November 2009.

Obama's speeches were downloaded from www.barackobama.com with the first on June 26, 2007 and ending with that on November 3, 2008. In total Obama data contains 107 speeches, for a total data size of 1,6 Mb (283 837 words).

McCain's speeches were downloaded from www.johnmccain.com beginning on June 20, 2007 and with the last one on November 11, 2008. McCain corpus contains 78 speeches, for a total data size of 1,06 Mb (176 695 words).

Obama's and McCain's sample texts were converted into plain texts and joined into two files, one called "McCain" (used for all McCain's speeches) and the second called "Obama" (used for all Obama's speeches).

Wmatrix2 was used to conduct a statistical analysis necessary to generate a list of keywords in McCain and Obama corpora. Then a detailed, manual analysis of the list of keywords was conducted and attention was focused on those words/categories which have LL values equal or greater than 15.13 ($p < 0,0001$; 99,99% confidence level) and frequency higher than 10 overall in at least one of the two corpora. Moreover, the set of words was reduced down to a manageable number by getting rid of those which do not seem to be interesting to this analysis.

Consideration of space limit in this paper prevent us from a detailed analysis of all keywords significant for this presidential election campaign, therefore, attention was paid to two keywords *government* and *Washington* (the first one overused by McCain and the second overused by Obama) which can be classified to a group of words expressing power. Additionally, they are closely related to the presidency in the USA.

Table 9.1: The differences at the word level between McCain's and Obama's speeches

	McCain data		Obama data			
Keyword	**Frequency**	**Relative Frequency**	**Frequency**	**Relative Frequency**	**O/U Use**	**LL**
Government	496	0.29	308	0.11	+	179.82
Washington	147	0.09	491	0.18	-	67.34

The penultimate column points out overuse (+) and underuse (-) of the word in McCain data with respect to Obama data.

Discussion

The Keyword *Government*

The keyword ***government*** occurs 496 times in McCain data and 308 times in Obama data, and is used 2.64 times relatively more frequently by McCain (0.29% compared to 0.11%). The most frequent left collocates of this keyword in McCain data are: *the government, of government, our government, their government, federal government, a government, that government, big government, Iraqi government, in government, states government*.

Let us analyse some of the above presented collocations in more details. The first chosen collocation ***federal government*** occurs 23 in McCain data and 17 in Obama data. Analysing the relevant concordances it is easily noticeable that in McCain data we can find that ***federal government*** is followed mainly by modal verbs:

can (4occurrences)

```
1.  ind most promising . The federal  government  can help fund this effort , but i
2.  ion infrastructure , the federal  government  can support towns through governm
3.  ten the best service our federal  government  can render is to do these things
4.  gies that often only the federal  government  can provide . And one of the most
```

which suggests that McCain highlights ability of the federal government,

can't (1 occurrence)

```
1.  lish our goals . But the federal  government  can't just summon those talents
```

and

shouldn't (1 occurrence)

```
1.  ities for others and the federal  government  shouldn't make your work any har
```

which suggest some disapproval of the federal government and its actions.

On the other hand, in Obama data ***federal government*** collocates immediately to its right with ***will*** (6 occurrences).

```
1.  tainable goals , and the federal  government  will provide half of the funding
2.  thin several years . The federal  government  will lead by making all of its bu
3.   self-employed . And the federal  government  will match savings for working fa
4.  ou change jobs , and the federal  government  will match the savings for lower-
5.  ou change jobs , and the federal  government  will match the savings for lower-
6.  ms . Under my plan , the federal  government  will pay for part of these catast
```

Using the Future Simple tense suggests that Obama wants to present his plans for the future and shows that he recognizes the need for changes. It is worth mentioning that, there are no such occurrences in McCain data.

Closer analysis of the second chosen collocation ***their government*** (27 occurrences in McCain data, including 14 occurrences ***in their government*** and 13 occurrences in Obama data, including 4 occurrences ***in their government***) shows that the personal pronoun ***their*** relates mainly to Americans which can be supported by the following examples:

1. *The pattern of reckless government spending has caused Americans to lose trust in **their government.***
2. *My friends, this is one more reason that Americans have lost faith in **their government**.*
3. *Americans have lost trust in **their government** and I intend to win it back, so help me God.*

As the above presented examples (quoted from McCain data) show, sentences in which collocation ***their government*** appears, relate to the past times, the times before elections. Moreover, ***their government*** is preceded mainly by ***lost trust in*** (8 occurrences):

```
1. ericans have lost trust in their  government  and that trust must be restored .
2. xpayers have lost trust in their  government  . Politicians refuse to talk stra
3. ericans have lost trust in their  government  to spend their hard earned money
4. ericans have lost trust in their  government  . We must restore that trust by d
5. ericans have lost trust in their  government  and I intend to win it back , so
6. ericans have lost trust in their  government  to spend their hard earned money
7. ericans have lost trust in their  government  and I intend to win it back , so
8. people have lost trust  in their  government  . I am running for President to r
```

and ***lost faith in*** (1 occurrence):

```
1. ericans have lost faith in their  government  . I 'm not going to make promises
```

Looking at the context it can be easily found that McCain tries to persuade the USA citizens that he understands their negative attitude towards the government and he also highlights that they have right to feel disappointed with the actions taken by the current authorities. We may suppose that in this way McCain wants to show the potential voters that he is able to change this situation and their negative attitude towards the government, which can be supported by the following sentence:

4. *I am running to restore the trust of the American people in **their government**.*
5. *I am running for President to restore the trust of taxpayers in **their government**.*

In the case of Obama data, ***their*** also relates to the citizens of the USA as in the following examples quoted from Obama data:

6. *It was rooted in the principle that the voices of the people can speak louder than special interests; that citizens can be connected to **their government** and to one another; and that all of us share a common destiny, an American Dream.*

7. *It is because of these failures that America is listening, intently, to what we say here today – not just Democrats, but Republicans and Independents who've lost trust in* ***their government****, but want to believe again.*

Analysing context in which ***their government*** appears, it can be noticed that Obama, similarly to McCain, recognises the lack of people's trust in the government, and a necessity to change it, to regain the trust, as in the sentence:

8. *It would require a renewed trust in the market and a renewed spirit of obligation and cooperation between business and workers; between people and* ***their government****.*

Their government, like in the aforementioned analysis of McCain data, is preceded by ***lost trust in*** (3 occurrences):

```
1.   ents who've lost trust in their  government  ,but want to believe again. And
2.   ents who've lost trust in their  government  ,but want to believe again. So
3.   ents who've lost trust in their  government  ,but want to believe again. And
```

Both candidates by using expression ***their government*** are distancing themselves from the current authorities and at the same time from all negative actions taken by them. They probably want to show that they are not responsible for the failure of the current government. Such 'post hoc reasoning' tactic is quite popular among politicians and sometimes employed in their rhetoric.

Let us now concentrate on the third selected collocation ***our government*** which occurs 50 times in McCain data and 22 times in Obama data (in McCain data there are also single occurrences like ***our system of government***, ***our own government*** and ***our federal government*** (3 occurrences)). Analysing McCain data, it is easily noticeable that ***our government*** is mainly used in a negative context, probably to highlight its drawbacks and weaknesses, it should be stated that such context refers to the current government, e.g.:

9. *And when* ***our government*** *forgets to honor the country's debts to you, it is a stain upon America's honor.*
10. ***Our government*** *has failed to meet some of its most basic responsibilities and the American people have lost trust in their leaders.*
11. *Even as we increase our military capacity, we must also increase our civilian capacity so that an undue burden does not again fall on our soldiers as it has in Afghanistan and Iraq, where the civilian agencies of* ***our government*** *have too often been missing in action.*

The usage of a possessive determiner ***our*** before the keyword ***government*** is a tricky political tactic as it makes all Americans partially responsible for the actions taken by the government. In this way McCain distances himself from all the negative aspects connected with the current government being under Republican control and tries to sidetrack voters attention by highlighting the fact that this government belongs to all citizens.

In the case of Obama data collocation ***our government*** also means that all Americans should identify with this institution, however, contrary to already described McCain data, Obama does not use it in a negative context and does not refer to the current government. He rather uses it in a context referring to the future and to a vision of a better tomorrow under his leadership.

12. *It's time to make tough choices so that we have a smarter government that pays its way and makes the right investments for America's future. It falls to us to shape a new century. Every aspect of* ***our government*** *should be under review. We can ill-afford needless layers of bureaucracy and outmoded programs. My Administration will open up the doors of democracy.*

Obama tries to defend the government and highlights Americans' expectations towards it:

13. ***Our government*** *cannot guarantee success and happiness in life, but what we can do as a nation is to ensure that every American who wants to work is prepared to work, able to find a job, and able to stay out of poverty.*
14. *We don't expect* ***our government*** *to guarantee success and happiness, but when millions of children start the race of life so far behind only because of race, only because of class, that's a betrayal of our ideals.*

Obama in his speeches employed a rhetorical figure, 'anaphora', by repeating ***a government that*** to emphasis the role and duties of a government:

15. *I trust the American people to realize that while we don't need big* ***government****, we do need a* ***government*** *that stands up for families who are being tricked out of their homes by Wall Street predators; a* ***government*** *that stands up for the middle-class by giving them a tax break; a* ***government*** *that ensures that no American will ever lose their life savings just because their child gets sick.*

Another rhetorical figure, ‘exemplum’ is used by Obama to have the audience make an association between him and Franklin Roosevelt. Such an association will invoke a memory of a respected and valued president and as a result make potential voters believe that Obama will be a similar politician.

16. *Amid a crisis of confidence Roosevelt called for a “re-appraisal of values”. He made clear that in this country, our right to live must also include the right to live comfortably; that* ***government*** *must favor no small group at the expense of all its citizens; and that in order for us to prosper as one nation, “... the responsible heads of finance and industry, instead of acting each for himself, must work together to achieve the common end.”*

The Keyword *Washington*

The second keyword ***Washington*** occurs 491 times in Obama data and 147 times in McCain data, and it is used twice relatively more frequently by Obama (0.18% compared to 0.09%).

Washington, similarly to the already analysed keyword ***government,*** can be classified as a group of words connected with power and authority. A brief investigation of the concordances of this keyword shows that in Obama and McCain data ***Washington*** refers to a center of power. Preliminary analysis of its context also demonstrates that in the Obama corpus we can find examples of ‘metonymy’ – Washington is substituted for elites, establishment. Moreover, in McCain data we can find references to Washington as the first president of the USA.

Let us now move on to a closer analysis of this keyword. As the relevant concordance shows, the keyword *Washington* appears in the pattern *V + (sb) +* ***to Washington*** (13 occurrences in Obama data, 15 occurrences in McCain data) where preceded verbs are mainly connected with movement, for example ***went***, ***go***, ***come, move***:

Concordance of keyword *Washington* from Obama data

1.	It was there before they got **to**	**Washington**	, and if you and I do n"t stand u
2.	I will invite the world back **to**	**Washington**	and let it be known that the Unit
3.	hange when everyone goes back **to**	**Washington**	. Because the lobbyists just writ
4.	icies .. But then they go back **to**	**Washington**	when the campaign "s over . Lobby
5.	nts of the country „ who come **to**	**Washington**	year after year to make your voic

Concordance of keyword *Washington* from McCain data

1.	along to get along . I went **to**	**Washington**	to get something done for the peo
2.	ople angry . But I did n't go **to**	**Washington**	to win the Mr. Congeniality award
3.	d proud . They do n't send us **to**	**Washington**	to take more of their money , and
4.	s what happens when people go **to**	**Washington**	to work for themselves and not yo
5.	hat will shortly take me back **to**	**Washington**	. Following September 11th , our

As already mentioned, in the Obama corpus we can find ***Washington*** substituted for elites and establishment. In such a usage Obama employs the rhetorical figure of 'personification' and creates a negative association with the analysed keyword ***Washington***. The examples presented below can support this claim:

1.	ake action on climate change But	**Washington**	**hasn't acted ;** and that is the r
2.	reason why America has n't led .	**Washington**	**'s failure** to lead on energy is t
3.	able has the chance to beat what	**Washington**	**said was inevitable** . And that 's
4.	become a day when George Bush 's	**Washington**	rewards its friends on Wall Stree
5.	tes . When this campaign began ,	**Washington**	**didn't give us much of a chance**
6.	alked about these problems while	**Washington**	**has done nothing** , or tinkered ,
7.	use . You know what happens when	**Washington**	**makes promises it doesn't keep** a
8.	not come from government alone .	**Washington**	**can't solve all our problems** . T
9.	rt a renewable energy industry .	**Washington**	**hasn't done that** . What Washingt
10.	. Because for eight long years ,	**Washington**	**hasn't been working for ordinary**
11.	that you know what happens when	**Washington**	**fails to do its job** . It may be e
12.	arts with energy . For decades ,	**Washington**	**has failed the American people** on
13.	ection , and that 's exactly why	**Washington**	**has failed to do anything** about o
14.	you . You know what happens when	**Washington**	puts out economic policies that w
15.	use . You know what happens when	**Washington**	listens to big oil and gas company

Looking closer at McCain corpus we can find references to the first president of the USA as in the following sentences:

17. *A distant ancestor served on General **Washington's** staff, and it seems my ancestors fought in most wars in our nation's history.*
18. *As **Washington**, Lincoln, and other great leaders reminded us, Americans who fought to defend this nation should always rank among the highest of national priorities.*

A detailed analysis of a context in which ***Washington*** appears in Obama data shows that Obama, while criticizing actions taken by Washington in the past years, highlights strong associations between them and McCain. In this way he draws voters' attention to McCain's failures which can be supported by the below quoted sentences:

19. *Now, a few days ago, Senator McCain said, "Our dangerous dependence on foreign oil has been thirty years in the making, and was caused by the failure of politicians in* ***Washington*** *to think long-term about the future of the country." I couldn't agree more. The only problem is that out of those thirty years, Senator McCain was in* ***Washington*** *for twenty-six of them. And in that time he has achieved little to help reduce our dependence on foreign oil.*

Obama employed all possible techniques to present his opponent in a bad light by listing different cases and issues in which McCain failed or presented a negative attitude, for example:

– environmental issues

20. *And now he's talking about a tax credit for more efficient cars even though he helped George Bush block these credits twice in the last year. After all those years in* ***Washington****, John McCain still doesn't get it.*

– controversial war in Iraq issue

21. *I opposed going to war in Iraq; Senator McCain was one of* ***Washington's*** *biggest supporters for war.*
22. *It's a* ***Washington*** *where politicians like John McCain and Hillary Clinton voted for a war in Iraq that should've never been authorized and never been waged – a war that is costing us thousands of precious lives and billions of dollars a week that could've been used to rebuild crumbling schools and bridges; roads and buildings; that could've been invested in job training and child care; in making health care affordable or putting college within reach.*

– tax issues

23. *And that's how we'll solve the problem of $4 a gallon gas not with another* ***Washington*** *gimmick like John McCain's gas tax holiday that would pad oil company profits while draining the highway fund that Michigan depends on.*

Obama clearly and openly demonstrates his negative attitude towards Washington's government and politics. He uses a political strategy of highlighting disadvantages and showing an old-fashioned way of governing in Washington. In his corpus majority of sentences in which ***Washington*** occurs are negatively marked by the usage of collocations: ***conventional thinking in Washington*** (7 occurrences), ***Washington is broken*** (5 occurrences), ***broken politics in Washington*** (4 occurrences), ***Washington has failed*** (3 occurrences), ***conventional Washington thinking*** (2 occurrences), ***Washington's conventional thinking*** (1 occurrence), ***distraction in Washington*** (1 occurrence), ***arrogance in Washington*** (1 occurrence), ***failure in Washington*** (1 occurrence), ***Washington gimmicks*** (1 occurrence), ***failure of politician in Washington*** (1 occurrence), ***destructive habits of Washington*** (1 occurrence), ***dysfunctional politics of Washington*** (1 occurrence), ***dysfunction and cronyism in Washington*** (1 occurrence), ***Washington's failure*** (1 occurrence).

In addition to this, Obama repetitively uses a context in which ***Washington*** co-occurs with ***change:***

1.	ake action on climate change but	**Washington**	has n't acted ; and that is the r
2.	the White House , but change in	**Washington**	that the American people can beli
3.	out who 's most likely to change	**Washington**	. Because that 's a debate we can
4.	't stop until there 's change in	**Washington**	. And tonight , we 're on our way
5.	eight , or fundamental change in	**Washington**	. People may be bitter about thei
6.	party will bring about change in	**Washington**	- the question is , will we ? Bec
7.	y who desperately want change in	**Washington**	. I have no illusions about how f
8.	we need to fundamentally change	**Washington**	if we want change in America . I
9.	, it 's about the need to change	**Washington**	. There are young people , and Af
10.	And few know better than you why	**Washington**	needs to change . But the truth i
11.	against women , and that 's why	**Washington**	has to change . Now Senator McCai
12.	ids . That 's why it 's time for	**Washington**	to change . And year after year ,
13.	ids . That 's why it 's time for	**Washington**	to change . Now , Senator McCain
14.	ream slipping away , this time ,	**Washington**	had to change . That 's what it '
15.	rom Washington . Change comes to	**Washington**	. Change happens because the Amer
16.	s time for fundamental change in	**Washington**	and a President who puts the midd
17.	rom Washington . Change comes to	**Washington**	. This election is our chance to

The main aim of Obama's campaign is to persuade potential voters about the need for change. He frequently uses the word ***change*** in various collocations, what we can observe in the above presented concordance, to make people believe that this change is the most effective solution to their problems. Interestingly, Obama does not define what changes he wants to introduce, he just highlights the need for change which is a political strategy of sidetracking voters' attention from details and creating an illusion of a better future. People usually subconsciously associate change with something new, better, more efficient and hopeful, hence, persuading them about having the ability to introduce needed changes in the current system, government and every domain of their lives is a key to victory in the presidential election.

McCain, similarly to already described Obama, wants to convince voters that he recognizes the necessity that also Washington needs some changes. He tries to persuade people that only he is able to introduce a real, right and possible change which can be supported by the following sentences:

24. *If we are going to change* ***Washington****, we need a President who has actually fought for change and made it happen. The next President won't have time to get used to the office. We face many challenges here at home, and many enemies abroad in this dangerous world. Senator Biden warned that Senator Obama would be tested with an international crisis. I have been tested. Senator Obama hasn't .*
25. *Both Senator Obama and I promise we will end* ***Washington's*** *stagnant, unproductive partisanship. But one of us has a record of working to do that and one of us doesn't. Americans have seen me put aside partisan and personal interests to move this country forward. They haven't seen Senator Obama do the same. For all his fine words and all his promise, he has never taken the hard but right course of risking his own interests for yours; of standing against the partisan rancor on his side to stand up for our country.*

Analysing the McCain corpus in more details we can notice that he is trying not to criticize Washington understood as a governing body, he also avoids using negative usage of this keyword. Even if he recognizes some of its negative actions, he presents it in a diplomatic and careful way. Such a tactic seems to be necessary taking into consideration McCain's indisputable connections with Washington and a close partnership with president George W. Bush.

McCain also tries to sidetrack potential voters attention from his associations with Washington (commonly disapproved and criticized by ordinary people) by presenting Obama in a negative way as an indifferent politician who talks a lot but does a little, and the following sentences can support it:

26. *My friends, this is the problem with* ***Washington****. People like Senator Obama have been too busy gaming the system and haven't ever done a thing to actually challenge the system. We've heard a lot of words from Senator Obama over the course of this campaign. But maybe just this once he could spare us the lectures, and admit to his own poor judgment in contributing to these problems.*
27. *Clear answers are hard to come by in* ***Washington****. As Senator Obama's leader in Congress memorably put it the other day and I quote – "no one knows what to do".*

As the above quoted sentences suggest, McCain chooses a tactic of persuading voters that an experienced candidate will be a better president because America affected by the international crisis does not have time for an inexperienced president who will be learning everything. It hints that van Dijk's positive self presentation and negative other presentation is a political strategy employed here by McCain.

McCain reminds his past obligations and promises which he fulfilled and mentions them now to show voters that he is a reliable and trustworthy politician who will not disappoint or disillusion them. Additionally, as it is presented in the below quoted sentences, McCain employs 'anaphora' and repeats *When I say I will (...) you know/you can see/you know I'll (...)* to emphasize that he always keeps his word. Again McCain takes the advantage of his political experience to convince others that he is a better candidate, as in the below presented sentences

28. *When I say I will defend taxpayers, you know it's true because it's what I've always done. When I say I will work across the aisle, you can see it in the results I've delivered. And when I say I will change* ***Washington****, you know I'll do it, because for me change isn't a political slogan, it's what I've been doing my whole career.*

Conclusions

To sum up, a keyword analysis can reveal features which are less obvious and often overlooked (Culpeper 2009). Keywords are a good indicator of the 'aboutness' of a text (Scott 2000) and they can be used to conduct a comparative analysis of two corpora. Additionally, a keyword analysis can also be used as a starting point to a collocational analysis and a phraseological analysis.

A keyword analysis conducted in this paper revealed rhetorical techniques employed on voters by Obama and McCain. Both politicians employed van Dijk's strategy of positive self-presentation and negative other presentation. Also both Obama and McCain recognized the need for changes but did not define what changes they want to introduce. In addition to this, closer keywords analysis shows that Obama frequently referred to the future whereas McCain often referred to his own experience. The keyword *Washington* was used by Obama to attack McCain who refuted his opponent's arguments highlighting Obama's lack of experience.

Consideration of age, origin, education, social status and belonging to a certain political party suggests that Obama is a better, more enthusiastic, charismatic and future oriented speaker with many plans for the future who concerns about the poor and the lower middle class of people, especially minority groups. On the other hand, McCain seems to be older and more experienced politician who has a great respect for history and patriotism which is a great value for him as he used to be a soldier. He is not likely to have a modern vision of the future USA, he would rather continue a former president G.W. Bush politics with some minor, unavoidable exceptions and focus on the middle and the upper middle class of voters.

References

Culpeper, J. (2009). "Keyness: Words, Parts-of-speech and Semantic Categories in the Character-talk of Shakespeare's 'Romeo and Juliet'", International Journal of Corpus Linguistics 14(1): 29-59.

Rayson, P. (2009). Wmatrix: a Web-based Corpus Processing Environment, Computing Department, Lancaster University.
Available at: http://ucrel.lancs.ac.uk/wmatrix/

Scott, M. (2000). "Focusing on the Text and Its Key Words". In Rethinking Language Pedagogy from a Corpus Perspective, Volume 2, Burnard, L. and McEnery, T. (eds.), 103-122. Frankfurt: Peter Lang.

Tuman, J. S. (2008). Political Communication in American Campaigns. Los Angeles: Sage Publications, Inc.

van Dijk, T. A. (2002). "Political Discourse and Political Cognition." In Politics as Text and Talk. Analytical approaches to political discourse, Chilton, P. A. and Schäffner, Ch. (eds.), 204-236. Amsterdam: Benjamins.

van Dijk, T. A. (2006). "Discourse and manipulation", Discourse & Society, 17(2): 359–383.

The Media in Transforming Audiences and Societies

Barbara Lewandowska-Tomaszczyk and Frauke Zeller

Abstract

The main aim of the paper is to present research and activities within a European Concerted Research Action designated as COST Action IS0906: *Transforming Audiences, Transforming Societies*, and in particular, main assumptions and studies conducted in the working group (WG3), which focuses on the Information Communication Technology and the use of computer-mediated communication with reference to the identification of new types of the Author(s) – Audience(s) relationships, as well as evolving social relationships.

The paper presents a contribution of corpus linguistics to the study of processes which take place in Computer-Mediated Communication, in particular email texts, blogs and posts. The qualitative content analysis is complemented with the investigation of the statistical data, which reflect the Interconnectivity Value and and on-line discourse activities of the users. On the basis of these findings the behaviour of the respective audiences is analysed and discussed.

Keywords

Audience, blogs, Computer-Mediated Communication (CMC), CMC linguistic functions, e-mail, Interconnectivity Value (IV), internet fora, On-line Discourse Activity (ODA), posts, social transformations, traditional media

Transforming Audiences, Transforming Societies

The present paper is part of the activities related to COST Action IS0906 whose main objective is to advance knowledge of the transformations of European audiences within a changing media and communication environment. Furthermore, the Action aims at the identification of the interrelationships between these changes and the social, cultural and political areas of European societies. Our project falls within tasks of Working Group 3, which focuses among other aspects on the Information Communication Technology and the use of computer-mediated communication with reference to the identification of new types of the *Author(s) – Audience(s)* relationships, as well as evolving social relationships.

Aim of the paper

Audiences have been recently experiencing transformations of their media and communication environment particularly with respect to new technologies, intercommunicative platforms and the boundaries between written and spoken language modes, between the private and the public and between the communicative roles of the author and the recipient of a message (cf. Alheide and Snow 1991).

The aim of the present paper is to present a contribution of corpus linguistics to the uncovering of some of the processes which are taking place in Computer-Mediated Communication (CMC), and more precisely in email exchanges on the one hand and blogs and discussions on the internet for a on the other. What will be firstly presented is a CMC Activity model embracing qualitative and quantitative activity factors, with a special emphasis on the Users' Interconnectivity Values (Lewandowska-Tomaszczyk forthcoming).

In the discussion of e-mail messages a method mix including quantitative content analysis and corpus analysis, combined with qualitative discourse studies is being used in order to analyse CMC interaction. A particular focus is put on how interaction and collaboration is being structured and carried out throughout the usage of the asynchronous communication medium email. The introduction of a non-typical corpus analysis instruments – that is content analysis as it is being traditionally used by scholars of media and communication, as well as discourse analysis – should enable to approach large corpora from a somewhat different, pragmatic-strategic angle, and at the same time to go into detailed (qualitative) analysis when needed.

In the sections involving blogs, Usenet, and other social networks, quantitative data as well as a description of the users' sentiments and attitude towards real life events will be identified and discussed.

Blurring the boundaries

A prototypical communicative act involves two participants: an author and an addressee engaged in a face-to-face spoken interaction. Computer Mediated Communication provides a prototypical instance of the *interchangeability* design feature of language and human communication: the speaker interchanges his/her role with the addressee and the exchanges develop dynamically during the interaction. However, what is observed in this form of communication is blurring the boundaries between the author and audience with the new concept of 'audiencing' i.e. active authoring and exchanging the messages and massive user-generated content.

An extension of the communication prototype are cases in which a single author addresses a community of addressees as for example in the case of books, press or film and theatre performances. What is witnessed at present is a further extension of the prototype towards multiple authors and multiple addressees possible in CMC in the forms of social networks, blogs, or internet fora, online chats, and multiplayer online games. This extension (i.e. boundary blurring) is often related to the notion of *prosumption* (a blending of "prosumer" and "consumption") and *produser* (a blending of "producer" and "user"), which was originally brought up by the Toffler (1980), and has been applied to CMC in connection with the so called Web 2.0 by Bruns (2008). The concept describes the active content production of the audiences/users by means of Web 2.0 applications. This also means that the role of the addressor and the addressee, or the sender and the receiver, is being blurred and leading to the need for new creative approaches to CMC.

The new forms require and impose new ways of communicating. They embrace both technical criteria (cf. Herring 2010, 2007) such as the size of the message and its persistence, temporal synchronicity, as well as content oriented ones such as the possibility of private messaging, anonymous messaging and message filtering.

Private messaging involves particularly such modes of CMC as e-mail contacts, while anonymous messaging and message filtering have their function and significance in the Usenet, blogs and internet fora. Connected with this is a *participation structure* in these forms of communication. While e-mail communication is traditionally more private and hence non-anonymous, with a group of participants more limited, typically to two participants, fora enable more massive participation with larger groups of active participants, entirely or partly anonymous. Blogs fall in between. The authors are either well-known celebrities or other users who, to a larger or lesser extent, shape and construct their Internet identities, more or less congruent with their authentic selves. The question of anonymity has been found to have important effects on increased self disclosure (Kiesler et al. 1984), vulgar behavior and building fake identities, in which truth merges with fiction (Donath 1996, Danet 1998).

The amount and rate of participation also varies. E-mail contacts can be frequent or sporadic, depending on more practical needs. Blogs are most engaging for their authors, while fora, posts, and the like group participants of various needs and frequencies of contacts.

Topics taken up in CMC are partly mode-related. Email exchanges are often one-to-one (or one-to-many while using most of the time a concrete set of addressees) discussions about, business, personal or semi-personal information, while blogs and Usenet posts are concentrated on various more general themes such as politics or feminism as well as involve commentaries of current global or regional events, or else they involve exchanges of a more personal type about participants such as vacation, cooking recipes, etc, in which the linguistic style and register can vary from formal and serious to more friendly and jocular or sarcastic and hostile. Each of these correlates with different discourse activities in terms of language and visual codes. In this respect, Jensen (2009) postulates a "Three-Step Flow of Communication," which is meant as an extension to Lazarsfeld's and Katz's "Two-Step Flow of Communication" (1955). Jensen's "Three-Step Flow" integrates three modi of communication – one-to-one, one-to-many, and many-to-many – in one concept of communication practices, and with that tries to overcome the classic distinction between interpersonal and mass communication.

Methods of analysis

What is proposed in this paper is the engagement of a new methodology in CMC analysis, preferably an integration of qualitative and quantitative methods as well as a combination of the cognitive and pragmatic perspectives on language. The analysis is linguistic in nature and involves the use of *language corpora*, i.e. balanced and representative collections of computer-readable authentic language texts. It employs both corpus-based and corpus-driven techniques, i.e. a more deductive analysis in the former and more inductive, language usage-based data in the latter.

The deductive analysis is on the one hand theory-driven, but on the other hand also based on preceding quantitative content analyses. The results of the content analyses allow for example to build adequate sub-corpora for subsequent corpus analyses, and also provide a more concise picture of the collected data/corpus which also results into new, i.e. more specific, research questions.

CMC Activity Model

It was proposed in Lewandowska-Tomaszczyk (forthcoming) that a *Model of Overall Online CMC Activities (OCA)* should cover quantitative and qualitative parameters of this type of communication (see (2) below). *The quantitative parameters* comprises what Lewandowska-Tomaszczyk calls an *Inter-connectivity Value (IV)*, which equals the number of interacting participants and the number of jointly linked turns. Furthermore, OCA is additionally estimated by the length of an utterance in each turn measured in terms of a number of words, their type : token ratio, the keyness of each author's lexical repertoire, i.e. the frequency of the words used in all posts by a given author measured with respect to a reference corpus, (in Lewandowska-Tomaszczyk forthcoming the reference corpora used are the British National Corpus and the National Corpus of Polish (www.nkjp.pl)). *The qualitative parameters* explore the lexical patterns, syntactic structures and discourse behaviour preferences of a given user, his/her figurative language uses, and, together with the quantitative values of each of the qualitative factor, they constitute a CMC user's *Online Discourse Activity (ODA)*.

Apart from the linguistic discourse behaviour, CMC users employ various visual and acoustic codes which are all responsible for a user's overall CMC activity (OCA). *OCA* then covers both a user's *ODA* as well as other semiotic codes (vocal, visual), which complement the former.

Interconnectivity designates the strength of connection of each individual user with all other users in the same topic domain (thread). Interconnectivity can be calculated from raw quantitative blog data as a sum total of turns with respect to each participant. The visualization software which can be used is *Gephi* – an open source graph visualisation and manipulation software (see one type of model shown below in (1), generated on 2 April, 2011 from a complete blog of a Polish rightist politician, Janusz Korwin-Mikke[1]) or other visualisation software available at www.wordle.net, which generates so-called *word clouds* from a document. Data analysis can be performed using *Public Comment Analysis Toolkit (*PCAT), developed at Amherst, MASS, US and originally used to streamline the federal notice and comment process and make it more easily available to US government and officials as well as to enable citizens to search, view and comment on US regulations (http://pcat.qdap.net). PCAT uses the 'cloud' computing and codes, validates, and analyses large digital textual data sets.

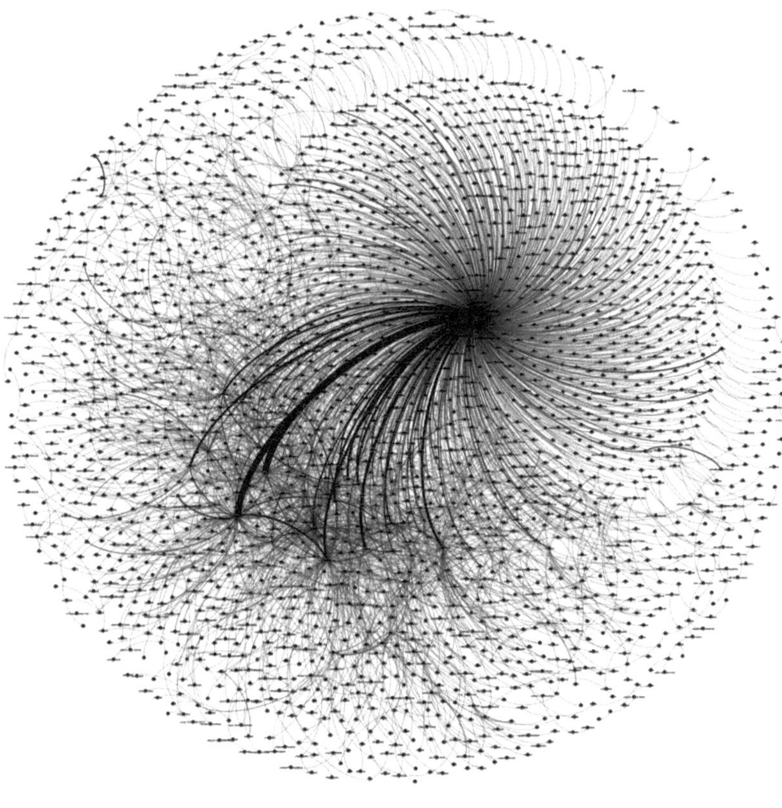

Figure 10.1.

1 The visualisation was generated by Piotr Pęzik (University of Lodz)

- ***QUANTITATIVE Parameters***
  Online Discourse Activity (ODA)
  - ***INTECONNECTIVITY Value (IV)***
  - ***The length of utterance in each turn (number of words),***
  - ***Type/token ratio [repetitions]***
  - ***Frequency/keyness (vs. a reference corpus)***

  Online Other Codes Activity (OAA)

- ***QUALITATIVE Parameters***
  Online Discourse Activity (ODA)
  - ***Lexical Patterns/ Syntactic structures/Discourse behaviour***
  - ***Figurative uses (absolute frequencies, variance)***

  Online Other Codes Activity (OOA)

- ***OVERALL Activity:***
- ***TYPOLOGICAL and NUMERICAL values of participant ONLINE DISCOURSE ACTIVITY and ONLINE OTHER CHANNELS/CODES ACIVITY***

Figure 10.2: Model of Overall Online CMC Activities (OCA) (Lewandowska-Tomaszczyk forthcoming)

What will be presented below are samples from an email-corpus of English in section 5, and a contrastive analysis of English and Polish comparable blog and Usenet data in the sections to follow.

E-mail corpora and properties of e-mail discourse

Email as an electronic, asynchronous communication form had been made available to the general public in the mid-1990s (Frehner, 2008). Whereas it used to be the communication means mostly employed, it has now been overtaken by other electronic communication forms such as Instant Messaging which particularly holds true in private life and among the younger generations (ibid.). Nevertheless, email still makes up one of the most important ways to collaborate and interact in work-related environments. This might be one reason for why there have been many studies on language usage in emails and emails as a tool for interaction, identity building, etc. (see for example Kavada, 2009; and also Biber and Conrad, 2009). Another reason for its attractiveness as an object of analysis is that emails are pre-structured – i.e. header, body, signature – which facilitates quantitative and computer-supported analyses. On the downside, however, it is difficult to obtain large samples of emails, due to privacy reasons. After all, email used to be (and still is very often) a so-called one-to-one communication medium, hence strongly connected to interpersonal communication.

From a linguistic point of view, email analyses have taken many different directions since the introduction and usage of emails in the general public. In its beginnings, concerns were stated regarding the somewhat 'careless' usage of language in electronic communication and its drawbacks on the by then conventional language usages in letters, newspapers, etc. Crystal was among those who then systematically had analysed 'Net Language' (Crystal, 2001; also see Baron, 2003) and came to the conclusion that language used on the Internet and its various applications (such as email) is in a certain perspective richer than offline-language, since its users develop means that substitute the missing cues conveyed in face-to-face conversation. This of course resulted into different approaches as to how to analyse email conversation, drawing for example onto conversation analysis (e.g. Harrison, 2008), or including the technological aspects of emails into the analysis (Herring, 2004a; 2004b).

Analyses of email usage in business/work settings are again vast, albeit often lacking a quantitative linguistic approach. Vasileiadou and Vliegenthart (2009) provide a concise overview of the existing literature/studies in this field, including the aspect of online collaborations and the influence of Internet use on identity building, productivity, etc.

Harrison provides a useful summary of the general characteristics of email discussions, that also hold particularly true for email usage in professional interactions: "E-mail discussions have their own specific attributes in addition to the general attributes of CMC. E-mail discussions are asynchronous, multiparty discussions, and although there are many active contributing participants in each sample within the data, there is an even greater number of participants not active in the samples but potentially reading the messages. " (Harrison, 2008, p. 759). This also resonates with Barjak's study of European scientists of five acaemic disciplines (2003). One of his results was a clustering of the researchers in terms of their communication activity and email use: silent researchers, email communicators, and communicators. Whereas the first type of researchers communicates least and mostly only follows up email-discussions, the second type mainly uses email as communication medium, and the third type communications most frequently, that is "who use all communication media above average" (Vasileiadou and Vliegenthart, 2009, p. 1261). Another relevant characteristic of email usage in work settings is that there are often several topics (threads) under discussion simultaneously (Harrison, 2008).

These characteristics challenge any analysis of email usage and discussions insofar that for example register usage (see Biber and Conrad, 2009) of certain groups are more difficult to obtain, given that there is no even distribution of utterances from each participant. Also, particularly regarding email discussions, certain threads might be dominating, and – from a temporal point of view – email exchanges might sometimes occur sporadically and then again rather concentrated, so that insights into collaboration patterns demand the integration of temporal analyses.

Sources

In this paper, the proposed methodological approach to email analysis will focus on emails from a professional/work background that had been collected in the course of a project funded by the European Commission (OPAALS Network of Excellence, 6th Framework Programme). The project ran 4.5 years, with an additional preceding year of the project proposal writing process, and included researchers from two main disciplines (social sciences/humanities, natural sciences/computer science), as well as administrative staff.

The email corpus for this study contains all emails sent on the general mailing list of the project, to which all members had access and could also send messages. Additionally, there are emails from two discipline-specific mailing lists: the social scientists' mailing list and the computer scientists' mailing list. Those two lists comprise comparatively few emails, however were included in the sample due to their specific target groups.

All in all, the corpus contained 1,209 emails, sent in the course of approximately 5.5 years. This sample is not representative in terms of all work setting email exchanges, nevertheless it is one of the very few samples that integrates a large number of emails. As already mentioned above, the availability of large data sets of emails is usually rather restricted[2].

Quantitative data

The following table provides a detailed overview on the email corpus. It shows the general corpus statistics before and after the corpus cleaning. The reason for this is that there are remarkable differences in terms of numbers of the tokens, which is again partly due to the specific communication medium email. As Harrison states: "The amount of text generated in e-mail discussions is very large, but some of this text is quotation, which is facilitated by e-mail software, and some text is added automatically by the software (some header and archive data, and signatures that have previously been set up by participants)" (Harrison, 2008, p. 759). For the analysis of emails in this study all quotations (i.e. prior messages) were deleted in the corpus cleaning process, including the typical usage of a stop-word-list and a lemmatisation process. So for example the difference of the number of tokens of

---

2 One example for another large data set is the well-known ENRON email corpus, however which is also restricted to one specific source/community and therefore not representative (see for example Klimt and Yang, 2004; Carvalho and Cohen, 2007).

the emails in Phase I (PI)[3] in the project results in almost one fifth of the original number of tokens after the corpus cleaning. This remarkably high difference derives mainly from the aforementioned quotation phenomenon in emails, which is not given in the analysis of for example newspaper articles.

	Texts	Types	Tokens	TTR	Types cleaned	Tokens cleaned	TTR cleaned
Emails before Project	136	3,120	51,878	54.47	2,769	16,310	56.47
Emails PI	248	5,310	233,875	57.45	4,896	59,287	61.78
Emails PII	316	5,570	277,115	53.55	5,028	69,956	58.15
Emails PIII	194	4,170	84,783	52.78	3,561	33,383	60.91
CompSci	236				3,914	45,488	52.38
SocSci	79				2,335	12,306	57.70
All	***1,209***				***22,503***	***236,730***	

Figure 10.3: Overview of the email corpus

In order to find a way to deal with the aforementioned challenges of email analysis (see page XY), a method mix of a quantitative content analysis followed by a linguistic corpus analysis was applied. This combination firstly aimed at providing a systematic approach to the corpus, regarding the analysis of relevant points/dates in the projects, where for example a high interaction (i.e. email exchange) took place. Secondly, the content analysis provided input as to whether there had been any threads – that is longer email discussions on the same topic – in the course of the project. Those threads could then be analysed in detail regarding the content and language usage. A third reason for the preliminary content analysis refers to the aforementioned challenge as to the irregular contribution of individual members to email communication in groups.

Figure 3 shows the result of the content analysis in a temporal representation of the amounts of emails in the general mailing list sent over the course of the project (beginning with the official project start in June 2006). Included are the annual reviews of the project. Those reviews were face-to-face meetings, where the project's progress was being assessed by external reviewers. As can be seen, in

3 The allocation of the emails into the three main phases of the project had been carried out in order to provide the means for a rough temporal analysis. All three phases had a duration of approximately 18 months.

those months when project reviews took place, a high amount of email exchanges took place, whereas for example months with general meetings scored less.

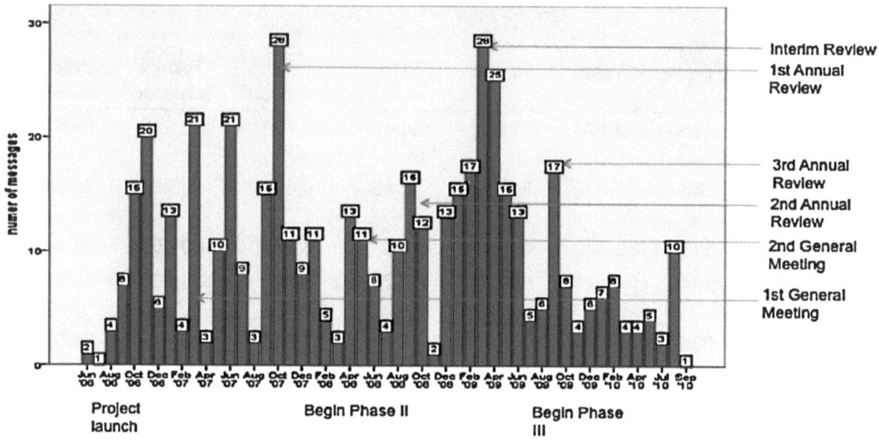

Figure 10.4: Results of the content analysis – temporal perspective

In turn, the content analyses of the discipline-specific mailing lists show a very different picture. Emails were sent on the social scientists' mailing list only from August 2007 to March 2009, whereas most of the emails were sent in September 2007 (23 emails), May 2008 (29 emails) and in the following month June 2008 (20 emails). The active usage of the computer scientists' mailing list was with one year (July 2009 to June 2010) even shorter, however with a more regular interaction.

Analysis

The content analyses showed that the amount of emails sent on general mailing list of the project is to a certain extent dependent on concrete face-to-face meeting. Hence, it can be assumed that the general mailing list was then used for administrative issues than, for example, for project content related discussions. The discipline-specific mailing lists in contrast were not used during the whole project life span and differed also among them strongly in terms of time-span and regular/irregular email exchange.

A subsequent analysis step was now to pursue the question whether concrete interaction or collaboration took place by means of each mailing list. This was again facilitated by content analysis, specifically regarding the question whether the emails sent were part of a dialogue or discussion, i.e. whether a question-answer structure could be detected or not. Figure 3 shows that the discipline-specific mailing lists contained significantly more emails which were answers to preceding questions. On the other hand, the low percentage of answers on the general mailing list underlines the assumption that this mailing list had not been used predominantly for discussions.

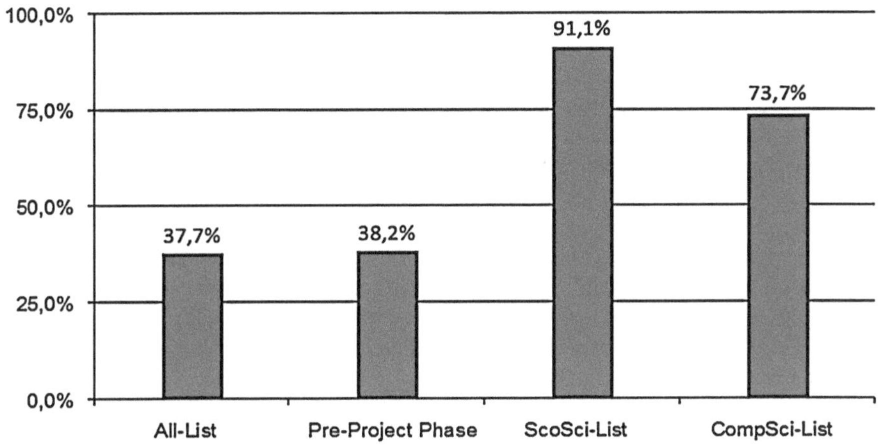

Figure 10.5: Amount of emails which were an answer to preceding questions

Following up on the results depicted in Figure 5, a linguistic corpus analysis was conducted regarding the usage of directives in the emails of the general mailing list. Rationale is here that if this mailing list had been used mainly for administrative purposes – for example as a tool to prepare review meetings – the communication should contain directives indicated by the usage of modal verbs such as 'should' or 'must'. In order to also hold to the discipline-specific perspective, the corpus had been divided into emails sent by social scientists and computer scientists. The corpus analyses showed that 'should' was the modal verb mostly used in both domains/disciplines. The comparatively strong modal verb 'must' was also used, however (referring back to the results from the content analysis) in both domains mainly related to the preparation of conferences or other meetings.

Additionally two outstanding cases where the usage of 'must' was even emphasized by bold face type were analysed in more detail. The discourse analysis showed that the first case was an email sent by the project coordinator, which contained a rather personal view upon the participation rate of the project members in the preparation of an upcoming workshop. The email starts with "I am a bit concerned" and then focuses (in nine lengthy paragraphs) on the expected results regarding the development of a specific, project-related software application.

Finally it finishes with the sentence: "I hope it is now clear to everyone that we **must** deliver the goods." Hence, one finds here an explicit directive, introduced however by a long explanation or justification of the urgency.

The second email was sent by the coordinator of the computer science domain. In contrast to the first example, the emphasized usage of 'must' appeared here in a meta-comment regarding the work routine/practice that the domain coordinator is used to, or rather expects: "I spent seven years of my life teaching system developers in various divisions of [company name] that they **must** define 'what' before they design the 'how'." This sentence shows that the occurrence of the modal verb 'must' is here on the one hand not part of an explicit directive, but on the other hand also in a rather personal context, like in the first example. This is also underscored by the fact that both sentences start with the first person personal pronoun 'I'. Another interesting result from this discourse analysis is that both examples derive from project members that have a coordinating/management role in the project, which could be an indicator for the role of hierarchies in the project.

Taking up this last point, further results from the quantitative content analysis can again provide more insights: Table 6 shows indeed a clear dominance of members from the project management as senders of emails. Almost 52% of the emails from the general mailing list (all-list) was sent by work package leaders[4], and more than 35% by the project coordinator. Furthermore, the results regarding the domain-specific mailing lists show that the social scientists list had a clearly stronger hierarchical structure with almost 42% of the emails sent by work package leaders (in contrast to the computer scientists list with only 15 %).

	Social Scientists List	Computer Scientists List	All-List
Work package leader	41.8	15.1	51.7
Project coordinator	10.1	11.6	35.7

Figure 10.6: Percentage of emails sent by work package leaders and/or project coordinator

A second course of analysis that demonstrates the application of a mixed methods approach relates again to domain specific differences in language usage (register analysis). One results of the preliminary content analysis was the aforementioned irregular usage of the social scientists mailing list. Furthermore,

4 The work carried out in the project was structured by means of work packages that in turn contained single tasks on which one or more partner institutions worked. The category „work package leader" includes all members who were in charge of the management of one of the altogether 14 work packages of the project, as well as the domain coordinators (who were always also work package leaders), as well as the project coordinator who was also leading one work package.

most emails were sent in only three months, whereas the content analysis also showed that the emails sent in the last two months belonged mainly to one and the same thread. This thread dealt with the planning and discussion of an interdisciplinary report, and hence included participants from both domains (social scientists and computer scientists). The content analysis results therefore pointed towards the assumption that this was a significant thread/discussion, which could reveal interesting facts regarding the collaboration inside this project and particularly between the two disciplines.

Figure 7 shows the number of emails sent in this thread, together with the general results from the corpus analysis.

	No. of Emails	Types	Tokens	TTR
SocSci	23	1,388	4,390	59.13
CompSci	24	1,176	3,810	55.00

Figure 10.7: Thread corpus

This first rough view on the linguistic interaction already shows a difference regarding the Type-Token-Relationship of the two domains. A word frequency analysis then showed that the work 'understand*' had been used very often, which is why a plot analysis was carried out.

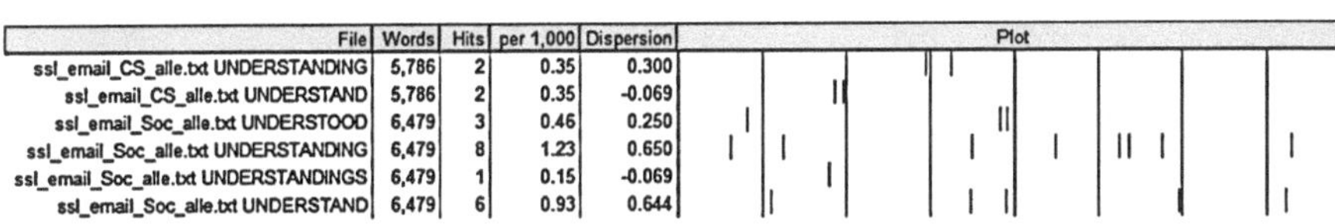

File	Words	Hits	per 1,000	Dispersion	Plot
ssl_email_CS_alle.txt UNDERSTANDING	5,786	2	0.35	0.300	
ssl_email_CS_alle.txt UNDERSTAND	5,786	2	0.35	-0.069	
ssl_email_Soc_alle.txt UNDERSTOOD	6,479	3	0.46	0.250	
ssl_email_Soc_alle.txt UNDERSTANDING	6,479	8	1.23	0.650	
ssl_email_Soc_alle.txt UNDERSTANDINGS	6,479	1	0.15	-0.069	
ssl_email_Soc_alle.txt UNDERSTAND	6,479	6	0.93	0.644	

Figure 10.8: Plot analysis of "understand"*

The first two lines in figure 8 show the usage of the different forms of the lemma 'understand' within the computer science domain, whereas the last four lines reveal the usage of 'understand*' in the social sciences domain. A first interesting result is that the social scientists use the lemma 'understand' more often than the computer scientists, albeit all emails analysed here were sent on the social science mailing list. Hence, one would assume a discursive "dominance" of the social scientists in terms of them explaining something to the computer scientists (who might use therefore the term 'understand' in the context of trying to understand a new topic/different disciplinary views). The results however indicate a reverse picture.

A different indicator regarding the perceived dominance of one group is the usage of strong modal verbs such as 'must' in contrast to 'should' or 'could'. The results here show that indeed the social scientists regularly use the comparatively weaker modal verbs 'should' and 'could', whereas they only once use 'must'. On the other hand, the computer scientists use 'must' seven times, and even once 'ought to'.

The results show an interesting reverse picture as to the linguistic dominance of a specific mailing list. Despite the fact that the analysed list was initiated by social scientists – and even called 'social science mailing list' – in most emails the few participating computer scientists dominated the discourse. Nevertheless, a further detailed discourse analyses revealed that the overall tone was very polite on both sides, which is shown in the following examples:

Social Scientists:

- "The highlights you have selected from the DOW are really insightful and appropriate, and they map over very well to some of the social science areas of interest"
- "Dear B2 many thanks for all these excellent explanations you are sending
- "Thank you again for the explanation"

Computer Scientists:

- "Thanks for your email; your questions are quite good (and technical)"
- "This is a great document, I really enjoyed reading it"
- "I am learning a lot from social scientists"

Figure 10.9.

Blogs and Usenet

Sources

Other internet sources used in the present study come from five different sources. Three Polish sources are blogs, a Polish open forum and the Polish Usenet. The English data are samples of the English blogs and the English Usenet, all accessed between 1 January and 31 March 2011 at the following websites:

1. Polish blogs from *blog.onet.pl* and those accessed at http://frazeo.pl/catalogue_by_date.jsp
2. Polish open forum www.forumowisko.pl
3. Polish Usenet
4. English blogs [search via top topics of a day with the advanced search function]: http://frazeo.com/catalogue_by_date.jsp and those accessed at http://blogsearch.google.com/
5. English *Usenet*

Out of the source domains, those on politics were searched and eventually those relevant to the current North African, and more precisely, Libyan, conflict, were investigated.

For the sake of completeness the materials from the Usenet were also identified and investigated. The name *Usenet* is used to refer to a distributed and heterogenous system of computer discussion groups. Its users participate in discussions by sending emails, i.e. *posts*, to one or many named newsgroups, initiating a discussion on a new topic or replying to posts by other users. It is important to note that the newsgroups, while divided in thematic hierarchies – eg. *soc.politics.uk* or *sci.physics* - they are not moderated in any way, and no other message filtering is used. This enables frankness as any user can post any content, not necessarily related to the name of the group. On the other hand, anonymity encourages identity construction not necessarily reflecting the users' real selves.

Quantitative data

The following amounts of Polish blog data were examined for the purposes of the present work:

Type	Texts	Authors	Words
Post	12,828	1,195	4,786,048
Comment	120,796	34,508	5,231,211

Figure 10.10.

What should be noted at this point is the phenomenon of possible *complex interchangeability* of communication, which presupposes a possibility of a user to employ more than one nick. Our assumption concerning the authorship here is that by an *Author* we understand a person using the same nick. The blog data shows the following regularity with reference to the word frequency per one post and per one comment:

1 author – average 10 posts
Average 400 words per 1 post
Average close to 40 words for 1 comment

Figure 10.11.

The Usenet structure (newsgrupa pl.soc.polityka accessed from 01/12/2010 – 03/30/2011) shows significant quantitative differences as in (12) below:

Texts: 23 952
Words: 1 921 185
Authors: 686

1 author – average 30 posts
(Average – 85 words for one text)

Figure 10.12.

A conclusion is that in the Usenet there is a small number of authors, talking to one another. The data also shows clearly that the Usenet is in retreat while other modes of CMC are advancing.

Topics and emotions

On 28 February 2011 the two prevailing topics both in the traditional media (press, radio, TV) as well as in CMC were:

1. Oscar for King's Speech
2. Libya; American/European intervention

The two themes made the top titles in the media. In the Polish Usenet data on this day there were identified 67 concordances for 'Libi*' and 49 for 'Kadaffi*' using Wordsmith Tools. The form *Kaddafi* serves as the base for word-formation processes such as abstract nominalization *kadafizacja* 'Quaddafisation' and Agentive nominalization *kaddafiści* 'Quaddafists'. Some of the examples are given below:

	N	Word	Freq.
–	*99 994*	*LIBIA*	*59*
–	*99 995*	*LIBIĄ*	*7*
–	*100 013*	*LIBIJCZYCY*	*5*
–	*100 014*	*LIBIJCZYKA*	*1*
–	*100 015*	*LIBIJCZYKAMI*	*4*
–	*100 016*	*LIBIJCZYKOM*	*2*
–	*100 017*	*LIBIJCZYKÓW*	*11*
–	*100 018*	*LIBIJSCY*	*2*
–	*100 019*	*LIBIJSKA*	*7*
–	*100 020*	*LIBIJSKĄ*	*1*
–	*100 021*	*LIBIJSKI*	*9*
–	*100 022*	*LIBIJSKICH*	*3*

- *100 023 LIBIJSKIE 4*
- *100 024 LIBIJSKIEGO 5*
- *100 025 LIBIJSKIEJ 9*
- *100 026 LIBIJSKIM 4*

*Figure 10.13. LIBI**

- *78 663 KADDAFI*
- *78 665 KADDAFIEGO*
- *78 666 KADDAFII*
- *78 667 KADDAFIM*
- *78 668 KADDAFISTAMI*
- *78 669 KADDAFI-STRASZY-ZACHOD-SOJUSZEM-Z-AL-KAIDA*
- *78 671 KADDAFIZACJI*

*Figure 10.14. Kadafi **

Threat and fear

North African events are most frequently presented in the media in terms of FIGHT and direct THREAT and FEAR (see concordance 78 669 in (14) above). In popular culture and media, both traditional and new, fear is a steady element used as a political weapon and ideology, contributing to the *negativity* of the content to "keep the audiences in the state of constant arousal" (see Altheide and Snow 1991) and meant to increase the media political and business profits.

Media incite fear in terms of different *event scenarios*, in the time of the analysis it was the North African conflict. There are three different outcomes in the FEAR scenarios possible: FIGHT, FRIGHT and FLIGHT (Lewandowska-Tomaszczyk and Wilson in press). The CMC samples discussed in this section uncover additional dimensions of the 'culture of fear' scenarios. The first one to be observed in the Polish blogs and posts () is much lower emotional involvement, so the perlocutionary effect of the FEAR scenario does not hit the target. No threat is recognized, so there is no FEAR effect.

- #11 Kenobi
- ***Napisano 21 marzec (21 March) 2011 - 19:14***
- ***Lobo - twoj ulubiony PiS postuluje ze polskie wojsko powinno byc w Libii***
  'your beloved Law and Justice [i.e. a rightist political party] postulates that the Polish military should be in Libya'
- ***Bać się raczej nie boję. Przynajmniej na razie. Cieszę się natomiast, że ktoś to w końcu załatwi. A kto i jakie miał naprawdę powody, to mi gancegal. Oby tylko szybko poszło, żeby wakacje nad Morzem Śródziemnym można było spokojnie spędzić. Bywalec***

'As for fear, I' m not particularly frightened, at least for the time being. And I am happy though that someone will eventually take care of this. And who and for what reasons – it ' s all the same to me. Let it only be fast so that one could spend one's holidays at the Mediterranean, unbothered by anything'.

Figure 10.15. Source: Open forum (FORUMOWISKO)

- 102 "ein Reich, ein Volk, ein Gaddafi" powstańcy wyobrażają sobie życie bez p. Kaddafiego, ale naród libijski i państwo libijskie traktują jako całość. polityka.txt
  ' "ein Reich, ein Volk, ein Gaddafi", the insurgents imagine life without Mr Gaddafi but they treat the Libyan nation and state as a whole'

- 103 Nie twierdzę wcale, że Kadaffi powinien zostać, ale to wewnętrzna sprawa Libii i powinni sobie to sami załatwić
  'I don't say Gadaffi should stay but it's an internal thing for Libya – they should deal with that themselves.'

Figure 10.16. source: Usenet

The English data contains significantly different reactions (). They show higher arousal, more polarization of the positions taken, summing up they are more involved and more emotional.

- 28 Feb 2011
- ***What next for Gaddafi and Libya?***
- (...) What next for Gaddafi and Libya? (...)
  19:52 | **EURONEWS.NET** |
- ***VIDEO: What next for Libya with Gaddafi defiant?***
- The BBC's Frank Gardner analyses what the future may hold for Libya, as Col Gaddafi clings to power despite mounting international pressure. (...) VIDEO: Whatnext for Libya with Gaddafi defiant? The BBC's Frank Gardner ana(...)

Figure 10.17. English EuroNews and blogs [search: LIBYA]

- ***28 luty 2011, 01:45 | BBC.CO.UK |***
- **3. Global pressure mounts on Gaddafi**
- British and Canadian prime ministers seek Gaddafi's ouster as Hillary Clinton prepares for talks on Libya in Geneva. (...) Global pressure mounts on GaddafiBritish and Canadian prime ministers seek Gaddafi's ouster as Hillary Clinton prepares for talks on Libya in Geneva.(...)

Figure 10.18. English BBC [search: LIBYA]

Quite a number of English reactions on the other hand involve sarcasm, rhetorical Qs, and/or provocation:

- *Something Stinks* **03/03/2011 01:50 PM**
- ***How many countries has Libya invaded recently?***
- ***If the people in this country got out in the streets and revolted do you think they would not be shot and killed?***
- ***Let's demonize Qaddafi, after all, we pay that guy and anyway, he has OUR oil. It isn't like it is THEIR country.***

Figure 10.19. English blogs

Direct, emotional talk is part and parcel of the THREAT scenarios.

- *Something stinks*
- ***Pay no attention to our wars of imperialism for dope, oil and Israel.***
- ***Qaddafi? He SOOOOO bad.***
  and Obama is SOOOOO Teflon.
  How many has he killed so far?

Figure 10.20. English blogs

The users resort to other painful events in the British history of the eighties (Lockerbie bombing in which a PAN AM plane crashed in 1988) to invoke a conspiracy theory of history:

- ***As for Lockerbie, it was CIA baggage that DID NOT get inspected because it was supposed to be drugs, but someone burned them on that deal, didn't they?***
  Stuff happens when you cross folks in the international drug trade. Let's blame Libya instead of blaming the CIA's drug running operations.

Figure 21. English blogs

Discussion of the data

Emotions are expressed visually, verbally and paralinguistically. In CMC emoticons, punctuation marks, idiosyncratic symbols or emotional language[5] are used for this purpose.

---

5 In linguistic literature a distinction is made between the language of emotions (e.g. John hates Mary) , in which language is used to describe or refer to emotions, and emotional language, in which language used expresses emotions, not necessarily by using emotion terms (e.g. You stupid bastard) cf. (cf. Lewandowska-Tomaszczyk and Wilson in press).

Emotional language can comprise sarcasm, ridiculing, parabole, and other figures of speech, all of which are present in regular face-to-face interactions as well as in CMC.

The users clearly recognize the manufacturing of fear in the traditional media. Their sarcasm and irony express a distrust to official politicians and, particularly in the English blogs, they convey clearly anti-American, and anti-government sentiments.

The spontaneous reaction to fear is an extension of FEAR scenario, where the cause is identified as fake, etc. so the FIGHT reaction, mentioned above, does not include one of the prototypical reactions to FEAR but refers rather to the *fighting of the FEAR presupposition*, conveyed in the texts published in the traditional media. Additional dimensions of the manufacturing of FEAR scenarios make a distinction between what can be called fear as a 'rational' emotion, and other, 'irrational' types of fear which cannot be considered fear proper but rather phobias.

The users estimate then the *plausibility of the THREAT and DANGER stimuli* involved in a realistic theory of danger and rational fear. Anticipation and awareness of danger as well as susceptibility, vulnerability to harm, risk, injury, creating a complex of realistic theory of FEAR meet with a ubiquitous reaction of British bloggers with sarcasm and irony as a type of FIGHT reaction. Another reaction is the rationalisation of the source of THREAT in terms of a conspiracy theory as a naive deconstructive model of history.

A comparison between the English versus Polish attitudes in the FEAR scenario shows divergence. The English blogs in majority involve pro-Libyan sentiments even though the clarification as to whether such attitudes are pro- or anti-Qadaffi, easier to uncover in the Polish data, is not easy to identify. On the other hand, their sentiments are clearly anti-(American) coalition with the FIGHT scenario reactions and unjustified threats recognized on the part of the American/European intervention. The bloggers are more directly involved, they tend to be provocative and sarcastic considering threats invoked in the media as ill-directed.

The Polish blogs show a much more balanced, less direct, clearly less involved and more careful attitude. This is understandable due to the much less active role Poland plays in the conflict.

As to the participation structure in these exchanges the users are either *instigators* and *opponents* or *followers* on the one hand or *provokers* on the other. Followers are the least likely to use emotional language and hyperbolic imagery, which is typical rather of instigators or provokers in particular.

An interesting observation can be that the CMC users we analysed can be considered relatively steady in their opinions. Their profiles drawn from their posts and comments show a certain rigidity in their opinions and lack of inclination to modify their positions.

Conclusions

The e-mail communication shows a number of differences when contrasted with blogs and Usenet posts and comments. The email communication analysed is first of all non-anonymous. In the analysed material the topics are from a project-related context, so the level of formality (hence politeness) is much higher than in the case of anonymous, much more emotional talks in the Usenet and posts. Also, the analysed general mailing list was mainly used for administrative reason, hence no concrete discussions could be detected. The results of also showed that a combination of different instruments enables a systematic approach to linguistic analyses of CMC. The content analysis as a first step provided relevant insights in terms of the existence (or non-existence) of dialogue-structures, the relations of email exchange quantities with certain events, and existing dominance or power structures. The corpus analysis subsequently showed results in terms of the frequency of certain terms, which was then further analysed by means of a discourse analysis. Hence, questions as to interaction structures etc. could be answered from different perspectives, providing finally a more conclusive picture than one would have obtained from the application of merely one analytic procedure/instrument.

The political topics discussed in blogs and fora arouse more emotion and enable taking a more polarized stand in the discussion. Nevertheless, the political themes involve different types and degrees of emotional arousal and appraisal in English as opposed to Polish bloggers and post authors. The reasons are external: a weaker involvement of the Polish government and Polish people with the North African conflict, contrary to the British side.

Another set of conclusions is more technologically-based and related to the methodology of the CMC research. The availability of user-generated content stored in the *CMC corpus data* makes it possible to conduct a qualitative and quantitative analysis of the attitudes of media audiences towards real life events and problems encountered. Since all such messages come with explicit annotation of the time they were first published, it is possible to correlate the predominant sentiments of CMC users with those expressed in the media contents published in the same or immediately preceding time period.

References

Alheide, D. and P. Snow (1991). Media Worlds in the Postjournalism Era. New York, NY: Walter de Gruyter Inc.

Baron, N. (2003). "The Language of the Internet". In Handbook for Language Engineers, Farghaly, A. (ed.), 59-128. Stanford: CSLI Publications.

Biber, D. and S. Conrad (2009). Register, Genre, and Style. Cambridge: Cambidge University Press.

Bruhn Jensen, K. (2010). Media Convergence: The Three Degrees of Network, Mass and Interpersonal Communication. Routledge Chapman and Hall.

Bruhn Jensen, K. (2009). "Three-Step Flow". Journalism 10(3): 335-337.
Bruns, A. (2008). Blogs, Wikipedia, Second Life, and beyond: From Production to Produsage. New York: Lang.
Carvalho, V. R. and W. Cohen (2007). "Recommending Recipients in the Enron Email Corpus", Machine Learning. Citeseer.
Crystal, D. (2001). Language and the Internet. Cambridge: Cambridge University Press.
Danet, B. (1998). "Text as a Mask: Gender, Play, and Performance in the Internet". In Cybersociety 2.0: Revisiting Computer Mediated Communication and Community, Jones, S. (ed.), 129-158. Thousand Oaks, CA: Sage Publications.
Donath, J. (1996). "Inhabiting the Virtual City: The Design of Social Environments for Electronic Communities". PhD dissertation. MIT.
Dziwirek, K. and B. Lewandowska-Tomaszczyk (2010). Complex Emotions and Grammatical Mismatches. Berlin: Mouton de Gruyter.
Frehner, C. (2008). Email - SMS - MMS. Bern: Peter Lang.
Harrison, S. (2008). "Turn Taking in E-Mail Discussions". In Handbook of Research on Computer Mediated Communication, Kelsey, S. and Amant, K. St. (eds.), 755-772. Hershey PA, London: IGI Global.
Herring, S. C. (2004a). "Computer-Mediated Discourse Analysis: An Approach to Researching Online Behavior". In Designing for Virtual Communities in the Service of Learning, Barab, S. A., Kling, R. and Gray, J. H. (eds.), 338-376. Cambridge: Cambridge University Press.
Herring, S. C. (2004b). "Online Communication: Through the Lens of Discourse". In Internet Research Annual, Consalvo, M. et al. (eds.), 65-76. New York, NY: Peter Lang.
Herring, S. C. (2007). "A Faceted Classification Scheme for Computer-Mediated Discourse". language@internet, 4.
Herring, S. C. (2010). "Digital media". In The Cambridge Encyclopedia of the Language Sciences, Hogan, P. (ed.). Cambridge: Cambridge University Press.
Kavada, A. (2009). "Email Lists and the Construction of an Open and Multifaceted Identity," Information, Communication and Society, 12(6): 817-839.
Kiesler, S., Siegel, J. and T. W. McGuire (1984). "Social Psychological Aspects of Computer-mediated Communication," American Psychologist, 39(10): 1123-1134.
Klimt, B. and Y. Yang (2004). "The Enron Corpus: A New Dataset for Email Classification Research," Machine Learning: ECML 2004, pp. 217-226.
Available at: http://www.springerlink.com/index/Q8G7BLQVQYXRPVAP
Lazarsfeld, P. F. and E. Katz (1955). Personal Influence. The Part Played by People in the Flow of Mass Communications. A Report of the Bureau of Applied Social Research, Columbia University. Glencoe: The Free Press.
Lewandowska-Tomaszczyk, B. and K. Dziwirek (eds.). (2009). Studies in Cognitive Corpus Linguistics. Frankfurt a. Main: Peter Lang.
Lewandowska-Tomaszczyk, B. and J. Tomaszczyk (in press). "We In the Union: A Polish Perspective on Identity".
Lewandowska-Tomaszczyk, B. (forthcoming) "Perception of Political Events in English and Polish Computer-Mediated Communication". InterCom 2011.
Lewandowska-Tomaszczyk and P. Wilson (in press). English Fear and Polish Strach in Contrast: GRID approach and Cognitive Corpus Linguistic methodology.
Toffler, A. (1980). The Third Wave. Bantam Books.
Zeller, F. and J. Wallmannsberger (2007). "Digital Ecosystems and Language". In Digital Business Ecosystems, Nachira, F. et al. (eds.), 56-59. Brussels: European Commission.
Zeller, F. and J. Wolling (2010). "Struktur- und Qualitätsanalyse Publizistischer Online-Angebote". Media Perspektiven 3: 143-153.

Investigating Semantic Sequences in Academic Legal Discourse. An Exploratory Study

Stanisław Goźdź-Roszkowski

Abstract

This study attempts to explore whether semantic sequences, a new type of recurring meaning-based elements, could be applied to investigate the construction of epistemology in legal discourse. A small-scale study of two nouns (*idea* and *notion*) frequently found in the pattern *the* + Noun + *that*-clause reveals their preference for co-occurring in evaluative semantic sequences. It is argued that semantic sequences of this type could be potentially very useful in describing evaluative language in academic legal discourse.

Keywords

Grammar pattern, epistemology, legal discourse, meaning, phraseology, semantic sequence

Introduction

It is now widely acknowledged that one of the greatest benefits provided by corpus linguistics is bringing phraseology to the fore of linguistic inquiry. The last three decades have seen a multitude of different types of recurrence proposed. Examples include lexical bundles (e.g. Biber et al. 1999), collocational frameworks (Renouf and Sinclair 1991), units of meaning (Sinclair 1991), grammar patterns (Hunston and Francis 2000), formulaic sequences (e.g. Wray 2002). One of the most recent additions is semantic sequence (Hunston 2009). The importance of repeated sequences of wordforms in specialized discourse can be hardly overestimated. Several corpus-based studies have recently begun to explore fundamental issues such as the way and extent to which patterns and phraseological items contribute to the creation and understanding of meaning, how such recurrent items shape beliefs, values and social structures and how specialized meanings and their relationships enacted through phraseology become linked to particular domains in which they are produced (cf. a useful overview in Schulze and Römer 2008)

Depending on a particular genre, word combinations can play a crucial role in legal discourse. In her analysis of word combinations in German legal language, Kjaer (1990: 28) argues that failure to employ prefabricated word combinations directly prescribed by the law may lead to "the invalidation of the whole text of which they form a part". In other cases, legal force or the security of law could be affected. Interestingly, there are relatively few studies that deal with phraseological issues in English legal language. Goźdź-Roszkowski (2011) demonstrates the central importance of phraseological patterns in text classification and the textual construction of different legal genres. For example, it appears that in legislation and contracts lexical bundles account for as much as 10% of the texts.[1] While extremely useful in studying relatively narrow, well-defined and repetitive genres, lexical bundles can be sometimes too inflexible to handle certain subtle phenomena in language. This study turns to a new concept of semantic sequence Hunston (2008) in order to begin exploring how different discoursal functions, especially those connected with evaluation can be expressed in judicial discourse. The paper first summarizes the methodology used to identify semantic sequences (Section 2). It turns out that the pattern N + *that* followed by appositive clauses can be highly productive in uncovering linguistic mechanisms used to express evaluation in legal academic discourse. Finally, the paper turns to a presentation and discussion of the preliminary findings on the frequency and function of semantic sequences in academic journals and textbooks (Section 3).

Methodology

What are semantic sequences?

The concept of semantic sequence is a new candidate for describing regularity in text. According to Hunston, semantic sequences are "recurring sequences of words and phrases that may be very diverse in form and which are therefore characterised as sequences of meaning elements rather than as formal sequences" (2008: 271). The sequence consists of a 'core item'(lexical word), the complementation pattern(s) associated with that word and a number of phrase types occurring before the core word which are consistent in terms of meaning. The concept of semantic sequence looks particularly promising for analyzing disciplinary discourses. Studies done by Charles (2004), Gledhill (2000) and Groom (2007) provide important evidence that disciplines may well be characterized by their unique phraseological profiles or templates. It appears that there are various ways of identifying semantic sequences. Both Gledhill and Groom argue that grammatical words, such as prepositions can be treated as a useful starting point for identifying semantic sequences in domain-specific corpora. As Hunston (2008) convincingly demonstrates, semantic sequences can also be found by starting with a phrase or a pattern. This stage is immediately followed by examining the relevant co-texts of a lexical item, grammatical words (e.g. prepositions) or a grammatical pattern.

This study starts with the grammatical pattern of *the* +Noun + *that*, where a noun is followed by an appositive *that*-clause. It is usually accepted that status nouns (with the pattern 'N *that*') are particularly significant in the construction of knowledge (Halliday and Matthiessen 2004). The noun in this pattern indicates the

---

1 The lexical bundles in that study were identified using fairly conservative criteria and they include only four-word sequences which appear at least 40 times per one million word in at least five different texts (See Chapter 4 in Goźdź-Roszkowski 2011 for a detailed discussion of the findings.

epistemic status of the proposition expressed in the *that*-clause. Projected clauses of this type are important to disciplinary epistemology. For example, Hunston (2008) investigates the phrase *the observation that* in the New Scientist Corpus. It emerges that it tends to follow an indication of consequence (e.g. *the argument is based on the observation that*); consistency (e.g. *this is consistent with the observation that*); an observation is confirmed by other observations (*our evidence, therefore, supports the observation that*). When the subject of a clause, observation is related to theory in a causal way. The phraseology can be related to the role that 'observation' plays in the construction of scientific knowledge. Observations lead to deductions. An argument might 'rest on' an observation or be judged as correct because it 'fits' an observation or be judged incorrect because an observation does not mean something. As a result, it is pointed out that the following semantic sequence emerges: *the observation* + *that*-clause + 'consistency' + 'theory / argument'. Inspired by Hunston's explorations of the N+*that* pattern in scientific discourse, this paper attempts to identify similar patterning in legal academic discourse. In doing so, a number of research questions could be posed. The most fundamental ones centre upon the method of semantic sequence identification and their discoursal function or functions.

Given the preliminary nature of this paper, the decision was made to start with the grammatical pattern Noun + *that* in an attempt to link the present investigation with the previous study of semantic sequences in scientific discourse (Hunston (2008). Adopting the same methodological step enables one to start addressing other important questions related to the degree of similarity between different types of specialized discourse. Ultimately, this line of research could lead to the discovery of semantic sequences unique to the construction of evaluation in legal discourse.

Corpus used for the study

Hunston (2008: 281) provides a list of 11 nouns (*assumption, belief, claim, conclusion, discovery, idea, impression, notion, view, suggestion, theory*) found in the *the* + Noun + *that* pattern "that best exemplify evaluation of epistemic status" in the New Scientist corpus[2]. As a first step, it was decided to examine whether these nouns are equally effective in marking evaluation of epistemic status in legal academic texts. The analysis was thus based on selected data from the American Law Corpus (ALC) compiled by the author and described in detail in Goźdź-Roszkowski (2011: 27-30). The ALC was constructed to represent major legal

2 These nouns were first identified on the basis of their frequency (5.1 occurrences per million words or more) in a corpus of about 8 million words compiled from the weekly journal New Scientist).

genres used in the US legal discourse. For the purpose of this analysis, only academic texts were used (Table 1).

Table 11.1: Composition of the sub-corpus used in the analysis (taken from the ALC corpus)

Genre	# of texts	# of words
Academic journals	71	552,487
Textbooks	104[3]	519,116
TOTAL	175	1,071,603

Discussion of findings

Each of the eleven nouns was subsequently investigated using the search sequence *the assumption + that*, *the belief + that*, and so on. Except for two nouns (*impression* and *discovery*), all the other nouns are found in this pattern with a frequency exceeding 5.1 occurrences per million words[4]. The absence of *impression* and *discovery* does not seem to be accidental. In fact, it appears to be linked to the specificity of the legal domain. *Discovery* is a legal term which denotes a significant concept in American legal procedure (Black 1990)[5]. For this reason, the word form *discovery* tends to be used in the technical rather than in its more everyday sense. On the other hand, *impression* is probably avoided in a discourse which favours categorical ways of expressing argumentation (Solan 1993).

The next stage was to identify phraseological patterns for some of the eleven nouns in order to arrive at a comprehensive set of discourse functions associated with the pattern. This was accomplished by studying the co-text of a few selected lexical items using the Concord feature of the WordSmith Tools (Scott 2008). The examples were arranged in groups depending on their co-texts. The number of instances found in each group was calculated. Figures 1 and 2 show the results.

The examination of the 'core' item *idea that* shows an extensive consistency of function. One clear function is associated with the expression of evaluation. Something referred to as 'idea' tends to be evaluated in negative terms. This is usually accomplished through the use of value-laden, highly evaluative adjectives such as *offensive, indefensible, rigid* or *preposterous*. However, as examples in Table 2 show, negative evaluation can also be evoked by means of nouns (e.g. *harshness*).

3 This number refers to text samples rather than full texts. Data collection focused on collecting ten different samples from ten different undergraduate textbooks on contracts and commercial law. Each sample contains 5000 words.

4 This search could yield even more occurrences if it allowed for words other than 'the' immediately preceding the noun.

5 The interested leader might want to refer to Goźdź-Roszkowski (forth.) for a detailed corpus-based study of this term in US Supreme Court opinions.

Table 11.2: The idea that totaling 22 instances

Group	Frequency	Sample environments
Idea that is the CAUSE	5 (23%)	*the whole model is suffused with ...* *all of these efforts are premised on ...*
Idea that is EVALUATED	7	*... encourages harshness* *...is offensive* *... is both in logic indefensible and in practice impossible of application* *...is far too rigid* *... was (...) preposterous*
Idea that is SUPPORTED	6	*empirical support for...* *regression results in this paper sustain ...* *This coincidence reinforces ...*
Idea that is CAUSED	1	*implicit in ...*
Idea that EXISTS	3	*one of the main strands which runs through this literature is...*

Idea that also co-occurs with lexical items indicating confirmation for findings obtained in the course of empirical research or conclusions reached through argumentation (e.g. *empirical support for the idea that*). The third distinct function is associated with *idea that* serving as a cause or basis for constructing some mental construct or as a stimulus for some kind of activity (e.g. *model is suffused with the idea that, these efforts are premised on the idea that*).

The three major functions identified for *the idea that* are also found in another 'N *that*' phrase *the notion that* (see Table 3). In this case, however, there is a markedly higher proportion of *notion that* co-occurring with evaluative elements. In more than 50% of all instances something that is referred to as *notion* is evaluated. This finding coincides with the results provided for *notion that* in Hunston (2008: 283) according to which "notions are predominantly evaluated" in scientific texts. More importantly perhaps, there is a qualitative difference between the evaluative items used in conjunction with the two phrases. *The notion that* tends to be used as a direct object for verbs indicating acceptance or rejection. Another observation is that it is usually courts that are the subject of the clauses containing this phrase (e.g. *The Supreme Court abandoned/accepted/rejected...etc.*).

Table 11.3: The notion that totaling 25 instances

Group	Frequency	Sample environments
Notion that is the CAUSE	3	*Article 6 is based on ...* *The neutrality norm derives from...* *adoption by English law of ...*
Notion that is SUPPORTED	6	*there is authority supporting ...* *There is evidence to support* *There is sufficient support for* *Justice Black advanced ...* *The notion (...) has been reaffirmed*
Notion that is EVALUATED	13	*The Supreme Court abandoned/ accepted/rejected ...* *The appellate court found unpersuasive...* *The court repudiated ...* *courts did not take kindly to ...* *uncomfortable with...* *happy to adopt ...*
Notion that EXISTS	3	*familiar with...* *... applies*

Both *the idea that* and *the notion that* co-occur with diverse forms indicating their confirmation. Examples collected in the *support* group are a fine example of a co-occurrence between a lexical item and meaning elements rather than formal sequences. The lemma *support* is found in various forms such as *supporting, to support* and *support.* The strength of its co-occurrence with *the notion that* comes from the cumulative frequency of all the occurrences of the individual word forms.

Just as in the previous case, *the notion that* is the basis or cause for legal constructs such as *norm* or *Article.* In addition, in both cases, there is a co-occurring group related to the existence or presence of *ideas* and *notions*. The findings provided above suggest that while these two 'N *that*' phrases may occur with a few semantic sequences, both *the idea that* and *the notion that* tend to show preference in terms of semantic sequence. In the case of *the notion that,* it is possible to propose a frequently-occurring sequence which consists of

'institution' + 'accept or reject' *the notion* + *that*-clause

As indicated above, *the notion that* tends to exhibit consistently the co-occurrence with evaluative elements. This seems to hold true across a range of different disciplinary discourses even if we acknowledge that the concept of evaluative language is problematic and it has been described in terms of various terminologies and approaches such as appraisal, stance, evaluative or affective language, to name just a few (see also Hunston 2011, Hyland and Tse 2004; Conrad and Biber 2000; Martin and White 2005).

Table 11.4: The notion that in judicial discourse (32 occurrences)

Group	Frequency	Sample environments
Notion that is **evaluated**	20	
AGREEMENT	12	*We discounted..., we rejected...*
APPRECIATION	8	*... absurd, ...is dubious,*
Notion that is SUPPORTED	4	*to support ...; dovetails ...*
Notion that is the CAUSE	5	*is based on.... is premised on...*
Notion that is CONSISTENT with other data	1	*... is reflected in our cases*

As Table 4 shows, *the notion that* as examined in judicial discourse[6] behaves phraseologically in much the same way as in the other genres. The co-occurrence between *the notion that* and evaluative elements is proportionally even larger than in the academic legal texts (62% and 52% respectively). Interestingly, in both academic and judicial texts, this phrase is found in clauses expressing agreement or rejection, with an institution or an institutional participant invariably found in the subject position. In judicial discourse, the personal pronoun *we* refers to the judges (see Table 3). At the same time, there seems to be some degree of similarity in the way both *the idea that* and *the notion that* co-occur with evaluative adjectives. Both these phrases tend to be used in legal discourse as a linguistic vehicle for the overt expression of criticism.

Conclusions

This brief study offers a mere glimpse into the potential of adopting a new methodological approach to the study of recurring phraseology. It seems evident that semantic sequences can be observed in large collections of naturally-occurring texts. Starting with a grammar pattern in search for such constructs appears to be an effective way of uncovering extensive phraseological patterns and it provides further argument for the close association between grammar pattern and meaning. This is a corpus-based rather than corpus-driven approach because the analysis is based on the prior knowledge that a particular pattern is significant in a given type of discourse. This study corroborates the claim made in Hunston (2008) that semantic sequences can be usefully employed to investigate epistemology in disciplinary discourses. The evidence (albeit limited) presented above suggests that

6 These findings are based on the examination of 114 opinions given by the US Supreme Court and totaling 1,182,246 words, collected between 2000 and 2006. The data is part of the American Law Corpus compiled by the present author.

the '*the* + Noun + *that*-clause' pattern is a productive way of addressing the issue of evaluation in legal discourse. This pattern tends to favour semantic sequences associated with evaluating function. At the same time, the pattern attracts nouns which often have the function of encapsulating the concepts and argumentation contained in a preceding or subsequent textual segment. Thus, the sequences appear to have both the evaluating and text-organizing function. Finally, semantic sequences could be useful in characterising disciplinary discourses. So far, we have noted a considerable overlap between scientific and legal discourses in the way this type of *that*-clauses is crucial to their epistemologies. Legal academic and judicial discourses might differ in the extent to which they employ subjective, value-laden words (e.g. *absurd, dubious, preposterous*) with negative polarity to evaluate concepts and argumentation in law. Yet, much more work is needed to find out whether legal discourse could be effectively described in terms of this type of recurrent expression. The present study is intended as a small step towards this goal.

References

Biber, D., Johansson, S., Leech, G., Conrad, S. and E. Finegan (1999). The Longman Grammar of Spoken and Written English. London: Longman.

Conrad, S. and D. Biber (2000) "Adverbial Marking of Stance in Speech and Writing." In Evaluation in Text: Authorial Stance and the Construction of Discourse, Hunston, S. and Thompson, G. (eds.), 56-73. Oxford: Oxford University Press.

Charles, M. (2004). The Construction of Stance. A Corpus-Based Investigation of Two Contrasting Disciplines. Unpublished PhD thesis. University of Birmingham

Goźdź-Roszkowski, S. (forthcoming). "Legal Terms and Meaningful Units. A Corpus-based Study of the Term Discovery in the United States Supreme Court Opinions".

Goźdź-Roszkowski, S. (2011). Patterns of Linguistic Variation in American Legal English. A Corpus-Based Study. Frankfurt am Main: Peter Lang

Gledhill, C. (2000). Collocations in Science Writing. Tubingen: Gunter Narr

Groom, N. (2007). Phraseology and Epistemology in Humanities Writing. Unpublished PhD thesis. University of Birmingham

Halliday, M. A. K. and C. Matthiessen (2004) An Introduction to Functional Grammar. London: Arnold.

Hunston, S. (2011) Corpus Approaches to Evaluation. Phraseology and Evaluative Language. New York London: Routledge

Hunston, S. (2008) "Starting with the small words. Patterns, lexis and semantic sequences". International Journal of Corpus Linguistics 13(3): 271-295

Hunston, S. and G. Francis (2000). Pattern Grammar: a Corpus-driven Approach to the Lexical Grammar of English. Amsterdam, Benjamins.

Hyland, K. and P. Tse (2004) "Metadiscourse in Academic Writing: A Reappraisal," Applied Linguistics 25: 156-176.

Kjaer, A. (1990). "Phraseology Research-state of the Art. Methods of Describing Word Combinations in Language for Specific Purposes." Terminology Science and Research 1 (1-2): 3-32.

Martin and White (2005) The Language of Evaluation: Appraisal in English. London: Palgrave.

Renouf, A. and J. Sinclair (1991)."Collocational Frameworks in English". In English Corpus Linguistics: Studies in Honour of Jan Svartvik, Aijmer K. and Altenberg B. (eds.), 128-143. London: Longman.

Schulze R. and U. Römer (2008) "Patterns, Meaningful Units and Specialized Discourses," International Journal of Corpus Linguistics, 13(3): 265-270

Scott, M. (2008) WordSmith Tools 5.0. Liverpool: Lexical Analysis Software

Sinclair, J. (1991). Corpus, Concordance, Collocation. Oxford, Oxford University Press

Solan, L. (1993). The Language of Judges. Chicago: University of Chicago Press.

Wray, A. (2002) Formulaic Language and the Lexicon. Cambridge: Cambridge University Press

Establishing Affirmation Modality as a Valid Grammatical Category in Serbian Through Internet-Based Research

Marcin Grygiel

Abstract

Recent studies on corpora have shown that the World Wide Web can be regarded as a representative language corpus, despite the fact that it is both unbalanced and uncontrolled for. In fact, Keller et al. (2002) claim that the gigantic size of the Web compensates for its deficiencies and makes it the largest language corpus available to us. This tool seems to be especially useful for linguists doing research on languages with no electronic corpora available or whose corpora are under construction and hard to get access to. In the paper I will report on my research on the semantics of affirmation modality in Serbian and give practical solutions I worked out searching for my data base on the Internet. I will argue that strong affirmation can be treated as a type of modality as it is marked consistently with the use of long forms of auxilliary verbs – the present imperfective forms of *biti* 'to be'and present forms of *hteti* 'to want'. A common assumption in Serbian grammar books is that the distribution of short and long forms is complementary and ruled by purely syntactic factors such as the position of these verbs in the sentence (Piper 2009: 402). Contrary to this, I will discuss examples with paradigmatic occurrence of the two variants showing that the long forms mark strong affirmation modality, perceived as an additional semantic component in the structure of the proposition. My conclusion is that in this type of research, qualitative linguistic analysis of Serbian webistites turns out to be more informative than the professional corpora of the Serbian language one can get access to, despite the fact that the latter can be also easily handled quantitatively.

Keywords

Affirmation modality, WWW, corpora in linguistic analysis, semantics of grammar.

Advantages of the Internet over the existing Serbian corpora

In Serbia there are two major academic projects whose aim is to build a large electronic *corpus* of the standard written Serbian. The oldest of the two projects is the Corpus of Serbian Language (henceforth CSL) initiated in the late fifties by Prof. Đorđe Kostić at the Institute of Experimental Phonetics and Speech Pathology in Belgrade. In 1996, through joint efforts of the Institute of Experimental Phonetics and Speech Pathology and the Laboratory of Experimental Psychology at the University of Belgrade, the corpus was reactivated and transferred into an electronic format. CSL comprises 11 million words and includes texts from the 12th century to the present day. The biggest advantage of CSL is the fact that each word is tagged for its grammatical status (at the level of inflected morphology), number of graphemes and syllables and phonological structure. The texts are also tagged for the beginning and end points of sentences and paragraphs. The system of tagging consists of about 2000 grammatical (inflected) forms.[1]

However, there are a number of weak points. First of all, CSL is not available online and in order to use it, one has to come to Belgrade in person, but even then you are not granted direct access to the corpus and all the research questions are handled by a technician who writes a special program adjusted to the needs of a particular analysis. Furthermore, work on the electronic version of CSL is still in progress and each of its subparts must be accessed separately. For the purposes of my analysis I used the corpus of contemporary language which includes texts written between 1945 and 1957. As a consequence, it could be easily argued that the corpus of contemporary language is not fully representative due to the fact that it is more than half a century old.

An apparent solution to this problem may seem an alternative project developed by the Mathematical Faculty of the University of Belgrade called Corpus of Contemporary Serbian (CCS). Nevertheless, CCS is grammatically mostly untagged and its size is still quite modest, not exceeding 23 million words. However, a newer version with a considerably bigger number of words is to be made available soon.[2]

By contrast, in the analysis I am going to present in the following sections, Serbian WWW pages serve as a rich source of revealing language material, allowing to formulate a number of theoretical genaralizations. This proves that the Internet could be regarded not only as an information resource, but also as a dynamic, multilingual, least controlled, easy to access and untagged language corpus. Unlike most traditional language corpora, it cannot be accused of being outdated by any means as it has an incredible growth day by day. Consequently, it becomes the best language model, reflecting a number of innovations and grammatical changes which may otherwise go unnoticed, be treated as inncorrect or even denied in most reference grammar books.

Linguistic status of affirmation

All natural human languages are sensitive to the affirmative/negative opposition (Lewandowska-Tomaszczyk 1996; Miestamo 2005). As a consequence, every language possesses linguistic means of expressing both negation and affirmation. Traditionally, affirmation is regarded as an unmarked – morphosyntactically invisible and semantically covert – counterpart of negation. Unlike negation, however, affirmation does not invoke any specific lexical items – such as negators – which have specialized for the expression of this function. Nevertheless, affirmation is far from being linguistically unrepresented. As I understand it,

---

1 See http://www.serbian-corpus.edu.rs/ns/digest.html

2 See http://www.korpus.matf.bg.ac.rs/

affirmation is a grammatical function which pertains to both syntactic and lexical forms, primarily used for other purposes, and exploits their meaning potentials. Out of their semantic properties, higher-level constructions are created, which are capable of affirmation marking.

Because of the fact that negative sentences use more uniform syntactic marking in comparison to their affirmative counterparts, the status of negation as a coherent, homogenous and universal category with linguistic validity has been generally recognized while that of affirmation is still questioned, widely avoided or confused with other categories such as assertion. In a nutshell, the diiference between affirmation and assertion resides in the fact that affirmation can express only positive values – not only convictions, but also doubts – while assertion stresses the veracity of both positive and negative statements. Thus, assertion is rather content-oriented, while affirmation – being thematically quite diverse – is more formally bounded. Obviously, there is a lot of overlap and criss-crossing between the two categories. For example, positive assertion is the focal point in the prototype structure of affirmation. Also, the opposition between affirmation and negation does not seem to be as stiff as it is traditionally assumed. This is evidenced by the existence of borderline cases such as examples of affirmative sentences expressed by means of negation and vice versa; negative contexts with no formal negators present. Moreover, there are some problematic examples which might be classified as being both negative and affirmative (e.g.: Srb. *nemoguće je* 'it's impossible', Srb. *neophodno je* 'it's necessary/indispensable', Pol. *nieznoszę* 'I hate', Srb. *nedostaje mi* 'I lack/miss', Srb. *Baš me briga* 'I don't care at all', Pol. *To mnie tak interesuje jak zeszłoroczny śnieg*/ Srb. *To me interesuje kao lanski sneg* 'It interests me like last year's snow, it doesn't interest me at all', Eng. *I dislike*, Eng. *it disappeared*).

The weakest form of affirmation is the affirmation by default represented both in English and Serbian by finite verb forms not accompanied by any kind of negator. This is the weakest form of affirmation marking because the same finite verb forms may be also used in the negative contexts (Eng. *we belong*: *we don't belong*, Srb. *pripadamo*: *ne pripadamo* 'we belong: we don't belong'). However, some finite verb forms are more closely associated with affirmative meaning and can be treated as better candidates for affirmation markers since their forms change in negative contexts, such as English 3rd person singular present and simple past forms (Eng. *he finished – he didn't finish*) In Serbian, on the other hand, all the future analytical forms with the auxilliary *hteti* 'want/will' placed after the verb are used exclusively in affirmative contexts (Srb. *uradiću* 'I'll do' – *neću uraditi* 'I won't do'). Furthermore, auxiliary verbs in Serbian are capable of expressing affirmation in a stronger way than ordinary verbs as they have developed separate affirmative and negative forms (Grygiel 2010b). Still further up the scale of affirmation spectrum, are special long forms of auxilliary verbs which do not have analogical negative counterparts and cannot be negated. Finally, towards the end of the gradation, affirmation may be strengthened by lexical intensifiers or a number of structural manipulations such as fronting of affirmation constructions, duplication of affirmative forms or introduction of conjunction which has a multiplying effect.

Expressing modality by means of auxilliation

Modality has been traditionally defined in terms of speaker' attitudes and classified as epistemic – expressing speaker's evaluation of the proposition – and deontic – expressing speaker's attitude towards possible actions. This bi-partite definition of modality has been taken over from logic. However, in linguistics the study of modality has a wider scope of application and is generally concerned with a speaker's expressed attitude to a proposition (Cruse 2006: 109). Consequently, modality – conceived in the broadest sense – is the modification of a whole sentence or clause by specifying the attitude of the speaker with regard to the content of the sentence (Palmer 2001: 24). In other words, modality is a semantic category which concerns the projection of the speaker's attitude onto what is being predicted.

From this perspective, the semantics of any sentence may be viewed as having a binary structure, with two main constituents: proposition and modality. On the one hand, it must include *dictum* – the propositional content, and on the other hand, it comprises – *modus* – judgment of its reality status expressed by linguistic means in the form of modality markers. Bobran (1996: 5) believes that *dictum* is the primary component of the sentential semantic structure and it is always obligatory. The second component – *modus* – is optional.

The speaker's judgment or altitudinal stance – modality – can be encoded at various levels of a linguistic system and by various linguistic means, such as grammatical marking, modal verbs, lexical expressions or intonation. A set of verb forms indicating one of a range of modal functions is a traditional grammatical category known as mood (Cruse 2006: 112). A basic three-way distinction of mood is between declarative (also called 'indicative'), interrogative, and imperative. Other types of mood include subjunctive, dubitative, reportative, evidential and so forth. The conditional form of the verb is also sometimes regarded as mood. Alternatively, rarer classes of this grammatical category are distinguished, for example those involving tentativeness of judgment, like: *He tends to…*, *He happens to…*etc. or politeness, as in: *Can you/Could you…?*, proposed by Skrzypczak (2006: 192), who defines modality as "an attitudinal state of mind about phenomenal reality".

Affirmation can be also viewed as a type of modality because, in most cases, it involves modification of an utterance by specifying the positive attitude of the speaker with regard to the content of the sentence. In the prosess, the speakers transform their utterances by stressing or attributing a positive value as an additional component to the semantic structure of a proposition. Generally, affirmation is triggered in opposition to negation or hypothetically negative contexts. A given sentence is considered to be affirmative only in the context of being potentially negative. As such, it is semantically marked due to the cognitive on-line processes accompanying it while formally it may be marked only by the absence of a negator (Grygiel 2011).

One of the characteristic features of modality is the fact that it makes part of the TAM (tense/aspect/modality) complex (Givón 2001: 337). Hence, the appearance of modality may be conditioned by the existence of TAM grammatical markers, for example, in the form of auxilliary verbs. In Serbian, there are two basic auxilliary verbs capable of expressing affirmation modality – the present imperfective forms of *biti* 'to be' and present forms of *hteti* 'to want':

Table 12.1: Present imperfective BE (biti) forms in Serbian

	strong affirmative forms	weak affirmative forms	negative forms
1.SG	*jesam*	*sam*	*nisam*
2.SG	*jesi*	*si*	*nisi*
3.SG	*jeste*	*je*	*nije*
1.PL	*jesmo*	*smo*	*nismo*
2.PL	*jeste*	*ste*	*niste*
3.PL	*jesu*	*su*	*nisu*

Table 12.2: Present WANT/WILL (hteti) forms in Serbian

	strong affirmative forms	weak affirmative forms	negative forms
1.SG	*hoću*	*ću*	*neću*
2.SG	*hoćeš*	*ćeš*	*nećeš*
3.SG	*hoće*	*će*	*neće*
1.PL	*hoćemo*	*ćemo*	*nećemo*
2.PL	*hoćete*	*ćete*	*nećete*
3.PL	*hoće*	*će*	*neće*

The distinction between short and long forms makes it possible to differentiate weak from strong/emphatic affirmative meanings. Notice that long forms are always stressed and therefore sometimes referred to as "full forms" (Kostić 1987: 194), while the short or "truncated" forms are unstressed and always used as clitics. The long forms cannot be negated in any way – **ne jesam*/**ne hoću* – while the short forms are also affirmative as they do not form negative counterparts with the negator *ne* in the same way as other verbs in Serbian.

Marking affirmation modality with long forms of auxilliary verbs

The long forms of auxilliary verbs are definitely less frequent than their short counterparts. For example, in the contemporary part of the CSL *jeste* appears in only 104 sentences, while the word *je* is used 34560 times as a verb and 1882 times as a pronoun. This shows that the use of short and long forms is asymmetric – the short forms are dominant and the long ones are used only sporadically. Most Serbian reference grammar books regard the formal criteria as decisive in the choice of either of the two variants and their distribution is believed to be ruled by purely syntactic factors such as the position of these verbs in the sentence. Thus, short forms are never stressed and therefore function as enclitics. The long forms, on the other hand, are claimed to be more restricted in their occurrence and generally only used in sentence initial position or on its own, for example in posing a question or in short affirmative responses (Stanojčić and Popović 2000; Stevanović 1980; Hammond 2005).

The Internet-based research conducted by me shows that the formal solution to the problem of distribution of short and long forms is not fully satisfactory, because there are occurrences which seem to break the formal rules. For example, long forms can be used as auxiliary verbs in all situations where short verb forms are used, i.e. in the past tense – both perfect and past perfect, future tense, passive voice and present tense copular predicates. On the other hand, short forms can be used with personal pronouns in short affirmative responses and one short form – the 3rd person singular *je* form – can be stressed and used with all persons in sentence initial position as a question marker.

In the examples given below the use of long forms, instead of the more frequent short forms, is semantically motivated. Speakers opt for longer forms because they cause a change in the modality. Namely, an additional meaning emphasizing the positive value of the proposition is introduced in this way. Using the Google search engine, which serves as a default means of access to the Web, I have collected a corpus consisting of sentences with the long 3rd person singular BE form *jeste*. The search was narrowed down to a specific language – Serbian – and the interrogative particle *li* was excluded from the search in order to eliminate questions. The sentences have been grouped in the following way:

Confirming, admitting and stressing that something is true or correct

In all of these examples the short and long forms may appear in paradigmatic variation. The use of *jeste* instead of *je* can be explained as a change in modality as the long forms mark strong affirmation modality, perceived as an additional semantic component in the structure of the proposition:

a) **Šminkanje** jeste **umetnost**
'Make-up is really art'

a') *Fotograf Iain Crawford nam je još jednom potvrdio, da šminkanje **jeste** umetnost*
'The photograph Ian Crawford has once again confirmed to us that make- up is really art'

b) *Nekada ćutanje **jeste** zlata vredno*
'Sometimes silence is really worth gold'

c) *Leni Kravic: Pesma sa Džeksonom **jeste** original*
'Lenny Kravitz: The song with Jackson is really original'

c') *Verzija koja se pojavila nije montaža. To **jeste** ta pesma, rekao je Kravic*
'The version which appeared isn't montage. It is really this song, said Kravitz'

d) **Rijaliti šou** jeste **realan život koji nam se dešava?!**
'Reality show is real life which is happening to us?!'

Confirming that something is true, but with reservations

In this group the positive value of the proposition is stressed by the use of affirmation modality, but it is shown as a relatively exceptional situation restricted by a more general context:

a) *Najavili ste da ćete od Krajine napraviti kanton broj 1 u FBiH. Unsko-sanski kanton nominalno i **jeste** kanton 1 u federalnom ustrojstvu, ali je po ekonomskoj snazi i političkoj nestabilnosti među posljednjima*
'You announced that you would make the Krajina canton no. 1 in FBiH. Unsko-Sana Canton nominally is really a canton no. 1 in the federal structure, but in the economic power and political instability it belongs to the last ones'

b) *Vlasnik ovog džipa se baš prevario, **jeste** ovo 4×4 mašina, ali ne može da prođe baš svuda gde on to ima nameru da je protera*
'The owner of this jeep has been mistaken, this is really a 4×4 machine, but it cannot go through all the places where he intends to take it'

c) *Nas rastanak **jeste** bolan, ali zivot ide dalje*
'Our parting is painful, but life goes on'

d) *Tržište naftnim derivatima – **Jeste** skupo, nije najskuplje*
'The market of petroleum products – is really expensive, it isn't the most expensive'

Confirming that something is true despite counterarguments

In these Internet-extracted examples, as in all the remaining ones given here, the original spelling has been preserved. This is the reason why in some words diacritic marks are missing or the Latin alphabet sometimes switches into the Cyrilic script. The second (b') sentence, extracted from the same context as the first sentence (b), explicitly defines the meaning of the long form *jeste*. It seems to show that the speaker can express the same meaning introducing additional lexical expressions (*potvrdio* 'confirmed') or, in a more economical way, by applying the affirmation modality as in the first example (b):

a) *Zdravlje ipak* ***jeste*** *u čokoladi*
'Health is really still in chocolate/it turns out that chocolate is healthy, in spite of earlier information'

b) *Ekrem Jevric ipak* ***jeste*** *Dolce&Gabbana maneken*
'(It turns out that) Ekrem Jevric is really Dolce and Gabbana's model'

b') *Pevac, Maneken, Youtube zvezda i jos stosta, Ekrem Jevric je potvrdio da je ucestvovao u snimanju nove reklame za kolekciju jesen/zima Dolce and Gabana*
'Singer, model, Youtube star and still other things, Ekrem Jevric has confirmed that he participated in shooting of new ads for the autumn/winter Dolce and Gabbana collection'

Explicit opposition to negation

Here the use of affirmation modality is determined by the introduction of the polarity opposition. The long form *jeste* seems to stress the positive value of the proposition and at the same time excludes negation. Notice that the long forms are affirmative par excellence – they cannot be negated in any way in Serbian:

a) Sudija nije video, ali UEFA jeste
'The judge did not see, but UEFA did'

b) ***Jeste*** *oprosteno, ali nije zaboravljeno!*
'It is forgiven, but not forgotten!'

c) *Prikazaću svoj život kakav zaista* ***jeste***, *a ne kakvim ga tabloidi prikazuju*
'I will present my life as it really is, and not as it is shown by tabloids'

Complex sentences including cleft and pseudo-cleft clauses

Affirmation modality is frequently applied in parts of complex sentences where the speaker wants to emphasize a given piece of information. As shown by the pairs of sentences given below, the grammatical construction itself does not trigger automatically the use of the long form *jeste*, because sometimes the short form *je* can be used in the same formal environment (a', b', c'). As a consequence, the rules of their distribution should be sought in the semantic criteria rather than be considered as a result of purely formal conditioning:

a) *Ono što sam hteo da kažem* ***jeste*** *da anketno istraživanje pokazuje više opredeljenih za pojedine kandidate nego odlučnih da izađu na birlalište*
'What I wanted to say is that the survey shows the bigger number of those wanting to vote for particular candidates than those who have decided to go to the polls'

a') *ono sto sam hteo da kazem* ***je*** da kratkih i jednostavnih domena ima, samo se treba potruditi naci ih
'what I wanted to say is that there are short and simple domains, you just have to make an effort to find them'

b) *Uloga portala* ***jeste*** da *svoje posetioce zadovolji kvalitetnim i pouzdanim informacijama*
'The role of the portal is to satisfy its visitors with quality and reliable information'

b') *moja uloga* ***je*** *da* pred kamerama ja budem – ja
'my role is that in front of the camera I will be – I'

c) *Čar sporta* ***jeste*** *da ne pobeđuju favorite*
'The charm of sport is that the favorites do not win'

c') *Jesu one favoriti, ali baš čar sporta* ***je*** *u tome da ne pobeduju uvek favorite*
'They are really the favourites, but the charm of sport is that the favourites do not always win'

The highest degree

Affirmation modality is opted for in cases where some piece of information is given prominence or considered to be the most important fact. Here the use of long forms is frequently accompanied by the co-occurrence of the superlative degree or the ordinal numeral *prvi* 'first':

a) *Porodicno seksualno vaspitanje* ***jeste*** *najvažnije*
'Family sexual education is really the most important one'

b) *Najvažnija stvar koju muškarac može učiniti za svoju ljubav* ***jeste*** da *je neguje*
The most important thing a man can do for his love is to take care of it/her'

c) *Trčanje.rs* ***jeste*** *najbolji sajt u kategoriji "sport"*
'Trčanje.rs (running) is the best site in the category "sport"'

d) *Prva stvar koju treba da pokažemo* ***jeste*** *da je Sveti Duh jedna od osoba Svetog Trojstva*
'The first thing we have to show is that the Holy Spirit is one of the persons of the Trinity'

e) *Grupa nam* ***jeste*** *teška i ne znam da li je mogla biti teža*
'Our group is really difficult and we do not know if it could have been more difficult'

The co-occurrence of existential quantifiers

The verb *biti* 'to be' in its primary use is associated with the expression of EXISTENCE and this quality predisposes it for the function of affirmation marker. Notice that one of the conceptual metaphors on which the semantics of affirmation is based may be phrased as AFFIRMATION IS EXISTENCE. By stressing that something exists, language users attach a positive value to it and contrast it with an opposite situation which may be metaphorically presented as NEGATION IS NONEXISTENCE. Here the meaning of EXISTENCE is further enhanced by the use of existential quantifiers such as *jedan* 'one' or *jedino* 'the only one':

a) *Jedna od navodnih glavnih prednosti formata MS-OOXML* ***jeste*** *osobina da omogućava kompatibilnost sa prethodnim standardima*
'One of the alleged main advantages of MS-OOXML format is its ability to allows compatibility with former standards'

b) *једино чудо Исуса Христа које се описује у сва четири јеванђеља* ***јесте*** *храњење мноштва људи с пет хлебова и рибом*
'the only miracle of Jesus Christ that is described in all four gospels is feeding many people with five loaves of bread and fish'

c) *Jedino što želim* ***jeste*** da *živim*
'The only thing that I want is to live'

d) *Jedini način da žena bude verna* **jeste**: *da bude zaljubljena ili ružna*
'The only way for a woman to be faithful is: to be in love or ugly'

e) *Jedna od čestih zabluda* **jeste** da *dečaci vole samo devojke nalik na filmske zvezde ili manekenke*
'One of the common misconceptions is that boys like only those girls who are similar to movie stars or models'

The co-occurrence of the universal quantifier

As a result of semantic extension, affirmation may receive alternative realizations based on the mental representations of COMPLETENESS, CONJUNCTION and EXISTENCE – all of which derive from the topological concept of COVERAGE (Grygiel 2010a). Thus, the universal quantifier *sve* 'all' can trigger the use of affirmation modality as it shows an action as being complete and at the same time expresses an affirmative meaning:

a) Sve *što mu je ostalo* **jeste** da *svoju igru razvlači koliko god je to moguće*
'All he can do is to take his time and play as long as it is possible'

b) *Sve sto treba* **jeste** *ljubav* da *potraje*
'All we need is that love lasts'

The co-occurrence of the conjunction *i* 'and'

Affirmation modality can be also motivated by the image-schema of ADDING/INCLUSION, realized linguistically in the form of conjunction. In grammar, a conjunction is a part of speech that connects lexical items, phrases, clauses or sentences together. In Slavic, the conjunction *i* combines non-contrasting items or ideas together, but in Serbian it is additionally employed as a marker of affirmation. For example, Partridge (1988: 120) notices that "in sentences which are not negative, emphasis or intensification of meaning may be given to any word by the use of the particle *i* immediately before it.":

a) *I* **jeste** *mi najteze nocu*
'It really is the hardest for me at night'

a') *Najteze mi* **je** *nocu*
'The hardest for me is at night'

b) I internet preljuba **jeste** razlog za razvod
'The Internet infidelity is also a reason for divorce'

c) *To što vidiš to i **jeste***
'What you see is what really is/exists'

Conclusions

The Internet is an excellent source of authentic language material and can be successfully applied as a corpus in the linguistic analysis – confirming or modyfing theoretical hyptheses. The fact that it contains a considerable amount of errors or the so called *noise* seems to constitute its potential strength rather than a disadvantage as it may reveal deeper linguistic patterns in the structure of language. The case of affirmation modality shows that this very quality of the Internet makes it extremely useful in the study of problematic grammatical categories which are still in the state of fluctuation and may be disregarded in the traditional accounts.

References

Bobran, M. (1996). Semantyka trybu składniowego w języku polskim i rosyjskim [The Semantics of the Syntactic Mood in Polish and Russian]. Rzeszów: Wyd. Wyższej Szkoły Pedagogicznej w Rzeszowie.

Cruise, A. (2006). A Glossary of Semantics and Pragmatics. Edinburgh: Edinburg University Press.

Givón, T. (2001). Syntax: An Introduction, Vol. 1. Amsterdam/Philadelphia: John Benjamins.

Grygiel, M. (2011). "Constructional Realizations of Affirmation in Slavic." In Slavic Linguistics in a Cognitive Framework, Grygiel, M. and Janda, L. A. (eds.), 175-198. Frankfurt/New York: Peter Lang.

Grygiel, M. (2010a). "Kwantyfikacyjne i egzystencjalne wykładniki afirmacji na przykładzie języka serbskiego" [Quantifiers and existentials as markers of affirmation in Serbian], Slavia Meridionalis 10: 103-120. Warszawa: Instytut Slawistyki PAN

Grygiel, M. (2010b). "Wyrażanie afirmacji za pomocą czasowników posiłkowych w języku serbskim i angielskim" [Expressing affirmation be means of auxilliary verbs in Serbian and English]. In Słowo i tekst w opisie porównawczym, Czapiga, A. and Czapiga, Z. (eds.), 56-64. Rzeszów: Wydawnictwo UR.

Hammond, L. (2005). Serbian: An essential Grammar. London/New York: Routledge.

Keller, F., Lapata, M. and O. Ourioupina (2002). "Using the Web to overcome data sparseness." In Empirical Methods in Natural Language Processing, Hajic, J. and Matsumoto, Y. (eds.), 230-237. Philadelphia: University of Pennsylvania.

Kostić, D. (1987). Operativna gramatika srpskohrvatskog jezika [Operative Grammar of the Serbo-Croation Language]. Beograd: Prosveta.

Lewandowska-Tomaszczyk, B. (1996). Depth of Negation: A Cognitive Semantic Study. Łódź: Łódź University Press.

Miestamo, M. (2005). Standard Negation: The Negation of Declarative Main Clauses in a Typological Perspective. Berlin/New York: Mouton de Gruyter.

Palmer, F. R. (2001). Mood and Modality. Cambridge: Cambridge University Press.

Patridge, M. (1988). Serbo-Croat Practical Grammar and Reader. Beograd: Prosveta.

Piper, P. (2009). Južnoslovenski jezici: gramatičke strukture i funkcije [South Slavic Languages: Grammatical Structures and Functions]. Beograd: Beogradska knjiga.

Skrzypczak, W. (2006). Analog-Based Modelling of Meaning Representations in English. Toruń: Nicolaus Copernicus University Press.

Stanojčić, Ž. and L. Popović (2000). Gramatika srpskoga jezika [Grammar of the Serbian Language]. Beograd: Zavod za udžbenike.

Stevanović, M. (1980). Gramatika srpskohrvatskog jezika [Grammar of Serbo-Croat]. Cetinje: Obod.

The Czech Preposition *na* and Its Polish Equivalents

Renata Novotná

Abstract

The paper explores the Polish equivalents of the Czech preposition na drawing on the data in the Czech-Polish and Polish-Czech parallel corpus in the Intercorp project. There were 34 698 instances of the preposition *na* found. It was impossible to study this material as a whole therefore 15 random samples of 100 sentences were extracted automatically, i. e. approximately 4% of the material, including 100 sentences in Czech and their Polish parallel counterparts. The resulting sample was analyzed to determine the most frequent types of Polish equivalent. All three functions of the preposition *na* – adverbal (V-N), adnominal (N-N) and adverbial (proposition – N) are taken into account, though the emphasis is mainly on the valency functions, i. e. adverbal and adnominal.

Keywords

Prepositions, valency, adverbial, adnominal and adverbial function, parallel corpus

Preposition *na* in frequency dictionaries

In this contribution a quite detailed analysis of one of the Czech prepositions (*na*) will be discussed in comparison with its Polish equivalents. This study is based on the Czech-Polish parallel corpus InterCorp.

In the Frequency Dictionary of Czech (2004, Frekvenční slovník češtiny, eds. F. Čermák – M. Křen) *na* is the second most frequent preposition (the most frequent being the preposition *v*). In the Frequency dictionary of Czech published at Routledge (2011, eds. F. Čermák – M. Křen), preposition *v* is the fifth most frequent and preposition *na* the sixth most frequent Czech word. In the Frequency Dictionary of Spoken Czech (2007, Frekvenční slovník mluvené češtiny, Čermák, ed.) *na* is the most frequent preposition (informal dialogues). This means that this preposition is used typically in spoken language and its usage also increases in contemporary written Czech. This expansion of the use of the preposition *na* can be seen in the shift from *v* to *na* as the most frequent preposition in the two author dictionaries which the Institute of the Czech National Corpus has published so far – while in Karel Čapek's vocabulary the prevailing preposition is still *v*, in the works of Bohumil Hrabal the preposition *na* is in first place (see Dictionary of Karel Čapek and Dictionary of Bohumil Hrabal published in 2007 and 2009).

Theoretical Considerations

Let us first briefly outline the theoretical background for this study, i.e. the sources used and the implications for the distribution of the preposition *na,* the object of this study.

The theoretical sources for this study are devoted to the problems of prepositions, word syntagmatics and valency. These are:

1. F. Čermák: System, Function, Form and Semantics of the Czech Prepositions (Systém, funkce, forma a sémantika českých předložek, 1996);
2. F. Čermák – J. Holub: Syntagmatics and Paradigmatics of the Czech Word: Valency and Collocability (Syntagmatika a paradigmatika českého slova: valence a kolokabilita, 2005)
3. F. Čermák: The Substance of Valency from the Lexicological Point of View (Podstata valence z hlediska lexikologického, 1991)

In the system of the Czech prepositions the preposition *na* is a one-word preposition in contrast to multi-word prepositions such as *na základě* (in the frequency dictionaries published in 2004 and 2007 mentioned above the prepositions *na* and *na základě* are treated separately; the frequency of the one-word preposition *na* as a part of the multi-word preposition *na základě* was subtracted (FSČ: *na* = 1012442, *na základě* = 6696, FSMČ: *na* = 7066, *na základě* = 20).

Czech prepositions can have three functions according to their position in the sentence:

1. adverbal (Verb – Noun) – expressing the relation between the verb and the noun (*vzpomínat na prázdniny* – to reminisce about the holidays)
2. adnominal (Noun – Noun) – expressing the relation between two nominal expressions, such as two nouns, adjective and noun etc. (*prázdniny u moře* – holidays by the sea)
3. adverbial (Preposition – Noun) – in contrast to the previous functions it does not express valency relations, only the relation to the preposition as a whole (e.g. *v létě* – in the summer).

In the present analysis all three functions of the preposition *na* were taken into account. The emphasis was mainly on the valency functions, i.e. adverbal and adnominal.

According to Syntagmatics and Paradigmatics of the Czech Word (Čermák and Holub 2005) the adverbal function was divided into two groups:

a) valency – cases such as *myslet na, čekat na - myśleć o, czekać na* etc., the preposition *na* expresses an abstract relation between the verb and the noun
b) complement – such as *jít na ples - iść na bal* (to go to the ball), *stát na/zemi - stać na ziemi* (to stand on the ground), in which the direction or the place, but not the abstract relation are expressed by the preposition; in this case the preposition *na* can be replaced by other prepositions, such as *do*, e.g. *jít do školy* (to go to school), *před*, e.g. *stát před domem* (to stand in front of the house) etc.

The adnominal function was concentrated on nouns and adjectives, i. e. their valency.[1] As the noun valency is slightly different from the verbal valency, abstract and concrete nouns were treated separately:

a) valency of abstract nouns, such as *myšlenky na vašeho bývalého partnera - myśli o twoim byłym partnerze* (thoughts of your previous partner)
b) valency of concrete nouns, e. g. *odborník na problematiku Ukrajiny - znawca spraw ukraińskich* (expert in Ukrainian problems)

The valency of the adjectives was studied as a separate group, e. g. *zvyklá na obdiv - nawykła do podziwu* (used to admiration)

While the valency of verbs, nouns and adjectives expressed by the preposition is the inherent attribute of the lexical item with the categorial feature[2] and therefore the verb/noun/adjective with the valency preposition can be taken as one lexical item or one lexeme; the adverbial function of the preposition is independent and forms a collocation, e.g. *na ulici – na ulicy* (in the street).

Besides the groups given above, fixed collocations and idioms were also studied, such as *na okamžik - na chwilę* (for a moment), *na rozdíl od - w odróżnieniu od* (with the difference of), *vůbec mu nepřišlo na mysl - nie przyszło mu do głowy* (he didn't take to mind).

Corpus Sources

The linguistic data for this study was searched in the Czech-Polish parallel corpus built as a part of the InterCorp project. As the corpus includes both Polish-Czech and Czech-Polish translations, there were 34 698 instances of the preposition *na* found. It was impossible to study this material as a whole, therefore 15 random

1 As F. Čermák states in his paper "The Substance of Valency from the Lexicological Point of View", all the parts of speech have their valency except for interjections, which form a separate sentence. (1991: 25)

2 This categorial feature is the part of the semantics of the word, cf. the metalanguage to buy = to get for somebody by paying the money where for somebody doubles the explicit valency. (Čermák, 1991: 21).

samples of 100 sentences each were extracted automatically, i. e. 4 % of the material. A similar study on English equivalents of the Czech preposition *na* has been already done so it is possible to do some further comparison with the Polish equivalents.

Czech-Polish Equivalence of the preposition *na*

According to the Polish equivalents given in the 15 extracted samples the original groups of lexical valency, collocations and idioms were extended to the following scheme:

I – lexemes

1) verb

a) valency – e.g. *když muž čeká na ženu - kiedy mężczyzna czeka na kobietę* (when man is waiting for a woman)
b) complement – e.g. *Jdu teprve na oběd - Dopiero idę na obiad* (I only go for a lunch)

2) noun

a) valency of the abstract noun – e.g. *čekání na smrt - czekanie na śmierć*[3] (waiting for death)
b) valency of the concrete noun – e.g. *nožík na brambory - nożyk do ziemniaków* (potato knife)

In the study on English equivalents the English equivalent was quite often expressed not by a preposition but by an adjective, where the essential meaning of the adjective-noun combination in English is the purpose:

c) valency of the concrete noun in Czech expressed by adjective in the attribute position in English, e.g. *koš na odpadky – trash can*

In Polish there appeared only three instances of this type, e.g. *komůrka na zásoby - zapasik zakamarkowy* (stores room)

3 A. Čermáková (2009: 71) gives the following most frequent abstract nouns with the preposition na (based on the SYN2000 corpus): ohled na, pohled na, náklady na, nárok na, návrh na, právo na, podíl na, vliv na.

3) adjective valency – e.g. *připravená na všecko - przygotowana na wszystko* [4] (prepared for everything)

Moreover, a separate group for mixed valency, i.e. valency of different parts of speech in each language, was established:

4) mixed valency – e.g. *pohled paní z Harrachu na slečnu Isabellu - spojrzenie pani z Harrachu skierowane na pannę Izabelę* (sight of madam from Harrach on lady Isabella)

II – collocations

1) adverbials – e.g. *na jaře - na wiosnę* (in spring)

2) fixed collocations – *nezávisle na - niezależnie od* (apart from)

III - idioms

This is also a separate group as it can include both collocations and sentences, e.g. *Co na tom? - I cóż w tym złego?* (What's wrong about it?), *na mou čest - daję ci słowo honoru* (upon my word)

IV – mixed group

This group incorporates the various possible differences in combinations of one-word and multi-word units between the two languages:

1) collocation – lexeme, e.g. *tady na místě – zaraz* (immediately), *uvádět na veřejnost - ujawnić publicznie* (to show in public)

2) idiom – lexeme – e.g. *já jí na to - ja mówię* (I say), *nebyl na pochybách - nie miał wątpliwości* (he had no doubts)

The last group is composed of quasi-idioms, i.e. combinations of verbs and abstract nouns having one-word equivalents in the other language:

3) quasi-idiom – lexeme – e.g. *činit si nárok na – pretendować do* (to trespass upon)

---

4 M. Kopřivová (2006: 41) gives the 10 most frequent adjectives with the preposition na (based on the SYN2000 corpus): založený, určený, zaměřený, závislý, postavený, umístěný, zvyklý, bohatý, náročný, nakrájený.

V – Particular differences

As a separate group, cases of particular differences were also studied, i.e. when the Polish equivalent was completely different from the Czech part.

A Quantitative Survey

Now we can give a survey of the percentage representation of each of the groups given above:

Table 13.1. Percentage representation of each of the groups

Group	Description	Percentage
I – 1a:	valency of the verb	30.7 %
I – 1b:	complement of the verb	16.7 %
I – 2a:	valency of the abstract noun	5.3 %
I – 2b:	valency of the concrete noun	3.6 %
I – 2c:	attribute as an English equivalent of Czech valency	0.2 %
I – 3:	valency of the adjective	2.0 %
I – 4:	mixed valency	1.7 %
II – 1:	adverbials	14.5 %
II – 2:	fixed collocations	4.5 %
III:	idioms	4.8 %
IV – 1:	collocation – lexeme	1.3 %
IV – 2:	idiom – lexeme	1.3 %
IV – 3:	quasi-idiom – lexeme	0.3 %
V:	particular differences	9.7 %
VI – 1	insufficient context	0.9%
VI – 2:	bad alignment	2.5 %

As it was stated above the group I-2c has a very low percentage for Polish, i. e. 0.2 %, for English the percentage was higher, 2.8 %. The same problem is in the groups IV 1, 2 and 3, where for English equivalents the percentage was higher – 3.7 %, 3.3 % and 2.5 % while for Polish this is not very typical and the percentage is low, i.e. 1.3 %, 1.3 % and 0.3 %.

Equivalent Types

To sum up the findings about the Czech preposition *na* and its Polish equivalents it would be useful to see the most frequent equivalents of the Czech preposition *na*, especially on the level of the valency and complement of verbs and of the valency of nouns and adjectives.

The group I–1a (verbal valency) contains 461 parallel sentences and the most frequent prepositions in Polish are *na* (248x), *do* (53x) and *o* (60x). There are also verbs in Polish without preposition (76x). Moreover, some other prepositions, such as *w* (15x) or *od* (4x) were found. The preposition *dla* appeared only twice, cf. *ze které dosti zbude na každého – z której dla każdego przypadnie część niemała, na té knize pracoval – dla tej książki pracował.* Some prepositions had only one instance, such as *po*, *za* or *wedlug*.The table gives the most frequent Polish prepositions and their representing verbs.

Table 13.2: Group I-1a

Valency	**Most frequent verbs**
na	*patrzeć* 48, *spojrzeć* 28, *czekać* 10, *spoglądać* 5, *grać* 4, *zależeć* 3, *gniewać się* 2, *poczekać* 2, *przygotować* 2
do	*uśmiechnąć się* 5, *zwrócić* 4, *wołać 3*, *uśmiechać się* 2
o	*myśleć* 25, *zapomnieć* 9, *pomyśleć* 5, *pytać* 3, *zapominać* 2, *pamiętać* 2
without prep	*pamiętać* 4, *przypomnieć* 4, *wskazać* 4, *wspominać* 4, *przyjrzeć* 3, *przyglądać 2*

The group I–1b (verbal complement) contains 251 parallel sentences. Most of the instances in Polish have the equivalent *na*, 12 instances have the equivalent *do* (*dojechać*, *przyjść*) and 7 instances *w*. The main difference in usage is the accusative and loccative case, i. e. *wejść na dworzec* x *leżeć na ziemi*. As the verbs were quite different, the repertoir of repeated verbs is rather low.

Table 13.3: Group I-1b

Complement	**Most frequent verbs**
na acc	*iść* 8, *jechać* 2, *paść* 5, *pojechać* 4, *wyjść* 3, *wybiegnąć* 3, *rzucać* 2, *biegnąć* 2, *odprowadzić* 2, *wejść* 2,*wrócić* 2, , *wychodzić* 2
na loc.	*stać* 22, *siedzieć* 13, *leżeć* 11, *położyć* 7, *usiąść* 7, *postawić* 3, *wisieć* 3, *klęczeć* 2, *mieszkać* 2, *spotkać* 2, *zostać* 2

The group I–2a (abstract noun valency) contains 76 parallel sentences. The Polish equivalents are preposition *do* (4x), *na* (36x with accusative and 13x with loccative case), *nad* (2x), *o* (2x), *pod* (1x), *w* (6x), and without preposition with genitive case (12x).

Table 13.4: Group I-2a

Valency	Most frequent nouns
do	different nouns, e.g. *przygotowanie do egzaminu*
na acc	*wpływ* 4x, *widok* 2x (e.g. widok na rzekę), *spojrzenie* 2x
na loc	different nouns, e.g. *uśmiech na ustach*
nad	*praca* 2x
o	different nouns, e.g. *myśli o twoim byłym partnerze*
without prep	*widok* 4x (e.g. *widok Delft*)

The group I-2b (concrete noun valency) contains 54 parallel sentences. The Polish equivalents are prepositions *do* (4x), *na* with the accusative (13x), *na* with the loccative (28x), *o, u, w* and *za* (1x) and genitive without preposition (5x). There are also different nouns so it is difficult to give the most frequent ones. The typical examples are:

Table 13.5: Group I-2b

Valency	Example
do	*szczotka do zębów*
na acc	*kandydat na najwyższy urząd*
na loc	*kłódka na drzwiach*
without prep – gen	*skala narzędzi pomiarowych*

The group I-3 (adjective valency) contains 31 parallel sentences. The prepositions used in Polish are *dla* (1x), *do* (4x), *na* with accusative (7x), *na* with loccative (11x), *nad* (1x), *od* (3x), *w* (2x), without preposition (2x). The most typical examples are:

Table 13.6: Group I-3

Valency	Most frequent adjectives
do	different adjectives, e.g. *nienawykła do tego tempa*
na acc	different adjectives, e.g. *więzień polityczny oczekujący na proces*
na loc.	*oparty* 2x
od	*zależny* 2x
w	different adjectives, e.g. *z oczami wbitymi w stół*

A summary

To sum up the findings about Czech preposition *na* and its Polish equivalents it can be concluded that the preposition *na* is used mainly as a verbal valency (30.7 %) and a verbal complement (16.7%) in both languages, which is 57.4% altogether, i.e within its adverbal function. However, the prepositions used as a verbal valency and as a verbal complement differ – for verbal complement the Polish preposition *na* is used either with accusative or loccative case, while for verbal valency *na*, *do* and *o* are the most frequent Polish prepositions. The adnominal function, i.e. noun and adjective valency, forms 10.9 %. Adverbial function represents 14.5 %. Fixed collocations and idioms with preposition *na* show 9.3 %. Particular differences appeared in 9.7 % of the parallel sentences studied. In comparison with a similar study on English equivalents of the Czech preposition *na* the group of valency of the concrete noun in Czech expressed by adjective in the attribute position in Polish was very low as well as group of mixed valency and also parallels of multi-word units to one-word units, i.e. idioms and collocations to lexemes, showed very low percentage of correspondence.

References

Čermák, F. et al.(1983, 1988, 1994). Slovník české frazeologie a idiomatiky I-III. Academia, Praha.

Čermák, F. (1991). "Podstata valence z hlediska lexikologického." In Walencja czasownika a problemy leksykografii dwujęzycznej, Rytel-Kuc, D. (ed.), 15-40. Wydawnictwo Polskiej Akademii Nauk, Wrocław-Warszawa-Kraków.

Čermák, F. (1996). "Systém, funkce, forma a sémantika českých předložek," Slovo a Slovesnost 57: 30-46.

Čermák, F. and M. Křen (eds.) (2004). Frekvenční slovník češtiny. Nakladatelství Lidové noviny, Praha.

Čermák, F. (2005). "Abstract Noun Collocations: Their Nature in a Parallel English-Czech Corpus." In Meaningful Texts. The Extraction of Semantic Information from Monolingual and Multilingual Corpora, Barnbrook, G., Danielsson, P. and Mahlberg, M. (eds), 143-153. Continuum, London, New York.

Čermák, F. and J. Holub (2005). Syntagmatika a paradigmatika českého slova I. Valence a kolokabilita. Nakladatelství Karolinum, Praha.

Čermák, F. (ed.) (2007). Frekvenční slovník mluvené češtiny. Nakladatelství Karolinum, Praha.

Čermák, F. (ed.) (2007). Slovník Karla Čapka. Nakladatelství Lidové noviny, Praha.

Čermák F. and V. Cvrček (eds.) (2009). Slovník Bohumila Hrabala. Nakladatelství Lidové noviny, Praha.

Čermák, F. and M. Křen (eds.) (2011). Frequency Dictionary of Czech. Routledge, London – New York

Čermáková, A. (2009). Valence českých substantiv. Nakladatelství Lidové noviny, Praha.

Kopřivová, M. (2006). Valence českých adjektiv. Nakladatelství Lidové noviny, Praha.

Novotná, R. (2010). "Czech Preposition na and its English Equivalents." In Intercorp: Exploring A Multilingual Corpus, Čermák, F., Corness, P. and Klégr, A. (eds.), 138-145. Nakladatelství Lidové noviny, Praha.

The Image of the Lexeme Based on an Analysis of Collocations

Milena Hebal-Jezierska

Abstract

The aim of this paper is to demonstrate a method for creating an image of lexemes based on collocations, especially with respect to problematic issues. The analysis has been performed on words referring to foreigners living in the Czech Republic. The starting point is a collocational quantitative analysis using a corpus-driven approach. The categories in which the examined words have occurred are based on statistics. Within this framework, a deeper contextual analysis has been made (inclusion of collocations in a broader context). Thanks to contextual and non-contextual analysis of collocations[1], an image of the lexemes has been created.

Keywords

Image of words, collocations, contextual analysis of collocations, non-contextual analysis of collocations, stereotypes of nationalities

PART I:
INTRODUCTORY

The aim of this article is to present the main problems which occur when creating an image of a lexeme on the basis of collocations. The definition of *collocation* is taken from Cambridge Dictionaries Online[2]. By this we mean "a word or phrase which is often used with another word or phrase, in a way that sounds correct to people who have spoken the language all their lives, but might not be expected from the meaning".

---

1 The non-contextual analysis of collocations is termed in corpora linguistics as collocation profile (Keibel 2011).

2 http://dictionary.cambridge.org/dictionary/british/collocation

The method

A quantitative corpus-driven approach is used to explore collocations. In general, the collocations are automatically extracted from the corpus data (with the help of software) and divided into semantic groups[3]. These semantic units/sets are arranged by frequency using the highest MI-score values. Afterwards the occurrences may be subjected to two types of analyses: non-contextual and contextual collocations. On this basis we attempt to construct the linguistics picture of the word[4].

The way of searching a lexeme

Key words were searched using the lemmatization function, e.g. [lemma= "Rom"]. This query finds all possible occurrences of the lexeme. Afterwards the findings were checked using the frequency distribution function (in the position 0), and potential homonymous forms were eliminated by using the option negative filter. The next step was the extraction of collocations from the corpus. In the software Bonito there are 4 statistical tests: MI score, T- score, relevant frequency, absolute frequency.

The research

The research, was carried out in the Czech and Slovak national corpora on words for foreigners living in the Czech Republic and in the Slovak Republic. The words which were studied mean: *foreigner, foreign*, (a) *Ukrainian*, (a) *Russian*, (a) *Vietnamese*, (a) *Slovak, Pole, Polish*, (a) *Romany/Gypsy*. The research[5] was conducted on the corpora of newspapers and magazines (there are c. 700m tokens) called SYN2006PUB[6], SYN2009PUB[7] and prim-5.0=inf[8]. These contain newspaper and magazine texts from 1995-2007.

---

3 McEnery in his book Corpus Linguistics suggests that "grouping similar collocates of words together to help to identify different senses of the word. For example, bank might collocate with words such as river, indicating the landscape sense of the word, and with words like investment indicating the financial use of the word". http://www.lancs.ac.uk/fss/courses/ling/corpus/Corpus3/3FRA1.HTM

4 In the article we attempt to adopt Bartminski's theory of the language picture of the word for corpus research/corpus linguistics.

5 The results of the research were published in Hebal-Jezierska, M. (2010), Hebal-Jezierska, M., (2011, in print), Hebal-Jezierska M. (2012, in print)

6 One of the subcorpora belonging to the Czech National Corpus, available from WWW: <http://www.korpus.cz>

7 One of the subcorpora belonging to the Czech National Corpus, available from WWW: <http://www.korpus.cz>

8 One of the subcorpora belonging to the Slovak National Corpus, available from www.korpus.sk

The image of non-contextual and contextual collocations

There are two types of collocation images. The first one can be called a *non-contextual collocation image*, and the second one might be termed a *contextual collocation image*. The main difference between these two kind of images is that a non-contextual collocation ariscs from dividing automatically extracted collocations into semantic groups without checking their meaning in context. The contextual collocation image involves putting the collocations into context.

Let us make a comparison of two kinds of images of the word *cizinec* 'foreigner'[9], which was created based the data from the Czech National Corpus. The first table presents the analysis of the collocations of this Czech word.

Table 14.1: Semantic sets of the non-contextual analysis of collocations of the Czech word cizinec 'foreigner'

Crime, criminal offence	Motion	Life	Work	Request	Buying	Other	
26%	11%	21%	9%	2%	2,5%	28,5%	100%

As you can see, collocations are divided into six main groups. The most frequent collocations are words referring to crime in general or a criminal offence (26% occurrences). Also quite frequent are words referring to life, motion, work, buying and requests.

But if the collocations are put into context, the collocation image changes.

Table 14.2: Semantic sets of the contextual collocations of the word cizinec 'foreigner'

A foreigner as a criminal, a lawbreaker	A foreigner as a Citizen	A foreigner as a Victim	A foreigner as a Tourist	Other	
44%	23%	9%	9%	15%	100%

The collocations put into context show the foreigner in the four main categories which create the contextual image of collocations.

The most frequent (almost half the occurrences of collocations) are words referring to a foreigner as a criminal (law breaker). After that come words referring to a foreigner as a citizen, a victim of crime and a tourist.

The words which create the category of a foreigner as a criminal/ a lawbreaker are the following: lexemes directly referring to the illegality of actions, adverbs with meaning of the illegality (*načerno, ilegalně, nelegálně* 'illegal'), verbs that in the context might have a meaning of crime offence (*pracovat* 'work', *zaměstnávat* 'employ', *pobývat* 'reside', *žít* 'live', *překročit hranice* 'cross the border', 'transport aliens, cigarettes'), lexemes that have a criminal meaning (types of

9 The analysis of the word foreigner is taken from Hebal-Jezierska 2010: 75-79

crime): *pašovat cigarety, narkotika, lahve vodky, cizince* 'smuggling cigarettes, narcotics, bottles of vodka, alien', *krást* 'to steal', *přepadnout* 'to rob', *oloupit, vydírat* 'to blackmail', *vyděrač* 'blackmailer', *dlužit* 'to owe'.

The category of a foreigner as a victim of crime is made up of words referring to crime; these are very often in the form of a past participle, *okradený* 'stolen', *přepadený* 'attacked/mugged'. In the contexts there are frequent occurrences referring to a foreigner as a victim of crime and a tourist and a foreigner as a victim of crime by other foreigners (connecting categories).

> *v srpnu roku 2000 ozbrojení pistolemi společně s dalším <cizincem přepadli> Vietnamce v jejich bytě v Kamenné ulici.* 'In August 2000, along with another foreigner armed with pistols, they attacked the Vietnamese in their apartment on Stone Street'.

In the frame of the category of foreigner as a victim of crime, words describing appearance are quite frequent, e.g. *tmavý* 'dark'. The contexts are related to victims of racist attacks.[10]

> *Soud uznal , že útok na <cizince tmavé> barvy pleti měl rasový motiv.*'The court acknowledged that the attack on dark-skinned foreigners had a racial motive'.

The category of foreigner as citizen is made up of the verbs *žít* 'live), *pracovat* 'work', *zaměstnávat* 'employ', *povolovovat* 'allow', *nabývat* 'acquire'.

> *Nejvíce <cizinců žije> v Praze.* 'Most (of the) foreigners live in Prague'.

The last category represents the foreigner as a tourist: verbs of motion: *přijíždět* 'arrive', *přicestovat* 'travel', *legálně* 'legal', *vylákat* 'elicit', *okradený* 'stolen', *valutový* 'with foreign currency'.

> *aby především od <cizinců vylákali> drobný peníz* 'First of all, to elicit from foreigners any small change'

On the basis of this type of analysis we have compiled the images of the most frequent nationalities living in the Czech Republic: Slovaks, Poles, Vietnamese, Russians, Ukrainians and Romany. The image of the Romany has also been elaborated in the Slovak press. From the non-contextual and contextual analyses, all the listed nationalities except Poles and Slovaks have a negative image in the press (the main category in which they occur is as a criminal). It is worth adding that these results are consistent with the results of the questionnaire[11] about acceptability of nationalities living in the Czech Republic. According the questionnaire the Vietnamese, Russians, Ukrainians and Gypsies are below the level of acceptability by Czech society; above the level are Poles and Slovaks.

---

10 It is estimated that in the Czech Republic 1% of the crime committed has a racial motive. It is very interesting to put the query "racism" into the corpus SYN2000. The first adjective which co-ocurrs most frequently is the word Czech.

11 Chludilová 2003

Making a profile of the word

We can make various profiles[12] of the image of the word using the collocations extracted from our corpora. For example, the noun *German* has different images in the press corpus and the corpus of imaginative texts. In the first one[13] the dominant category is a German as a victim of displacement, in the second one[14] the dominant category is a German as a persecutor and oppressor.

PART II:

CHOSEN PROBLEMS IN USING THE METHOD (THE MOST FREQUENT PROBLEMS WITH CREATING IMAGES BASED ON COLLOCATIONS)

The size of corpus

The main problem encountered when the collocation images are created arises from the inadequate size of corpus. If we want to use the method, the corpus we choose must be large. Let us compare two results from the noun *Ukrainian* carried out on two different-sized corpora. The first corpus we used for our research was the Czech-language corpus of imaginative texts and newspapers and magazines called SYN2005. It has 100m tokens. The total number of occurrences of the noun *Ukrainian* searched by lemma is 844 and there are only a few collocations. Too few collocations means it is impossible to classify them and create an image based on them. A completely different situation obtains when using a larger corpus. After using the SYN2009PUB corpus of newspapers and magazines, which has 700m tokens, the total number of occurrences of the noun *Ukrainian* is 8544, the amount of collocation is sufficient to classify them and create on that basis an image of a lexeme.

The size of the corpus is not the only quantitative problem of the method. A very important condition is that the word should be also very frequent and have a strong and clear stereotype profile. It means that creating an image of a word on the basis of collocations is not appropriate and possible for every word.

---

12 Profiling involves, firstly, the initial categorization, secondly, the selection made the corresponding aspects of categorization, thirdly, the qualitative characteristics of the object within the adopted aspects. All these operations are obviously more strictly linked, secreted them here only for description. Bartmiński 2009: 94

13 Czech National Corpus, and Slovak National Corpus, press subcorpora.

14 Czech National Corpus and Slovak National Corpus, subcorpora of the imaginative literature.

Disadvantages of non-contextual collocation images

Although creating a non-contextual collocation images is quite a fast and interesting way of working with large amounts of data, it gives only a preliminary glimpse of the image of the word. Common problems of the method are: non-reliable frequency values of categories; homonymy, synonymy and polysemy of collocations; avoidance of important contexts; and the danger of potential collocations.

To illustrate few of the aforementioned problems (especially of homonymy, synonymy and polysemy), a set of non-contextual collocations belonging to crime will be given as an example, as was shown in the tables illustrating the word *foreigner*. Collocations without reference to the context of crime constitute 26 percent of the total, but after reference to the context they constitute almost half of all occurrences. It means that the frequency value of non-contextual collocations is not reliable because there are many more that, in the wider context, refer to crime. In the case of the word *foreigner* it concerns words such as *work* and *live*, which only in the appropriate context are seen as referring to crime.

Another quite interesting example is the word *ghetto*, which collocates with the word *Romany* in the Slovak language. The word *ghetto* has several meanings according to Cambridge Dictionaries Online[15]: a) an area of a city, especially a very poor area, where people of a particular race or religion live closely together and apart from other people, b) old use in the past, an area of a city where Jews were made to live, c) a part of society or group that is in some way divided from the main part.

In our research the word *ghetto* refers to the Romany's place of living but the meaning appears only after putting the collocations into context.

Words we may have seemed to be avoiding can, after they are put into context, be very important for the picture of word. For example, synsemantic words such as linking words, prepositions, and conjunctions, often belong to longer phrases. A good example was the word *and* in the aforementioned picture of word *foreigner*.

To avoid making the aforementioned mistakes it is necessary to contextualize extracted collocations.

Too-different types of collocations – The case of a noun *Vietnamese*

It happens, even in the analysis of words which have strong stereotypes in the language, that it is difficult to group collocations because of their diversity (variety). This problem was encountered when the noun *Vietnamese* was being analysed. Although the stereotype of the Vietnamese in Czech Republic is strong

15 http://dictionary.cambridge.org/dictionary/british/ghetto?q=ghetto

and stable, the collocations extracted from the noun *Vietnamese* do not show it. This is due to the variety of collocations. The most frequent words or phrases which are often used with other words or phrases are so various that it is impossible to put them into semantic groups. Therefore the largest group is made up of words that are labeled as "other". The words which are important for creating the stereotypes are created by small, frequent groups. Words referring[16] to trade are 2.5 %, crime 11%. This type of case shows the necessity of extracting collocations from related words (in our case, for example, the adjective *Vietnamese*). The collocations of the main word and the related words are complementary.

Table 14.3: Non-contextual collocations of the noun Vietnamese

Age	Trade	Crime	Other	
17%	2.5%	11%	69.5%	100%

Table 14.4: Non-contextual collocations of the adjective Vietnamese

Trade	Army	Crime	Communism	Community	Other
51%	19%	1.5%	2.6%	14%	11.9%

It is worth noticing that neither the noun and the adjective *Vietnamese* shows the true image, which is seen after putting the collocations into context. If we do it, the Vietnamese is often presented as a criminal. Let us look at a few examples. The non-contextual Vietnamese salesman has been changed into a criminal.

Vietnamec prodával nekolkované cigarety. 'The Vietnamese sold illegal cigarettes'.

Vietnamci prodávali padělané kompaktní disky. 'The Vietnamese sold counterfeit compact discs'.

Vietnamci prodávali pirátské nahrávky. 'The Vietnamese sold pirated recordings'.

Present-day issues as a factor that blurs a stereotype image of the lexeme – the case of the noun *Pole* and the adjective *Polish* versus the case of the nouns and adjectives *Ukrainian* and *Russian*

It is quite difficult to create an image of the words that are frequent because of their occurrence in present-day issues. In the case of the Czech press, the noun and adjectives *Pole, Slovak, Polish* are mostly used in the context of political and social issues. It means that stereotype features (stereotypical traits) disappear in the words referring to the actual problems.

16 The analysis of collocation of word Vietnamese is taken form Hebal-Jezierska 2010: 88.

The collocations of the words *Pole*, *Slovak*, *Polish* seem to be not very interesting. The most frequent lexemes that co-occur are surnames and forenames or words related to present-day political issues. Any stereotypical features occur singly and are not very frequent, for example the adjective *opilý* 'drunk' does not belong to any semantic group, because of the lack of words with similar meaning which could create semantic groups. It is also interesting that the feature of Polish people (*opilý* 'drunk'), although it belongs to the classical stereotypical feature of Poles, is not very well represented statistically. The word *opilý* 'drunk' in the statistical tests has the following statistical values: MI- score 5, 09, test T 2.912, rel f. 0.1146, abs. F. 9.

In the case of stronger stereotypes in the Czech press, such as with the nouns and adjectives *Ukrainian* and *Russian*[17], it is easier find sterotypical features. Among the collocations referring to age of people, the names of towns, the names of occupations: *dělník, horník, zedník* 'worker, miner, bricklayer' the names of sportsmen, the names of artists, there is a large group of words referring to crime and categorizing Ukrainians as criminals e.g.: *vražda* 'murder', *vyhoštěný* 'deported, the detainee', *pobodaný* 'knifed', *střílející* 'shooting', *prchající* 'fleeing', *zatčený* 'arrested', *zastřelený* 'shot', *uprchlý* 'escaped', *zadržený* 'detained', *zavražděný* 'murdered', *obžalovat* 'accuse', *zraněný* 'wounded', *ozbrojený* 'armed', *přepadnout* 'raid', *obžalovaný* 'accused', *zadržet* 'detain', *gang* 'gang', *obviněný* 'accused of', *mafie* 'mafia', *mafián* 'mafioso'.

> *Opilý Ukrajinec se dokonce pomocí pistole rozhodl okrást tři své krajany.* 'A drunk Ukrainian even decided to rob three of his compatriots at gunpoint'. *Pět opilých Ukrajinců zbilo a zkopalo policistu* [...] 'Five drunk Ukrainians beat and kicked the policeman [...]'

The collocations of the noun *Russian* look quite similar. There are 5 thematic groups. Apart from sets of collocations referring to Russian reality, the age of people and their origin, the units of collocations referring to the wealth of Russians and to crime stand out.

> *Sám Nikolaj Ghiuri uvedl , že mu dříve vyhrožovali členové ruské mafie.* 'Nicholas Ghiuri said that he had previously been threatened by members of the Russian mafia'

The danger of domination of one theme/one book/one event – the case of the noun *Rom* 'Romanian' and *cizinecká policie* 'foreign police'

Quite often a non-contextual/contextual image of collocations may be disturbed by one event or one thing, making it statistically unreliable. In our research, this was

17 The analysis of collocations of words Ukrainian and Rusian is taken from Hebal-Jezierska 2010: 86

the case with the collocation "murder of a Romanian". It concerns four cases of murders of Romanians, although the MI-score values of this type of words was high. The second example concerns the non-contextual and contextual analysis of collocations of word *cizinecký* (adj. 'foreign'). The most frequent word which co-occurs with the adjective foreign is a word police[18], which is an institution.

PART III: CONCLUSIONS

It seems that the method of creating an image based on collocations might be helpful in creating a linguistic picture of words and stereotypes. It indicates central and peripheral categories but it is important to remember about the aforementioned problems, especially: when using contextual collocations, we must be aware of the possibility of domination of the collocations by one event or several events.

References

Bartmiński, J. (2006). Językowe podstawy obrazu świata, Lublin.

Corpus SYN2006PUB (2010). Český národní korpus – SYN2009PUB. Ústav Českého národního korpusu FF UK, Praha. Available at http://www.korpus.cz

Corpus SYN2009PUB (2010). Český národní korpus - SYN2009PUB. Ústav Českého národního korpusu FF UK, Praha. Available at http://www.korpus.cz

Corpus prim-5.0=inf (2010). Slovenský národný korpus, Bratislava. Available at www. korpus.sk

Chludilová, I. (2003) Cizinci v České republice, Naše společnost 1-2.

Gries, T., Stefanowitsch, A. (2006) Corpora in Cognitive Linguistics, Berlin-New York.

Hebal-Jezierska, M. (2010). "Obrazy kolokacyjne wybranych leksemów, należących do pola semantycznego cudzoziemiec (na materiale korpusu języka czeskiego SYN2006PUB)." In Res slavisticae, Goszczyńska, J. and Greń, Z. (eds.), 73-92. Warszawa.

Hebal-Jezierska, M. (2011). "Kolokační obrazy některých lexémů patřících do sémantického pole cizinec v českém tisku (s metodologickými úvahami)," Korpusová lingvistika, Prague (In print)

Hebal-Jezierska M. (2012). "Wizerunki kolokacyjne mniejszości romskiej w korpusach publicystycznych języka czeskiego i słowackiego," Zeszyty Łużyckie, (In print)

Keibel, H., Belica, C., Kupietz, M. and M. Perkuhn (2011). "Approaching grammar: Detecting, conceptualizing and generalizing paradigmatic variation." In Grammatik und Korpora 2009, Konopka M., Kubczak J., Mair Ch., Šticha F. and Wassner U. (eds.), 329-356. Mannheim.

Leontiyeva, Y. (2003). "Cizinci v ČR: ‚my' a ‚oni'?," Naše společnost 1(3-4): 22-25, 2003.

Mc Enery, T. and A. Wilson. (2001). Corpus Linguistics. Edinburgh University Press. Available at http://www.lancs.ac.uk/fss/courses/ling/corpus/Corpus3/3FRA1.HTM

18 In the Czech Republic, the "foreign police" is a special branch of the police only for foreigners. It is also an office, where you have to go, if you live in Czech Republic.

In Quest of a Multi-Purpose Multi-Corpus Service-Based Corpus Research Tool

Karlheinz Moerth and Matej Durco

Abstract

Over the past decades, sizeable amounts of authentic digital language data have been collected for many languages in many parts of the world. While the available data is continuously increasing in size, tools to access them and glean data from them have remained comparatively scarce. One such prototypical corpus access application has been developed at the Institute of Corpus Linguistics and Text Technology of the Austrian Academy of Sciences. The so-called *corpusBrowser* is a program that not only allows researchers to linguistically analyze the corpus at hand, but also has navigational tools that offer random access to the texts under investigation. This paper discusses concepts underlying the design of the central components of this freely available corpus front end and highlights recently developed additional features. The second part of the paper includes the outline of an enhanced requirement specification defining comparable tools and presents plans to transform this standalone application into a multi-purpose corpus front end that operates in a platform-independent manner in any internet browser. After discussing the *corpusBrowser* application, we will present our plans for a generic web-based application, a front end for heterogeneous text resources available across different locations and domains on the Internet, and discuss the first implementation steps, which the ICLTT already started to work on in early 2011. This content search system is being built largely on previous ICLTT activities (Korpus C4, CLARIN CMDI and CLARIN European Demo Case).

Keywords

Corpora, corpus access, corpus tools.

The Austrian Academy Corpus

The research presented in this paper has been connected to the Austrian Academy Corpus (AAC), which has been compiled over the past decade and is currently maintained by the Institute for Corpus Linguistics and Text Technology (ICLTT) of the Austrian Academy of Sciences.

The AAC is largely made up of retrodigitised texts reflecting authentic samples of written German language of the 19th and 20th centuries. In addition to creating digital texts, the AAC has also been working on methods to access this pool of data and has sought to develop adequate tools to enable researchers from different fields, in particular Social Sciences and Humanities, to work on these texts.

Originally, the work on this corpus proceeded from different starting premises than those assumed by many others in the field. The working group's endeavours were characterized by what one might describe as a holistic approach, focusing on texts in their entirety rather than excerpting and not restricting the project to particular types of text. Their interests circled not only around the texts but also around what made the digital versions they were producing different from their printed counterparts. These digitising activities were characterized by a strong connection to the physical objects: the physical appearance of the digitized objects was given as much importance as the semantic structures of the texts.

The data collected over the years amounts to roughly 500 mil. tokens. The selection was motivated by literary principles rather than linguistic criteria and guided by a number of topical foci (such as law, religion, social economy, socialism, language of science and research, literature in exile, expressionism, travelling) and by particular historical events such as the Revolution(s) of 1848, World War I or the July 1927 Revolt. In addition, type of text was an important criterion: the aim was to incorporate a varied range of text types to cover as many different manifestations of written language as possible.

Almost half of the data is made up of historical magazines of literary, political and scientific significance and what in the department's nomenclature is called *collections* (publications which cannot be attributed to single originators), which include almanacs, anthologies, commemorative publications, yearbooks, readers, etc. The corpus is not in any way restricted to what might be referred to as *belles lettres*. In setting up the collection, we have gone far beyond a narrow interpretation of what is traditionally understood by the term 'literature'.

The corpus is entirely based on XML and cognate technologies. Over the years, a number of tools needed to be developed to handle the ever growing volume of data. At the beginning of the project in the late nineties of the 20th century, hardly any usable software was available, a fact which caused the working group to embark on a number of their own development projects. Today, the ICLTT toolbox comprises tools to produce digital texts as well as tools to access them. The main encoding tool used at the department has been a program called *corpedUni*, an XML text editor developed in-house from the start of the project[1]. Users of this tool were for the most part scholars with a background in literary studies or history. This fact accounts for a number of rather unusual built-in features. When working on texts, the application can always offer an additional facsimile view of the particular documents to allow users to comfortably compare digital text and original. The program is also capable of changing XSLT stylesheets on the fly. Furthermore, stylesheet transformations can be applied to certain sections of documents, such as a particular paragraph, which is a very useful feature when working with large documents. In most XML editors, transformations of entire documents – there are usually no other options – are so cumbersome that users rather tend to avoid them.

1 The AAC started to work with XML as early as 1998 when there were practically no tools available.

Corpus access tools

Most applications in the field have been built for and around particular corpora. Thus, the name of the *British National Corpus* (BNC) has been associated for a long time with a software application called *SARA* (Aston and Burnard 1998; Lee 2001; Burnard 2007). Another tool to access the BNC is and an application called *SCoRE* (Purver 2001). The *Czech National Corpus* is accessed through the corpus manager software *Bonito* (Rychlý and Smrž 2004) and a Polish application is *Poliqarp* (Janus and Przepiórkowski 2006). The largest collection of German language corpora, hosted by the *IDS* (Institut für Deutsche Sprache) in Mannheim, Germany, is accessed through *Cosmas,* which stands for *Corpus Search, Management and Analysis System* (al-Wadi 1994). In the last few years, the trend has been towards web based interfaces (Rehm et al. 2008) and it is regarded as state of the art to provide publicly available corpora with such interfaces. Just to name two of many, there are *BNCweb* (CQP-Edition) (Hoffman et al. 2008) and *Cosmas II* (Perkuhn, Belica et al. 2006; Institut für deutsche Sprache 2009).

The *corpusBrowser* tool – a prototypical corpus access application

The *corpusBrowser* was created for the special purpose of accessing the digital holdings of the *Austrian Academy Corpus* (AAC). In terms of concept and design, both the access tool and the corpus were designed to meet the needs of various scientific communities, literary scholars and historians as well as linguists, which made it necessary to implement a number of functionalities that go beyond what other corpus access tools offer. To our knowledge, there are no out-of-the-box solutions for comparable text collections. Therefore, the work on this tool has, out of necessity, been exploratory and very experimental in nature.

Currently, *corpusBrowser* is a Windows standalone application. It is designed as a multi-purpose corpus access tool in the sense that it is not only used to perform linguistic queries, but also serves as a reading device offering random access to the underlying data. It communicates with the local data server through the HTTP protocol and all of the functionalities are based on XML and related technologies such as XSLT and XPath.

The current generation of *corpusBrowser* retrieves data from an indexer that is known by the name *ddc-concordance* (Sokirko 2003). This free open-source tool is hosted by the source-forge site[2], is little known, has proved to be very useful and is remarkably efficient. As outlined in the software's documentation, "The main purpose of ddc-concordance is to search for words or sequences of words together with morphological patterns." Actually, the software has a much wider applicability than linguistic queries, as it is also capable of performing general

2 http://sourceforge.net/projects/ddc-concordance/

purpose word form searches and handling any type of token attributes. It also offers neatly definable range operators and regular expressions as well as the ability to filter results based on defined (bibliographic) metadata fields. The built-in server is able to process queries retrieving data from other (identically configured) servers, which allows the establishment of distributed systems. The only additional software needed are some simple wrapping scripts written in Perl (or Python).

The working group's initial requirement specification for this prototypical corpus access tool consisted of six basic components:

1. A unit to input queries and to display the results in form of KWICs.
2. A unit to display the related pages of the results as digital text.
3. A unit to view facsimiles of the texts.
4. A unit to display metadata of the digital objects.
5. A unit to query the metadata database.
6. A unit to browse/page through the original text, which – in default of a more adequate term – was called navigational control.

The query control is the part of the system that allows for inputting and launching queries and that is subsequently responsible for offering a basic overview of the query results. Among the required features of the query input unit of the prototypical corpus access tool were supportive mechanisms that propose and explain options such as drop-down lists, validation of input, etc. Each single result also had to provide metadata, information such as source, author, date of publication, etc. Results of queries are delivered by the server in XML which makes it fairly easy to adjust the representation of the output. In principle, any XSLT stylesheet can be used to tailor the display of the output. Predefined stylesheets allow for various modes of display, data extraction and analysis. The software also provides direct access to the raw XML data. Stylesheet transformations open up many options for the user. For example, one can easily create statistical breakdowns of the data or produce sorted lists of authors on the fly.

The display unit works in a similar manner. Customisable stylesheets that can be selected from drop-down lists through simple clicking allow instant switching between different views. To enable users to adjust stylesheets, the interface also has to provide direct access to the XML source of the texts.

Another important component of the *corpusBrowser* is the facsimile viewer. All the texts of the corpus can be displayed in dual mode, offering simultaneous access to text and facsimiles of the pages displayed. This is regarded as an indispensible feature for all those who want to perform more extensive reading of the texts, an important aid for scholars who need information about the formal features of the underlying texts, which are often not captured by structural markup.

The navigational control is the user-interface component that allows users to access the corpus texts at random. In order to allow for both literary and historical research, corpus access tools have to offer access to the corpus not only through query result lists but also through a library unit that enables readers to navigate to any desired part of the digital object. The navigational unit was conceptualised as a simple 'book emulator', a window that fans out symbols representing the pages contained in the respective digital objects.

Generic web-based interface ...

The following paragraphs attempt to outline a project that is currently evolving along two lines: (a) building a web-based corpus access tool that implements more or less all of the *corpusBrowser* functionality, and (b) enhancing this tool with methods that allow for not only one digital resource to be accessed but for queries to be performed on heterogeneous data in a distributed manner.

Practically, the first part involves migrating the *corpusBrowser* application to the web. As large portions of the *corpusBrowser*'s technologies are grounded on web-based standards, the standalone application already contains a considerable number of reusable components. Therefore, this undertaking, which was started in 2010, is well under way now. In general, the new application should be at least as versatile as the stand-alone application. The new and enhanced wish-list for the basic application contains eight basic requirements:

1. Query input + result viewer (KWIC).
2. Full-text browser with page-navigation and synchronized facsimile viewer.
3. A generic mechanism for accessing the corpus texts via various indices, be it tables of contents, lists of proper nouns or other taxonomies.
4. Options to export (store) results (together with associated metadata).
5. Options to build subcorpora both explicitly by indicating particular collections of resources or implicitly through queries or bibliographic filters.
6. Means to create and visualize aggregated overviews of the corpus, sub-corpus or a specific result.
7. Service-oriented architecture.

In addition, the tool should be capable of accommodating various types of resources: not only simple texts, but also more complex objects such as parallel corpora, lexicographic, prosopographic, encyclopaedic and other such data. Varying language resources will require varying functionalities. Thus, the system will have to allow a sufficient degree of configurability with respect to the corpus at hand and with respect to the current task. This applies mainly to the user interface, which has to be versatile enough to accommodate various "perspectives", allowing to dynamically add or remove individual "functional blocks" on demand. To achieve this end, we have introduced the notion of a *resource viewer*, a generic UI-component (possibly a plugin/addon) that can be provided in varying form in accordance with the type of the resource to be displayed. For example, users would be able to have a specific resource viewer for facsimiles, allowing them to navigate through the pages, another one for a simple digital text and yet another for geo-located or prosopographic data.

... for distributed search

The second part of the project, which aims at accessing language resources at other locations, has been motivated by a number of factors. Building new corpora has not become considerably cheaper over the past few years and obtaining funds has grown ever more difficult. Many large-scale corpus projects have come to a halt and it appears that the focus has started to shift from accessing your own small or big corpus/corpora towards a more collaborative approach, which consists of accessing various corpora in a distributed manner.

Actually, there have been several initiatives in this direction. One such project has come up with the *corpusEye* interface, which offers access to such heterogeneous resources such as *euroParl*, *Wikipedia*, and the *British National Corpus*.[3] Our department, the ICLTT, was involved in another such experiment: the *Korpus C4,* which was started a couple of years ago and brought together four partners in four European countries to develop a common federated corpus of the German language.[4] The whole undertaking was primarily a feasibility study building upon the aforementioned *ddc-concordance*.

In pursuit of these kinds of activities, the department has also actively taken part in the development of the *European Demo Case* (EDC), a group of interested people working within CLARIN's WP2 (technical infrastructure)[5], which so far has been focusing on federated meta-data search. The task force started in early 2010 as a joint activity to deliver appealing demonstrations of the (future) possibilities of CLARIN as a research infrastructure. The contribution of our institute in cooperation with colleagues from DWDS, BBAW was *C4W – Content for Webservices* – a prototype bringing together *Corpus search and Content Processing*. Gradually, the EDC initiative evolved into a working group developing an architecture that would allow for combined distributed metadata and content search. In this framework, we are currently undertaking efforts to specify and develop *federated content search* as a distributed system for querying resources and corpora.

---

3 http://beta.visl.sdu.dk/corpus_linguistics.html
4 http://chtk.unibas.ch/korpus-c4/
5 http://www.clarin.eu

Corpus_shell is being designed as part of this evolving CLARIN technical infrastructure. It is characterized by a service-oriented architecture, a system consisting of individual interacting components with clearly defined competencies and interfaces. One main element is of course the corpus search engine (CSE). In our case, we have started with the *ddc-concordance*, which is already being used in existing solutions. The system will be able to support widely used alternative CSEs such as CQP (Corpus query processor) or *manatee*.

The basic requirement of accessing heterogeneous target repositories dictates the introduction of a harmonizing layer – a lingua franca of the federated system. A candidate for such a common protocol is the *SRU/CQL* (Search/Retrieval via URL, Contextual Query Language)[6] standard proposed by the Library of Congress standardizing body as the successor of the Z39.50-protocol. However, as this protocol is designed mainly for querying and retrieving bibliographic metadata records, a few extensions seem to be necessary to make it usable for full-text content search. In addition, this would require implementing a thin wrapper component for every CSE that would translate between the idiosyncratic interface of that engine and the common protocol agreed upon within the architecture.

However, in addition to this common protocol, the web-application could provide searching and browsing capabilities over different repositories independent of the specifics of every individual CSE. The main reason for this harmonising layer is the federated or distributed search. In any case, a system designed to perform distributed queries needs an aggregator, a service that dispatches users' queries to individual search engines and returns merged results. To achieve this end, it is indispensable to assure, that all the individual search engines can be addressed through one common 'language'. The aggregating service will have to concentrate on the one task of merging the results and not have to bother with the specifities of particular target engines. Of course, such a harmonization can only be partial, as there is no search engine that can support all possible features. Thus, another important aspect of the protocol and a crucial feature of the aggregating service has to be a robust handling of errors, preferably as graceful degradation.

Current Status and Outlook

As stated above, the work on *corpus_shell* is tightly embedded in activities being conducted as part of the CLARIN project. In recent months, the focus of this collaborative work lay on formulating the specification of the interfaces and individual components of the architecture for the federated content search. At the same time, prototypical applications have been built (both CSE wrappers and aggregating components) to test the usability of the specified interfaces and set up the connectivity between the distributed components. In our case, we contributed a

6 http://www.loc.gov/standards/sru/

component mapping between SRU and ddc-concordance and a simple aggregator based on the *pazpar2* component of the *Masterkey*-suite[7].

At the moment, the focus is on trying to interlink the work on *corpus_shell* with other interested projects in order to share resources and foster synergies. Next to having strong ties to the EDC/FCS working group of the CLARIN project, especially with the CLARIN-NL working group, we are also involved in an exchange with teams within D-Spin/CLARIN-D (especially the WebLicht working group lead by the ASCL group at Tübingen University[8]), where we plan to work on harmonizing the interface between the content search and content processing.

Projects such as ours can only thrive in a networked environment. That is why the Viennese working group has sought the cooperation of a number of other European researchers. In this respect, we should like to highlight the cooperation with the LinfoVis[9] team at EURAC, in Bozen who investigate methods of integrating visualization techniques for linguistic information into the system currently being designed.

While the idea of distributed access to tools and shared data swirling around in clouds and grids has become a very popular notion in all fields of computing these days, while the shift of paradigm from classic "client-server" architecture towards less centralised "software as a service" is gaining ground, we have to concede that we still have not arrived when it comes to digital language resources. However, we believe that our project will contribute significantly to narrowing the gap between aspirations and reality, bringing us a couple of steps closer to the goal of easier access to more and better data, allowing more researchers to make use of increasingly versatile scientific working spaces.

References

al-Wadi, D. (1994). Cosmas. Benutzerhandbuch. Mannheim, Institut für deutsche Sprache.

Aston, G. and L. Burnard (1998). The BNC Handbook: Exploring the British National Corpus with Sara. Edinburgh University Press.

Burnard, L. (ed.) (2007). Reference Guide for the British National Corpus (XML Edition). Available at: http://www.natcorp.ox.ac.uk/docs/URG/.

Hinrichs, E. et al. (2009). "WebLicht - Web-based LRT Services for German." Workshop on Linguistic Processing Pipelines. Tagung der Gesellschaft für Sprachtechnologie und Computerlinguistik, Potsdam.

Hoffmann, S., Evert, S., Smith, N., Lee, D. and Y. Berglund Prytz (2008). Corpus Linguistics with BNCweb - a Practical Guide. Peter Lang.

Institut für Deutsche Sprache (ed.) (2009). COSMAS II. Corpus Search, Management and Analysis System. Available at: www.ids-mannheim.de/cosmas2/.

---

7 http://www.indexdata.com/pazpar2/

8 Hinrichs 2009; v. also http://weblicht.sfs.uni-tuebingen.de/weblicht.shtml

9 http://www.eurac.edu/linfovis

Janus, D. and A. Przepiórkowski (2005). "POLIQARP 1.0: Some Technical Aspects of a Linguistic Search Engine for Large Corpora." In The Proceedings of Practical Applications of Linguistic Corpora, Waliński, J., Kredens, K. and Goźdź-Roszkowski, S. (eds.). Peter Lang.

Lee, D. (2001). "Genres, Registers, Text Types, Domains, and Styles: Claryfying the Concepts and Navigating a Path Through the BNC Jungle," Language Learning and Technology 5(3): 37-72.

Perkuhn, R., Belica, C., al-Wadi, D., Lauer, M., Steyer, K. and Ch. Weiß (2006). „Korpustechnologie am Institut für Deutsche Sprache." In Korpuslinguistik deutsch: synchron – diachron – kontrastiv, Schwitalla, J. and Wegstein, W. (eds.). Würzburger Kolloquium 2003. Niemeyer.

Purver, M. (2001). Score: A Tool for Searching the BNC. Available at: http://www.eecs.qmul.ac.uk/~mpurver/papers/score-1.0.pdf.

Rehm, G., Schonefeld, O., Witt, A., Chiarcos, Ch. and T. Lehmberg (2008). "A Web-Platform for Preserving, Exploring, Visualising, and Querying Linguistic Corpora and other Resources," SEPLN 2008: 155-162. Madrid

Rychlý, P. and P. Smrž (2004). "Manatee, Bonito and Word Sketches for Czech," Proceedings of the Second International Conference on Corpus Linguisitcs: 124-131. Saint-Petersburg.

Sokirko, A. (2003). "DDC – A search engine for linguistically annotated corpora," Proceedings of Dialogue 2003. Protvino, Russia.

i-Publisher, i-Librarian and EUDocLib – Linguistic Services for the Web[1]

Anelia Belogay, Diman Karagiozov, Damir Ćavar, Dan Cristea, Svetla Koeva, Roumen Nikolov, Maciej Ogrodniczuk, Adam Przepiórkowski, Polivios Raxis and Cristina Vertan

Abstract

This paper presents three linguistically-aware online services built on top of the multilingual framework prepared for the ICT PSP EU-co-financed project ATLAS (Applied Technology for Language-Aided CMS). The framework intends to use the state-of-the art text processing methods in order to extract information and cluster documents. These basic blocks provide the base for advanced CMS functions such as automatic categorization or text summarization.

The i-Publisher is a Web-based content management platform for visual website building which integrates linguistic features to improve content navigation e.g. by interlinking documents based on extracted phrases, words and names, providing short summaries and suggested classification concepts. Apart from comprehensive language analysis, the CMS supports data visualisation as well as large volume multilingual data storage and maintenance.

i-Librarian is a sample online service build with and on top of i-Publisher (as a content management layer) to illustrate the benefits of applying language technology to content administration. It allows visitors to maintain a personal workspace for storing, sharing and publishing various types of documents and have them automatically categorized, summarized and annotated with important words, phrases and names. It also allows similar documents in different languages to be found easily.

The EUDocLib service basing on the collection of EU legal documents illustrates how users can easily find similar documents, obtain the summaries of desired documents or extracted important phrases and words.

One of the innovative issues in project is the integration of linguistically and technologically heterogenous language tools within a common framework. Certain level of uniformity has been achieved by establishing the collective list of tools (tokeniser, sentence boundary detector, paragraph boundary detector, lemmatizer, part-of-speech tagger, noun phrase chunker, named entity extractor) to be used for all languages and sharing general annotation properties (minimal structure and features). To facilitate chaining, the language processing tools have been integrated into a common UIMA (Unstructured Information Management Application) framework.

Currently all three services and their underlying language processing chains are available for English (the reference language), but will be soon extended with integrated tools for Bulgarian, Croatian, German, Greek, Polish and Romanian, making the first framework offering uniform solutions for languages of Central and South-Eastern Europe.

---

1 The work reported here was carried out within the Applied Technology for Language-Aided CMS (ATLAS) project co-funded by the European Commission under the Information and Communications Technologies (ICT) Policy Support Programme (Grant Agreement No 250467). The authors would like to thank all representatives of project partners for their contribution.

Keywords

Linguistic tools, language resources, Web services, content management system, online services, UIMA.

Introduction

During the last years, the number of applications which are entirely Web-based, or offer at least some Web front-end has grown dramatically. As a response to the need of managing all this data, a new type of system appeared: the Web content management system. In this article we will refer to these type of system as WCMS.

Existent WCMS systems focus on storage of documents in databases and provide mostly full-text search functionality. These types of systems have limited applicability, due to two reasons:

1. data available online is often multilingual and
2. documents within a CMS are semantically related (share some common knowledge, or belong to similar topics).

Shortly currently available CMS systems do not exploit modern techniques from information technology such as text mining, semantic Web or machine translation.

The recently launched ICT PSP EU project ATLAS – Applied Technology for Language-Aided CMS – aims to fill this gap by providing three innovative Web services within a WCMS. These three Web services: i-Librarian, EUDocLib and i-Publisher are not only thematically different but offer also different levels of intelligent information processing.

The ATLAS WCMS makes use of state-of-the art text technology methods in order to extract information and cluster documents according to a given hierarchy. A text summarization module and a machine translation engine are embedded as well as a cross-lingual semantic search engine.

The cross-lingual search engine implements Semantic Web technology: the document content is represented as RDF triples and the search index is built up from these triples.

The RDF representation of documents collects not only metadata information about the whole file but also exploits linguistic analysis of the document and store as well the mapping of the file on some ontological concept.

This paper presents the architecture of the ATLAS system with particular focus on the language processing components to be embedded aiming to show how robust NLP (natural language processing) tools can be wrapped in a common framework.

The paper is organised as follows: Sec. 2 describes briefly the added-value of the NLP tools for Web applications. Sec. 3 is dedicated to the description of language processing chains in a multilingual setting, while Sec. 4 presents the Web services embedded in the ATLAS platform which make use of the described language processing chains. Finally Sec. 5 describes the more complex language processing tools to be built around the language chains within the ATLAS platform.

Linguistic Tools for the Web

A Web-based CMS for advanced language processing should support comprehensive language analysis, data visualisation, and information sharing for diverse languages (at the moment seven languages are envisaged, namely Bulgarian, Croatian, German, Greek, English as a reference language, Polish, and Romanian, but more languages should be expected) – thus combining automatic linguistic annotation that enable more sophisticated language analysis and advance technologies for large volume multilingual data storage, maintaining and processing. The more extensive, consistent and sophisticated the linguistic annotation is, the more useful the multilingual data will be for a whole range of Web services provided. The lower level annotation marks values of attributes such as part-of-speech, grammatical categories of the lemma and word forms, as well as lemma itself, allowing homographs to be distinguished, and word forms of the same lemma to be grouped together. The annotation process of large amount of data should be automated, thus the minimum set of language processing tools (either rule, or statistical, or mixed-approaches based) integrated for each language are: tokenizer, tagger, and lemmatizer (which presupposes a morphological analyser as well). The benefit of having morphological and lexical information in a domain of humanities, i.e. cultural heritage digital libraries, has been demonstrated by the success of the Perseus Digital Library, oriented for wide user community.

Language Processing Chains in a Multilingual Setting

As mentioned in Sec. 1, the ATLAS platform provides Web services involving advanced language technology components for seven languages. The linguistic diversity in the project is a challenge not to be neglected: the languages belong to four language families and involve three alphabets. To our knowledge it is the first WCMS which will offer solutions for documents written in languages from Central and South-Eastern Europe. Whilst the standardised development of tools for wide-spread languages as English and German is more common, the situation is quite different when involving languages from Central and South-Eastern Europe (see http://www.c-phil.uni-hamburg.de/view/Main/ LrecWorkshop2010). Tools with different processing depth, different output formats and sometimes very particular approach are current state of the art in the language technology map of the above-mentioned area (Vertan et al. 2009).

One of the innovative issues in project ATLAS is the integration of linguistically and technologically heterogenous language tools within a common framework.

The following description presents the steps taken in order to provide such common representation.

- Starting from the fixed desiderata to include text summarisation, automatic document classification, machine translation and cross-lingual information retrieval the minimal list of tools required by such engines which can be provided by all languages involved in the project has been collated and includes:
  - tokeniser,
  - sentence boundary detector,
  - paragraph boundary detector,
  - lemmatizer,
  - PoS tagger,
  - NP (noun phrase) chunker,
  - NE (named entity) extractor.

Some of these tools are not completely available for particular languages (e.g. NP chunker for Croatian) but can be developed within the project. Regarding the NE extractor the following entities has been agreed upon: persons, dates, time, location and currency.

- The annotation levels in the texts and the minimal features to be annotated have been defined: *Paragraph*, *Sentence*, *Token*, *NP* and *NE*. In order to provide a common representation all linguistic information regarding lemma, PoS etc. have been agreed to be provided at the token level. For a token following features will be retained:
  - `begin` – an integer representing the offset of the first character of the token,
  - `end` – an integer representing the offset of the last character of the token,
  - `pos` – a string representing the morphosyntactic tag (PoS, gender, number) associated with the token,
  - `lemma` – a string containing the lemma of the token.
- For each of the above-mentioned tools the list of additional linguistic features to be represented (if necessary and available) have been defined, for example `antecedentBegin` and `antecedentEnd` representing the offset of the first and respectively the last character of the referent in an NP. This feature is necessary for processing German NPs and is therefore included as optional in the NP annotation frame.

A glossary of tagsets delivered by each tool is also maintained, ensuring cross-lingual processing.

Each of the language tools can be included as primitive engine, i.e. part of an UIMA aggregate engine, but also as an aggregate engine. In this way any language component can reuse results produced by a particular tool and exploit its full functionality if required.

One of the goals of the ATLAS WCMS is to offer documented language processing chains (LPCs) for text annotation. A processing chain for a given language includes a number of existing tools, adjusted and/or fine-tuned to ensure their interoperability. In most respects a language processing chain does not require development of new software modules but rather combining existing tools.

Most of the basic linguistic tools (sentence splitters, stopword filters, tokenizers, lemmatizers, part-of-speech taggers) for languages in scope of our interest have already existed as standalone offline applications. The multilinguality of the system services requires high level of accuracy of each monolingual language chain – simple example is that a word with part-of-speech tag ambiguity in one language may correspond to an unambiguous word in the other language. The complexity grows at the level of structure and sense ambiguity differs among languages. Thus the high precision and performance of language specific chains predefines to the great extend the quality of the system as a whole. For example the Bulgarian PoS tagger has been developed as a modified version of the Brill tagger applying a rule-based approach and techniques for the optimization leading to the 98.3% precision (Koeva 2007). The large Bulgarian grammar dictionary used for the lemmatization is implemented as acyclic and deterministic finite-state automata to ensure a very fast dictionary look-up.

The language processing chains have been fine-tuned and adjusted to facilitate integration into a common UIMA[2] framework. Other tools (such as noun phrase extractors or named entity recognizers) had to be implemented or multilingually ported. The annotation produced by the chain along with additional tools (e.g. frequency counters) results in higher-level functions such as detection of key words and phrases along with improbable phrases from the analyzed content, and utilisation of more sophisticated user functionality deserves complex linguistic functions as multilingual text summarisation and machine translation.

Integration of the Tools into UIMA Framework

UIMA is a pluggable component architecture and software framework designed especially for the analysis of unstructured content and its transformation into structured information. Apart from offering common components (e.g. the type system for document and text annotations) it builds on the concept of analysis

2 Unstructured Information Management Application. See http://uima.apache.org/.

engines (in our case, language specific components) taking form of primitive engines which can wrap up NLP (natural language processing) tools adding annotations and aggregate engines which define the sequence of execution of chained primitives.

The Annotation Model

Making the tools chainable requires ensuring their interoperability on various levels. Firstly, compatibility of formats of linguistic information is maintained within the defined scope of required annotation.

The UIMA type system requires development of a uniform representation model which helps to normalize heterogeneous annotations of the component NLP tools. With ATLAS it covers properties vital for further processing of the annotated data, e.g. lemma, values for attributes such as gender, number and case for tokens necessary to run coreference module to be subsequently used for text summarisation, categorization and machine translation.

To facilitate introduction of further levels of annotation a general *markable* type has been introduced, carrying subtype and reference to another markable object. This way new annotation concepts can be tested and later included into the core model.

WebCMS and its Online Applications

The language chains are used in order to extract relevant information such as named entities and keywords from the documents stored within the ATLAS WCMS. Additionally they provide the baseline for further engines: *Text summarization*, *Clustering* and *Machine translation* and as such they are the foundation of the enhanced ATLAS platform.

The core online service of the ATLAS platform is i-Publisher, a powerful Web-based instrument for creating, running and managing content-driven Web sites. It integrates the language-based technology to improve content navigation e.g. by interlinking documents based on extracted phrases, words and names, providing short summaries and suggested categorization concepts.

Currently two different thematic content-driven Web sites, i-Librarian and EUDocLib, are being built on top of ATLAS platform, using i-Publisher as content management layer. i-Librarian is intended to be a user-oriented web site which allows visitors to maintain a personal workspace for storing, sharing and publishing various types of documents and have them automatically categorized into appropriate subject categories, summarized and annotated with important words, phrases and names. EUDocLib is planned as a publicly accessible repository of EU legal documents from the EUR-LEX collection with enhanced navigation and multilingual access.

An important aspect of ATLAS System is that all three services operate in a multilingual setting. Similar functionality will be implemented within the project for Bulgarian, Croatian, German, English, German, Greek, Polish and Romanian. The architecture of the system is modular and allows anytime a new language extension.

i-Publisher

The i-Publisher service (see Fig. 1):

1. is mainly targeted at small enterprises and non-profit organizations,
2. gives the ability to build via point-and-click user interface content-driven Web sites, which provides a wide set of predefined functionalities and whose textual content is automatically processed, i.e. categorized, summarized, annotated, etc.,
3. enables publishers, information designers and graphic designers to easily collaborate,
4. saves authors, editors and other contributors valuable time by automatically processing textual data and allows them to work together to produce high-quality content.

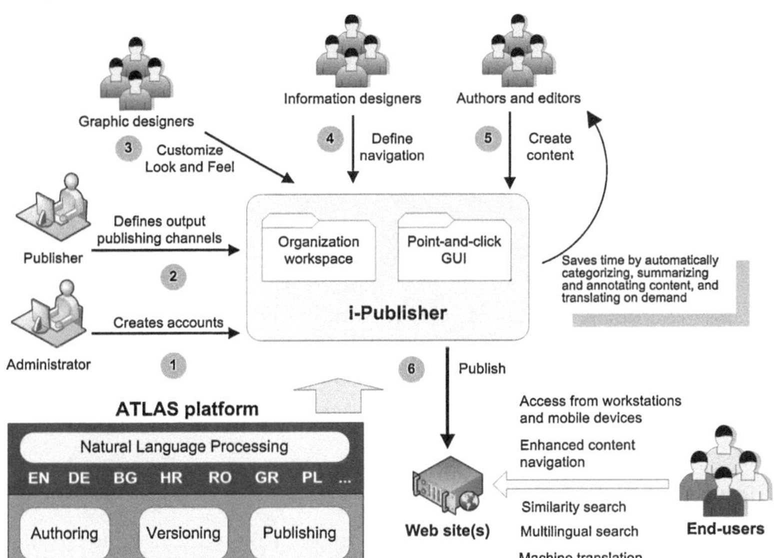

Figure 15.1: i-Publisher architecture

i-Librarian

The i-Librarian service (see Fig. 2):

1. addresses the needs of authors, students, young researchers and readers,
2. gives the ability to easily create, organize and publish various types of documents,
3. allows users to find similar documents in different languages, to share personal works with other people, and to locate the most essential texts from large collections of unfamiliar documents.

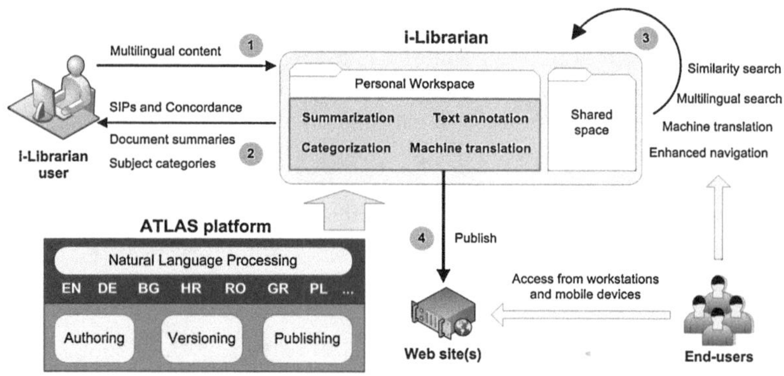

Figure 16.2: i-Librarian architecture

EUDocLib

The EUDocLib service:

1. addresses the needs of people who require easier access to EU documents in their own language,
2. enables users to easily find similar documents, read the summaries of desired documents, or read extracted important phrases and words.

Further Steps

The project outlines numerous directions to be followed, ranging from novel approach to advanced linguistic topics through building on user's opinions on to improve their usability up to sustainability issues. From the Semantic Web point of view the most innovative research areas to be covered in the project in the next 1.5 years are connected with integration of Machine Translation engine, Cross-language retrieval engine, Summarization engine and Categorization engine.

According to the project schedule, public versions of these online services will be launched in the beginning of 2012, after their evaluation is completed.

Machine Translation and Cross-lingual Retrieval

Machine translation ensures integration of foreign-language content, achieved by means of using the EuroMatrix technology (Koehn et al. 2007), improving existing translation models and incorporating them in the proposed online services. The users will be offered a computer-aided translation service based on the database with existing translations in the form of a translation memory tool. As a next step, the system to process user-submitted translations will be implemented to further improve the quality of existing models.

Cross-lingual retrieval is intended to give users the opportunity to rapidly access content made available by the online content services independently of its language. Existing concept-based cross-lingual search engine together with its underlying ontology, both developed during the LT4eL project (Monachesi et al. 2006; Degórski et al. 2008)[3], will be adapted and further improved. Basing on categories and keywords a conceptual space will be constructed and integrated into a conceptual search mechanism (Vertan et al. 2007).

Text Summarization

Summarization tools will be prepared by adjusting and fine-tuning existing software components for the project target languages basing on a discourse-parsing based method.

After the text is segmented into elementary discourse units (mainly clauses), a discourse tree is composed for each sentence based on cue-phrases recognized by the parser. The sequence of sentence trees is arranged into discourse tree by maximizing a score contributed from centering transitions and anaphoric links. The discourse tree is in turned used for computing the summaries, both general and focused, with the support of specialized resources and tools such as a collection of discourse markers and (optionally) an anaphora resolver.

Automatic Categorization

A language-independent text categorization tool fine-tuned to work with each project language will be prepared and tuned to heterogeneous domains. Its ultimate goal will be effective organization of content in the online services by using vector space models (VSMs) with lexical distribution patterns or alternative features

---

3 Language Technology for eLearning FP6 Specific Targeted Research Project (Information Society Technologies), contract number 027391. See http://www.lt4el.eu/.

selected from the documents. Initial VSMs will be generated on the basis of lexical distribution in documents, using various lexical windows, of 1 to n N-grams, as well as normalization methods for matrix reduction (i.e. by elimination of specific lexical classes of elements, or elimination of lexical covariation etc.). Finally, classification of documents will be performed by applying similarity measures over the vector space models of classes and particular documents. For the particular classification algorithms, we will use k Nearest Neighbours, Support Vector Machines and Latent Semantic Analysis.

Conclusions

The ATLAS platform opens the doors to standardized multilingual online processing of language and it offers localized demonstration tools built on top of the linguistic modules. We intend it to be a contribution to the development of text processing chains for the Web, especially for underrepresented languages.

The framework is ready for integration of new types of tools and new languages to provide wider online coverage of the needful linguistic services in a standardized manner.

References

Banerjee, S. (2002). Adapting the Lesk algorithm for word sense disambiguation to WordNet. University of Minnesota, Duluth. Master's thesis.

Degórski, Ł., Marcińczuk, M. and A. Przepiórkowski. (2008). Definition Extraction Using a Sequential Combination of Baseline Grammars and Machine Learning Classifiers. In Proceedings of the Sixth International Conference on Language Resources and Evaluation, LREC 2008, Marrakech. ELRA.

Erkan, G. and D. R. Radev. (2004). "LexRank: Graph-based Centrality as Salience in Text Summarization," Journal of Artificial Intelligence Research 22.

Monachesi, P., Cristea D., Evans D., Killing A., Lemnitzer L., Simov K. and C. Vertan. (2006). Integrating Language Technology and Semantic Web Techniques in eLearning. In Proceedings of The International Interactive Computer-Aided Learning Conference (ICL 2006), Villach, Austria, September.

Tsoumakas, G., Katakis I. and I. Vlahavas. (2010). Mining Multilabel Data. In Data Mining and Knowledge Discovery Handbook, Maimon O. and Rokach, L. (eds.). Springer, 2nd edition.

Tsoumakas, G., Vilcek J., Spyromitros E. and I. Vlahavas. (2000). "Mulan: A Java Library for Multi-Label Learning," Journal of Machine Learning Research 1.

Vertan, C., Monachesi P., Simov K., Osenova P., Lemnitzer L., Killing A. and D. Evans. (2007). "Crosslingual Retrieval in an E-Learning Environment." In Proceedings of The 10th Congress of the Italian Association for Artificial Intelligence (AIIA 2007), Basili, R. and Pazienza, M. T. (eds.), 839-847. Berlin, Heidelberg. Springer-Verlag.

Translation Quality Checking in LanguageTool

Marcin Miłkowski

Abstract

In large computer-aided translation (CAT) projects, especially in software localization, one of the main problems is to maintain the consistent style of the translated text. To tackle this problem, translators have to follow different guidelines defined in style guides for different translation jobs. Yet, in the case of conflicting guidelines (for example, terminological) for various projects it is very easy to make mistakes, and quite hard to find them because they are neither obvious nor glaring errors. Automated translation quality assessment (QA), on the other hand, are usually quite costly compared to other CAT tools and/or do not have any comprehensive natural-language processing features. Usually, their use is not really beneficial for languages other than English. Because of that, the proofreading process is costly and time-consuming, or the translation quality is negatively impacted.

In this paper, I will present the translation QA features available in LanguageTool, an open-source proofreading tool (Miłkowski 2010). LanguageTool currently (as of version 1.4 released on June, 26, 2011) supports 22 languages and is able to use the standard target language rules to check for the mistakes in the translated text, including false friends in translation, as well as specially designed translation QA rules. These rules may be specially crafted to conform to informal style guides and include the most frequent mistakes found by human proofreaders (using the method specified in Miłkowski, forthcoming). I will show some examples of such bilingual rules. It is hoped that thanks to XLIFF standard support the proofreading tool will be easily introduced to the standard translation QA workflow of translation agencies and individual translators.

Keywords

Computer-aided translation, quality assessment, grammar checking.

Quality Assessments in Translation Jobs

In the real translation world, especially in the field of technical, business and legal translation, translators have to follow different style guides.[1] While they might be of great help to maintain the terminological and stylistic consistency of the resulting translation, they also contribute to problems for individual translators. This is especially the case when the advice offered by a style guide differs from the widely accepted language use. For example, Microsoft recommends “strona sieci web” as the translation for “web page” (thereby making “web” a proper name, left

1 For example, see the style guide for Polish EU translators at: http://ec.europa.eu/translation/polish/guidelines/documents/styleguide_polish_dgt_pl.pdf. In software localization, Microsoft style guides are the state-of-the-art documents for most languages: http://www.microsoft.com/Language/en-us/StyleGuides.aspx.

in the English form in the Polish text), whereas the more popular version is "strona internetowa". Such specific and often conflicting requirements make quality assessment harder, as the proof editors may simply not see that there is a non-standard translation of a term.

Another problem stems from translating technical text in a tagged form, which is usual for technical applications, such as software localization, web pages, help pages, DTP-ready text. Translators have to be careful to preserve the format (and other) tags from the original in the translation. For example, formatting tags abound in software strings ("%s" etc.), and they need to be preserved. Similarly, numbers in general should remain the same, yet there are exceptions such as unit conversions, different date formats or currency conversions. In other words, some of the numerical content should remain as is in the translated text, whereas some of it should be translated. As numerical content is rarely read with much attention, simple errors may creep in.

Automated Quality Assessment Tools

For these reasons, it is a good idea to automate the chores of proofreading. It is especially easy when the text to proofread is already in a bilingual form, which is what all current computer-aided translation (CAT) tools provide. Yet, the standard translation quality assessment (QA) tools that support bilingual formats are usually limited. For example, QA Distiller[2] has the following features:

- detect untranslated segments,
- detect inconsistency,
- detect formatting problems (spaces, commas...),
- detect language-dependent formatting problems (date format etc.),
- detect terminology errors,
- use regular expressions for customized rules.

Such features help find many obvious, yet hard-to-find problems in the translation. However, for morphologically rich languages, regular expressions are usually not enough to specify the inflected form, especially for consistency checking. In other words, QA Distiller, though arguably one of the leading QA tools, is mostly blind to the grammar of the natural language. It can easily support only languages that are similar to English with relatively stable word order and limited morphological variation.

While QA Distiller is a commercial tool for translation agencies, there are also free applications that gain popularity among individual translators. The most

2 http://www.qa-distiller.com/

notable of them are ApSIC Xbench,[3] featuring most of the checks offered by QA Distiller (with the exception of the date formats etc.), and CheckMate,[4] and open-source QA tool from the Okapi tool set, which offers even more. Figure 1 shows the dialog box of CheckMate. As can be seen, it displays several kinds of possible errors detected by the tool: untranslated segments, translated content with hidden content, special tags not found in the source, and suspicious ratio of the target text to the source text (too short or too lengthy). Some of the errors might be trivial for most uses (like adding or removing "http://" part in the URL addresses), but for financial data, any change of numbers should be highlighted.

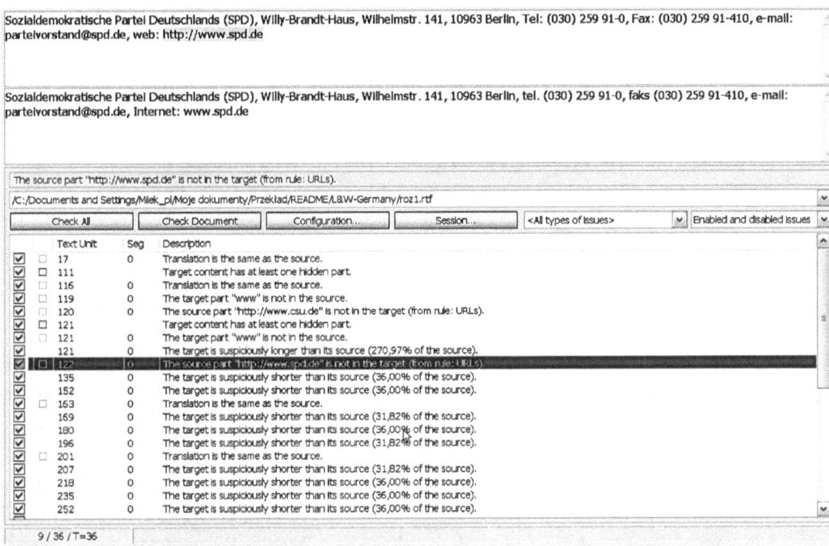

Figure 17.1: Screenshot of CheckMate

Yet neither commercial nor free tools really support linguistic technology. None of them uses part-of-speech (POS) tagging of text to build rules that detect grammatical problems. They also do not support stemming, and custom rules rely exclusively on regular expressions on strings. Moreover, words in the sentence are specified as linear sequences, and that is acceptable only for languages with strict word order.

---

3 http://www.apsic.com/en/products_xbench.html

4 http://www.opentag.com/okapi/wiki/index.php?title=CheckMate

Out of the three standard QA tools, CheckMate is special in one regard: not only does it support custom regular-expression-based rules, but it also uses external proofreading engines, such as LanguageTool, and that greatly enhances its abilities.

LanguageTool

LanguageTool is an open-source proofreading tool, used for example in OpenOffice.org and LibreOffice (Miłkowski 2010). As of June 2011, it supports 22 languages to a different degree, described in Table 1, and more are in preparation (during the current Google Summer of Code project, Tao Lin is preparing support for Chinese, and there are also preliminary prototypes for Filipino).

Table 17.1: Languages supported by LanguageTool.

Language	XML rules	Java rules	Rule maintainers
Belarusian	7	0	Alex Buloichik
Catalan	213	1	Ricard Roca
Danish	22	0	Esben Aaberg
Dutch	311	0	Ruud Baars
English	490	3	Marcin Miłkowski, Daniel Naber
Esperanto	177	0	Dominique Pellé
French	1891	1	Agnes Souque, Hugo Voisard (2006/2007), Dominique Pellé
Galician	166	0	Susana Sotelo Docío
German	150	8	Daniel Naber
Icelandic	39	0	Anton Karl Ingason
Italian	86	0	Paolo Bianchini
Khmer	22	2	Nathan Wells
Lithuanian	4	0	Mantas Kriaučiūnas
Malayalam	18	0	Jithesh.V.S
Polish	1028	4	Marcin Miłkowski
Romanian	418	1	Ionuţ Păduraru
Russian	129	3	Yakov Reztsov
Slovak	55	2	Zdenko Podobný
Slovenian	58	0	Martin Srebotnjak
Spanish	70	1	Juan Martorell
Swedish	26	1	Niklas Johansson

Figure 2 shows the dialog box of OpenOffice that uses LanguageTool as its backend to check text.

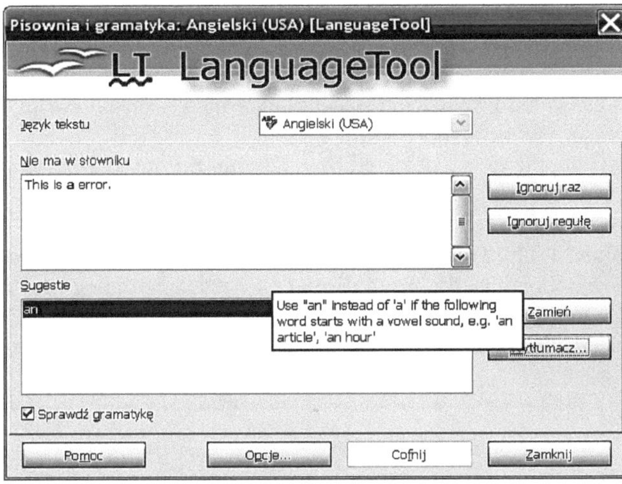

Figure 17.2: LanguageTool checking an English sentence in OpenOffice.org

LanguageTool (LT) is based on surface text processing, without deep parsing, not to mention semantic analysis, yet, it manages to get significantly better results (for some languages) than commercially available products (see Miłkowski 2010 for comparison for Polish). Some rules in LT are built semi-automatically from corpora (Miłkowski forthcoming). Most interestingly for the translation QA, LT is used as the grammar-checking engine in several tools, such as the aforementioned CheckMate or the open-source CAT tool OmegaT. Figure 3 shows how LT is supported in OmegaT.

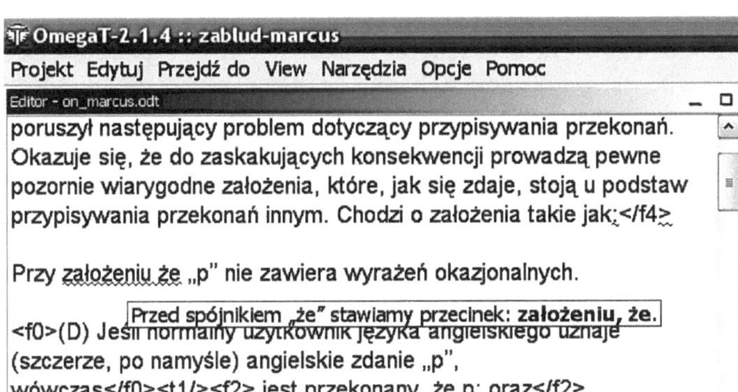

Figure 17.3: LanguageTool in OmegaT displays an error in a Polish sentence

The API of LT allows its integration via simple HTTP requests in different software packages, as well as direct use of its methods in Java. LT can also natively support bilingual text files in tabbed format (where the first field is the source segment, and the second field – the target one), which makes it useful for inclusion in batch processing workflows.

In CheckMate, the errors detected by LT might fall into two categories: target-text errors, which are supported in a monolingual mode, and bilingual-mode errors. CheckMate itself supports numerous bilingual input formats, such as XLIFF, TMX, PO, TTX, tagged RTF (Trados-style) *etc.*, which means that LT does not have to duplicate this functionality. Figure 4 displays CheckMate dialog box including the errors found in the target-text error mode.

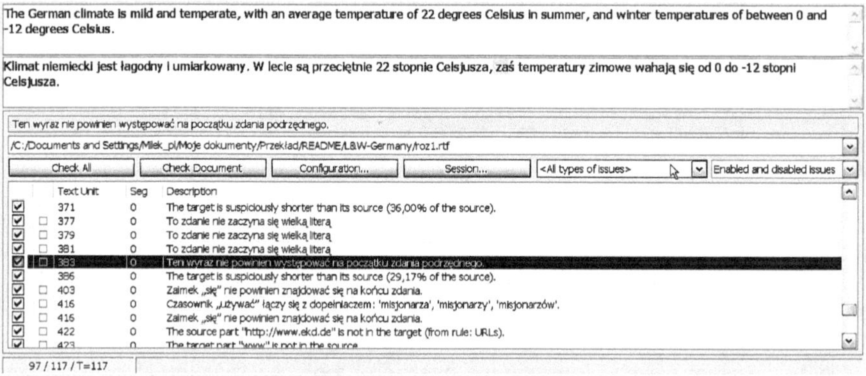

Figure 17.4: CheckMate uses LanguageTool to check target text

As can be seen on the screenshot, the errors in this mode are much more related to linguistic structure of the text than previously: usage of capital letters, pronouns, valence of verbs etc. However, only the bilingual mode of LT shows its real strength in checking translations.

In bilingual (bitext) mode, LT uses:

- false friend rules: the rules are matched only when both source and target contain the false friend terms (to avoid false alarms);
- rules for target language;
- generic bitext rules (in Java);
- XML bilingual rules for target language (if any).

False friend rules

In LT, there are many rules that detect possible false friends in translation (in different language combinations, mostly for English, German, Polish, Italian, and

French). They are useful for non-native speakers writing documents in a foreign language. In bilingual mode, these rules are triggered less frequently because the source text is also checked, so the number of false alarms is much lower. Table 2 shows the number of false friend rules per language (the languages not included do not have them defined at all). The number of rules per languages is the sum of all rules in which the language is mentioned (in all combinations). In other words, if there are 4 rules for Catalan, it does not mean that they all support Polish-Catalan false friends. At the same time, English words have usually false friends defined for multiple languages ("actually" is a false friend in all languages in Table 2).

Table 17.2: False friend rules in LanguageTool

Language	Number of false friend rules
Catalan	4
English	231
French	5
Galician	6
German	88
Italian	36
Polish	140
Spanish	27
Swedish	5

Rules for target language

These are standard target-text rules, which include declarative rules (saved in XML format), and procedural rules written in Java. Most of them are XML rules as they are much easier to write for people without programming experience, as well as they allow focusing on the linguistic content of rules (for the detailed description of the formalism, see Miłkowski 2010). The Table 1 under **XML rules** includes the number of such rules per language, and the column **Java rules** displays the number of generic Java rules per language. Note that some of the generic Java rules work for multiple languages (for example, rules to detect word repetition and unpaired brackets).

Generic bitext rules

As of writing, there are only two such rules: one checks if the translation length is roughly the same as the source, and another if the translation is the same as source. Both are written in Java. Obviously, using them in CheckMate makes no sense, as CheckMate already includes this functionality.

XML bilingual rules

The XML bilingual rule files specify errors found for many source languages and one target language, and their format is based on the formalism used already in monolingual rules. They declare language-aware specific checks and corrections, including, but not limited to:

- terminology, even in complex phrases (and with rich morphology);
- incorrect syntax patterns (copying original grammar structure to a target language with a different syntax);
- inconsistency in terminology;
- dates, currencies, number formats...

LT includes lemmatization for most languages it supports, and declaring that any form of the word should be detected is as easy as adding a single XML attribute *inflected* with a value "yes". Even though the XML rules are restricted to shallow parsing, their expressive value, is, as we believe, roughly comparable to that of the Constraint Grammar (Karlsson et. al 1995).[5] Shallow parsing, moreover, is successful in many applications in computational linguistics (Przepiórkowski 2008), and it is easier to develop it step-by-step, starting from very simple resources, which is important for the success of open-source projects. Our XML notation allows specifying most errors in a concise way, mostly without recourse to cryptic regular expressions (though they are also supported).

In the current release of LT (1.4), there are only a handful of rules for English included. As the XML notation is documented and there are already thousands of examples in LT code base, it is however possible to formalize at least some of the advice offered in the translation style guides. This way, LT might become part of the QA workflow for complex translation jobs, where multiple translators and proofreaders collaborate. Using LT, the proofreader will be able to focus on important mistakes, not just mechanical and stupid ones.

Anatomy of a Rule

Let us take a real-world mistake: a translator uses Google Translate to make his job quicker and mistranslates "similar in kind" literally as "podobny w naturze". This is an obvious style problem in Polish. The pattern in XML rule for Polish would be:

---

5 One of the projects for the Google Summer of Code 2011 in LanguageTool is preparing a (hopefully lossless) conversion tool from Constraint Grammar to LT formalism.

```
<pattern>
<source lang="en">
 <token>similar</token>
 <token>in</token>
 <token>kind</token>
</source>
<target>
 <token inflected="yes">podobny</token>
 <token>w</token>
 <token>naturze</token>
</target>
</pattern>
```

The rule is processed in the following way: if LT finds an English sentence (or segment) with words "similar in kind" and the Polish sentence with words "podobny w naturze" (whereas "podobny" might occur in any of its inflected forms), it will match the rule. After the rule is matched, a suggestion may be offered (if it is defined in the rule). For example:

```
<message>
Czy chodziło o
  <suggestion>podobnego rodzaju</suggestion>?
</message>
```

In this case, LT will offer "podobnego rodzaju" as a correction in the Polish text. (If the automatic mode is used, LT may automatically apply this correction. This is especially useful in automated post-editing (see section 5) and in applying terminological changes to multiple files automatically.)

The last part of the rule are examples of correct usage (which are not detected, though usually similar to the source pattern), and examples of incorrect sentences that are detected as incorrect. For example:

```
<example type="correct">
  <srcExample>These apples are similar in kind.</srcExample>
  <trgExample>Te jabłka są podobnego rodzaju.</trgExample>
</example>
<example type="incorrect" correction="podobnego rodzaju">
  <srcExample>These apples are <marker>similar in
kind</marker>.</srcExample>
<trgExample>Te jabłka są <marker>podobne w
naturze</marker>.</trgExample>
</example>
```

These examples serve several purposes. First, they check if the rule was declared properly and it actually matches the incorrect sentence in the place identified with the tag "marker". They also check if the suggestion applied is actually the same as the developer of the rule intended (in this case, this is trivial, but suggestions may be created dynamically by inflecting words, changing them using regular expressions etc.). Second, they can be used as the internal documentation of the rule: if properly displayed on the screen, they can help to easily identify the purpose of the rule.

Note that the tokens in the source and target sentences are not aligned with each other: LT does not try to align words with each other, so it does not know which source word has "naturze" as its translation. If such alignment is required, it can be added in the generic Java rules. However, we found no need for it in our practice.

Other Uses and Future Work

The application of bilingual checking in LT is not limited to translation quality control. Another possible use is automatic post-editing of statistical machine translation.[6] For example, it may be used to make sure that financial data get translated in a consistent manner (i.e., that currency remains consistently translated). Such rule-based checks are useful when the translation itself was done statistically. It may also fix missing negation words, which is common in Google Translate in Polish.

Bilingual checks may also be used to validate syntactic correctness of complex multilingual structures. For example, custom rules for checking validity of abbreviations and notation in a large bilingual dictionary project were built by the present author.

In the future, there are several important rules that we plan to implement. The first is a smart number matching rule that uses textual way of translating figures ("one" gets translated into "1", or "1" gets translated into "jeden"). Standard QA tools cannot do that, but thanks to the NumberText library[7], it is relatively easy to convert numbers to text for multiple languages. The second rule will be partly based on the first: it will include smart currency and date conversion checks.

6 Usually, it is the rule-based machine translation (RBMT) which is post-edited using statistical methods to enhance the fluency of the translation (see Simard et al. 2007, Dugast et al. 2007). However, post-editing in the case I mention serves another purpose: applying strict, rule-based checks on statistical input in order to preserve certain strict translations (like currency conversions). It may also be used to remove false friends and translate idiomatic phrases that are underrepresented in corpora (instead of including the lexicon as part of the training corpus, one may simply apply lexicon-based translation on garbled statistical translation).

7 http://www.numbertext.org/

Another area of future development is inclusion of conversion tools to convert terminology bases in TBX and text format to the richer LT format (and, alternatively, direct support for glossaries in terminology checks but without special linguistic features). For this to work, it will be useful to add support for multiple custom rule files and rule file sets to LT user interface.

It is also possible to create some of the false-friend rule files semi-automatically by using terminology bases (especially for multiword expression) and machine translation to see which multiword expressions are usually mistranslated by default, and then supply the correct translation as the proper one.[8] This can enhance the capabilities of the QA system far beyond the style guides and mechanic mistakes.

Conclusion

Translation QA should be done in language-aware fashion, not just like pure text search (even with regular expressions). Otherwise, many mistakes will not be detected, though they are arguably mechanic in nature and hard to spot for human proof readers.

There are free and open-source tools that enable checks that go beyond what most commercial packages can do. We hope that their development will help the proof readers and translators to focus on the content of the translation. Otherwise, the proofreading process is costly and time-consuming, and the translation quality is negatively impacted.

References

Miłkowski, M. (2010). "Developing an Open-source, Rule-based Proofreading Tool," Software: Practice and Experience 40(7): 543-566.

Miłkowski, M. (2011). "Automating Rule Generation for Grammar Checkers." In Explorations Across Languages and Corpora, Góźdź-Roszkowski, S. 9ed.). Frankfurt am Main.

Karlsson, F., Voutilainen, H. J. and A. Anttila (ed). (1995). Constraint Grammar: A Language-Independent System for Parsing Unrestricted Text, Mouton de Gruyter, Berlin.

Dugast, L., Senellart, J. and P. Koehn (2007). "Statistical Post-editing on SYSTRAN's Rule-based Translation System," Proceedings of the Second Workshop on Statistical Machine Translation – StatMT'07: 220-223. Morristown, NJ, USA: Association for Computational Linguistics.

Przepiórkowski, A. (2008). Powierzchniowe przetwarzanie języka polskiego. Akademicka Warszawa: Oficyna Wydawnicza EXIT.

Simard, M., Ueffing, N., Isabelle, P. and R. Kuhn (2007). "Rule-based Translation With Statistical Phrase-based Post-editing," Proceedings of the Second Workshop on Statistical Machine Translation: 203-206. Prague: Association for Computational Linguistics.

8 This idea was suggested to me by Jimmy O'Regan (personal communication).

How DOES Google Translate?

Belinda Maia and Rui Sousa-Silva

Abstract

In this paper we shall look at how Google Translate is contributing to the world of professional translation. We argue in favour of training translators to accept machine translation, to learn how to use it as a tool and to revise the result for clients who need translations for urgent and more ephemeral use, like the background for tomorrow's meeting. We investigate whether Google actually uses the vast material at its disposal efficiently to obtain its results, and examine its claims to use only statistical means. The objective is to increase awareness of the strengths and weaknesses of machine translation as a tool.

Keywords

Machine translation, professional human translation and research.

Introduction

The background to this paper involves the EMT - European Master's in Translation Network[1] and the Academic Network OPTIMALE – Optimising Professional Translator Training in a Multilingual Europe[2], and the perceived need to understand how the demands on the professional translator and language service provider will evolve. Experience shows that revision of MT is becoming an essential skill for professional translators, and we shall consider how human translation – HT – can use Google Translate – GT – and other MT systems for professional language services. Our personal interest is in observing how online text resources are used for Natural Language Processing – NLP – generally, and Machine Translation - MT - in particular, and how training future translators to use MT can contribute to linguistic analysis and topics for research.

While the MT world debates the value of rule-based MT (RBMT) versus example-based MT (EBMT) versus statistical MT (SBMT), GT[3] claims to be doing what it can with statistical analysis, looking for "patterns in millions of documents to help decide on the best translation for you". It recognizes that it relies for quality on the HT documents at its disposal and that, as a result "translation accuracy will sometimes vary across languages". Although we have no access to the secrets of

---

1 EMT – European Master's in Translation network
Available at: http://ec.europa.eu/dgs/translation/programmes/emt/index_en.htm

2 OPTIMALE – Optimising Professional Translator Training in a Multilingual Europe - http://www.translator-training.eu/optimale/index.php

3 Google Translate – http://translate.google.com/about/intl/en_ALL/

the system, as outside observers we can see that it is exploiting enormous databases of text, and that is also probably using whatever language tools are at its disposal.

Machine Translation, translators and language services providers

In 1959 Bar-Hillel (1964) claimed that FAHQMT - Fully Automatic High Quality Machine Translation of 'unrestricted text' was impossible for philosophical and linguistic reasons. This will continue to be true until artificial intelligence reaches the same level as human intelligence, which, although no longer an impossibility, is still some time in the future. For the time being, human translation is still essential for High Quality Translation, but it is expensive.

Translation is in high demand as the world becomes increasingly globalized, while remaining multilingual, and MT is an important means of maintaining economic sustainability for HT and social sustainability for multilingualism. The alternative, as is already the case at the higher levels of communication, like conferences and academic and scientific publications, is English.

In order to train students to use MT as a tool as part of their training, we have used our own meta-MT tool, METRA, for this purpose for some time (Maia, 2008). The exercise of pre-editing draws attention to doubtful structures or redundancy in the original text and is good practice for revising and editing work, as it raises awareness of the quality of both source and target text. The task of post-editing is useful for teaching the complexities of language systems.

Pre-editing texts for MT takes several forms: some have advocated controlled language (Mitamura, 1999), or artificially simple language, that can be easily translated. This type of language has been implemented when dealing with repetitive texts like weather forecasts, as in the well-known METEO project for MT between English and French at the University of Montréal, or specific industries, such as Caterpillar (Kamprath et al, 1998). There have also been several attempts to produce software that performs simplification or summarization of texts, but few have been very successful., and space does not allow us to describe them here.

Some texts for localization are deliberately 'internationalized', in the sense that these texts contain the most commonly acceptable syntactic structures and minimum cultural content. Some systems use semi-automatic pre-editing of originals by creating more easily translatable paraphrases (Barreiro, 2007). This type of editing, however, requires extensive manual input by linguistically sensitive people. In a professional situation, pre-editing may have a limited application, unless the client also requires language services that permit improvement or modification of the original.

However, as MT improves, the ability to post-edit its results is fast becoming a useful and marketable language services skill. In the past, training someone to post-edit the results of an MT engine was a question of making the person aware of the flaws in the syntactic rules and the limited lexicon used by the system. The syntax could be improved, if one were allowed access to the 'black box', and special lexicons could be built for domain specific MT (Oliveira 2008). Our tool METRA[4], referred to above, collected English <> Portuguese MT and originally accessed 5 online free translation systems, most of them based on Systran[5], a rule based system with smaller or larger dictionaries, depending on the development of the version being used. By studying the results that were fed to the systems, we were able to establish that many of the mistakes were predictable as well as being similar to those of unskilled human translators translating into their foreign language.

The systems had problems with lexical ambiguity and hyponyms, and the dictionary 'solutions' were often idiosyncratic. On the other hand, simple syntactic structures, like the change of the English adjective + noun to the Portuguese noun + adjective, seemed to function quite well. There were even solutions for areas judged by programmers to be 'difficult', such as the English Present Perfect. When a word had multiple meanings in the other language, the tendency was to opt for the most common 'solution', as, for example, with the Portuguese preposition *em,* which is more frequently translatable by *in*, although it also means *on*. However, as should be expected, MT keeps very close to original language structures.

We also developed a further tool called Boomerang, which returned the MT solution to the systems for a series of back translations, which clearly showed that there was not necessarily any connection between the MT programming in both directions, and this fact was demonstrated more conclusively with our MT evaluation project (Sarmento et al. 2007).

Recent developments in MT and why Google Translate is different from previous online MT systems

However, the experience gained from experiments with the Systran based MT systems could not be applied to testing Google Translate and preparing exercises to train translators. As we have already indicated, systems like Systran are rule-based, and Rule Based MT – RBMT – always uses syntactic (+ semantic) rules and large dictionaries. Since RBMT has proved much more difficult than was previously believed, not least because of the conflicting theories of linguistics employed, and the very complexity of differences between most languages, computer specialists have argued for Example Based MT – EBMT, using parallel corpora and translation memories to establish databases of acceptable equivalent words and phrases, although the exact nature of this EBMT is debatable (see Hutchins 2003). On the far end of the spectrum from RBMT, through EBMT, comes Statistical MT

4 Linguateca – METRA - http://193.137.34.101/metra/
5 Systransoft – http://www.systran.co.uk/

– SMT – using statistical analysis over parallel, comparable and concurrent texts. SMT was originally expected to work at word equivalence level, but now it can be subdivided into Phrase Based SMT (PBSMT) and Syntax Based SMT (SBSMT). PBSMT can be seen to be a natural development of translation memory software, which suggests whole phrases or even (fuzzy matched) sentences from the existing database. SBSMT may well start by using part-of-speech annotated dictionaries, a shallow parsing system, and, possibly, some form of RBMT, and then aim to pick up on the syntactic regularities found statistically to correct and amplify the RBMT. All this implies a certain amount of what computer scientists refer to as machine learning, an area on which we cannot elaborate here.

GT claims to use purely statistical methods and exploits its enormous text resources – monolingual, bilingual, and multilingual for this purpose. It uses European Commission texts, official online text databases, Wikipedia, all (and any) online parallel corpora or text databases, comparable text collections, dictionaries, thesauri, encyclopedias and other reference material. It also acquires material via the GT toolkit, a translation memory + MT + terminology management that is 'free' for anyone who wants to use it, as well as GT users' "corrections". It claims "If Google displays your content to an end user, it will do so only according to the sharing rules below, and only on a translation unit basis." This 'translation unit' is not clearly defined and the same document warns that:

> By submitting or creating your content through the Service, you grant Google permission to use your content to improve or make available the Services pursuant to these additional terms, provided that Google will not disclose the subject matter of your content or make your content available on a standalone basis to any third parties without your consent.

So, by using their 'free' software and agreeing to correct the results the system produces, you are helping to improve the system itself.

Google Translate and some results

We have tested GT on various occasions to see how it performs, using Portuguese to English examples as these are the languages we usually compare, and the results in English will make more sense in the context of this paper. We realize that this will present only a partial view of what is happening, and that, since Portuguese is a major world language, thanks to the almost 200 million Brazilians, the results will reflect Brazilian rather than European Portuguese. By the same token, because of Brazilian input, the amount of online material in some form of Portuguese is probably much greater than with other 'smaller' European languages.

Although the sentence structures of GT, like any other form of MT, usually follow the original, the lexical usage can be good as it manages to retrieve the correct terms from parallel or comparable texts. However, the syntactic pattern choices are more difficult to predict than is the case with RBMT.

Sometimes the examples one tests need no correction. This is particularly true when translating international news from Portuguese to English, as in the following example:

1a. Com a ajuda do Exército francês, os apoiantes do presidente marfinense eleito, Alassane Ouattara, conseguiram esta madrugada tomar o controlo do palácio presidencial e da casa privada do Presidente cessante da Costa do Marfim, Laurent Gbagbo, que permanece agarrado ao poder e cujo paradeiro é agora desconhecido.

1b. With the help of the French Army, supporters of Ivorian President-elect, Alassane Ouattara, have managed this morning to take control of the presidential palace and the private home of the outgoing President of the Ivory Coast, Laurent Gbagbo, who is still clinging to power and whose whereabouts are now unknown.

The error-free result suggests that a Portuguese journalist put the internationally distributed news item through GT, possibly polished it up, and the system then memorized it. This is a good indication of plagiarism, as discussed in Sousa-Silva et al (2009).

However, the following example demonstrates the dangers involved in this sort of exercise:

2a. A Líbia está pronta para uma "solução política". Mas com Khadafi no comando. Foi esta a mensagem que ***transmitiu*** o porta-voz do Governo líbio, Mussa Ibrahim, aos repórteres que o questionaram sobre o teor das suas negociações com outros países.

2b. Libya is ready for a "political solution". But with Gaddafi at the helm. This was the message ***conveyed to*** the spokesman for the Libyan Government, Ibrahim Mussa ***told*** reporters who questioned him about the contents of their negotiations with other countries.

Here something similar has happened, but GT must have enough underlying shallow parsing to pick up on the verb *transmitiu* as belonging to *o porta-voz do Governo líbio* and to assume that *Mussa Ibrahim* is a different person who then needs the verb *told*, thus causing a serious error of misunderstanding!

When one tests local Portuguese news, which has probably been created by a local journalist, one gets rather less satisfactory results in English:

3a. O ministro da Agricultura desafiou hoje, no Algarve, os desempregados nacionais com capacidade para trabalhar no setor agrícola a aceitarem as propostas de emprego existentes em Portugal e recordou que os empresários estão a contratar mão de obra externa.

3b. The minister of Agriculture defied today, in the Algarve, the national unemployeds with capacity to work in the agricultural sector to accept the existing proposals of job in Portugal and remembered that the entrepreneurs are to contract hand of external workmanship. (A free RBMT online system).

3c. Agriculture Minister challenged today in the Algarve,_the unemployed nationals with ability to work in the agricultural sector to accept the job offers in Portugal and pointed out that entrepreneurs are hiring foreign labor. (GT)

GT does not change the Portuguese structure, which prefers a different position for its adverbs, and it preferred to omit the obligatory Portuguese definite article for the Agriculture Minister. However, GT's choice of lexical items such as *unemployed nationals, job offers* and *foreign labor* is a considerable improvement over the RBMT version, which suggests that GT is collecting more suitable phrases from databases on similar subjects, rather than relying on an integrated dictionary.

Sometimes GT produces mistakes that demonstrate that it is using clues from the context rather than named entities, as in:

> 4a. Em *Coimbra* "há hoje mais de uma centena de empresas de base tecnológica", a maior parte das quais ligadas à Universidade, sublinha Almeida Santos, antigo presidente da Assembleia da República, prevendo que, com "este rumo", a cidade terá "um futuro brilhante".
>
> 4b. In *London* "*is* now over one hundred technology-based companies, most of which related to the University, stresses Almeida Santos, former president of Parliament, predicting that*"(with) this* course, "the city will have" a bright future."

This translation of Coimbra by London probably owes something to the surrounding information but, given the NLP community's concentration on Named Entity Recognition, this is a surprising mistake.

One is left to wonder whether GT, despite its claims to use only statistical means, is using some RBMT, or at least basic shallow parsing, as the following example, where most of the translation is probably plagiarized, suggests:

> 5a. "Quando cheguei ao meu gabinete, no primeiro dia como secretário do Tesouro, encontrei uma carta do meu antecessor [Liam Byrne]. Pensei que se tratava de algum conselho ou recomendações quanto à melhor forma de desempenhar as minhas funções nos próximos meses", *contou Laws aos jornalistas.*
>
> 5b. "When I arrived at my office on the first day as Secretary of the Treasury, found a letter from my predecessor [Liam Byrne]. I thought it was some advice or recommendations as to how best to perform my duties in the coming months," *he told reporters Laws.*

The translation has not only given the reporting verb two subjects, it has moved the second one, *Laws*, to after the indirect object.

It is also clear that when the tone of the text is colloquial and the cultural references less than clear, GT tends to fail in its interpretation, as can be seen in the following example:

> 6a. Desde a antiguidade que o homem é seduzido pela descoberta de novas culturas e o conhecimento de novos locais. Mas viajar hoje é muito mais cómodo, fácil, simples e económico do que foi outrora. Já não precisamos de rumar par o Brasil a bordo de Caravelas movidas a vento. Actualmente, com a Internet, já estamos a viajar em nossas casas, mesmo antes de sairmos.
>
> 6b. Since antiquity man is seduced by the discovery of new cultures and learning about new places. But travel today is far more convenient, easy, simple and affordable than it once was. No longer need to head to Brazil to pair Caravelas board

powered by wind. Currently, the Internet, we are traveling in our houses, even before we left.

GT is meant to learn from the material it receives, but the following example belies the earlier examples where we showed how, when one uses GT shortly after the publication of a news item, one can track the original (and plagiarized?) version. In the following examples, we back-translated the Portuguese version a month after the first translation and it became clear that, at this distance, GT has gone on to randomize its phrases somewhat.

7a. At the beginning of the last century, the power of nations might have been measured in battleships and coal. In this century it's as likely to be graduates. There has been an unprecedented global surge in the numbers of young people going to university. **Original – February 2011**

7b. No início do século passado, o poder das nações poderia ter sido medido em navios de guerra e de carvão. Neste século, ele é tão susceptível de ser licenciados. Houve um aumento global sem precedentes no número de jovens que vão para a universidade. **GT - February 2011**

7c. At the beginning of last century, the power of nations could have been measured in warships and coal. In this century, it is as likely to be *licensed.* There *was* an unprecedented global increase in the number of youngsters going to university. **GT back-translation 15 March 2011**

Conclusions

Despite the errors of syntax, which occur even in RBMT because of the difficulty in coordinating syntactic and semantic information to a level that solves problems like ambiguity, and the occasional incorrect retrieval of information, GT would seem to be an improvement on other free online MT systems. This is true at least between major languages and English and at a lexical / phrasal level, and it would appear that many people, translators among them, use GT more frequently at these levels than at a sentence or textual level. This point is also made by Hutchins (2009). GT is also used by the more linguistically naïve to provide translation service. It is here that professional human translators need to intervene and show how their versions are better. But they also need to realize that using GT can help to accelerate their work when speed is more essential than quality.

Our intention with this paper was to call attention to the study of the use of MT in general, and GT in particular, as an instrument for training 9) in a practical skill that will be increasingly necessary in their future profession. We hope we have shown the difficulties involved.

References

Bar Hillel, Y. (1964). Language and Information. Reading, MA: Addison Wesley.
Barreiro, A. (2008). "Port4NooJ: Portuguese Linguistic Module and Bilingual Resources for Machine Translation." In Proceedings of the 2007 International NooJ Conference, Blanco, X. and Silberztein, M. (eds), 19-47. Cambridge Scholars Publishing.
Hutchins, J. (2003). "Example Based Machine Translation – a Review and Commentary." In Recent Advances in Example-based Machine Translation, Carl, M. and Way, A. (eds.), 482. Dordrecht: Kluwer Academic Publishers.
Hutchins, J. (2009). "Multiple Uses of Machine Translation and Computerized Translation Tools." ISMTCL: International Symposium on Data Mining and Sense Mining, Machine Translation and Controlled Languages, and Their Application to Emergencies and Safety Critical Domains, July 1-3, 2009, Centre Tesnière, University of Franche-Comté, Besançon, France (Presses universitaires de Franche-Comté, 2009); pp. 13-20.
Kamprath, C., Adolphson, E., Mitamura, T. and E. Nyberg (1998). "Controlled Language for Multilin- gual Document Production: Experience with Caterpillar Technical English," Proceedings of the Second International Workshop on Controlled Language Applications (CLAW-98).
Maia, B. (2008). "Machine Translation and Human Translation: Using Machine Translation Engines and Corpora for Teaching and Research." In Current Trends in Contrastive Linguistics, González, G., de los Ángeles, M., Lachlan Mackenzie, J. and González Álvarez, E. M. (eds.), 123-145. John Benjamins Pub. Co.: Amsterdam/Philadelphia.
Mitamura, T. (1999). "Controlled Language for Multilingual Machine Translation," Proceedings of Machine Translation Summit VII, Singapore, September 13-17, 1999.
Oliveira, D. (2008). O uso de terminologia na melhoria de sistemas de tradução automática para textos de especialidade – o caso dos patentes de invenção. Universidade do Porto: Master's dissertation.
Sarmento, L., Barreiro, A., Maia, B. and D. Santos. (2007) "Avaliação de Tradução Automática: alguns conceitos e reflexões." In Avaliação conjunta: um novo paradigma no processamento computacional da língua portuguesa, Santos, D. (ed.), 181-190. Lisboa, Portugal: IST Press.
Sousa-Silva, R., Maia, B. and T. Grant (2009). "When News Becomes a Forensic Issue," International Association of Forensic Linguists 9th Biennial Conference on Forensic Linguistics/Language and Law – VU University, Amsterdam, Netherlands.
Sousa-Silva, R. and T. Grant (2010). "'Reporter Fired for Plagiarism': A Forensic Linguistic Analysis of News Plagiarism," IAMCR – The International Association for Media and Communication Research Conference 2010 – Communication and Citizenship: Rethinking Crisis and Change, Universidade do Minho, Braga, Portugal.

A Corpus-Driven Comparison of Translational and Non-Translational Literary Polish

Łukasz Grabowski

Abstract

This article presents selected results of a corpus-driven comparison of the two custom-designed corpora of translational and non-translational Polish literary texts. The aim of the study was to find stylistic differences between the two corpora as well as identify traces, if any, of translation universals, namely T-universals (after Chesterman 2004) with emphasis on core patterns of lexical use, as proposed by Laviosa (1998, 2002). The results of the study revealed, among others, that translated texts are more varied lexically and have more repetitions and lower lexical variety among top-frequency words than non-translated Polish texts. On the other hand, the study showed that non-translational texts have higher lexical variety among bottom-frequency words, where usually one can find author-specific and creative vocabulary.

Keywords

Translational texts, non-translational texts, translation universals, corpus-driven analysis, literary Polish

Introduction

According to Baker (1993, 1995, 1996), descriptive Translation Studies (DTS) conducted today should not be limited to the comparison of source texts and their translations, but they should also be extended to comparisons of non-translated texts with translated texts, which are produced under different social, cultural and sometimes even political circumstances. In her seminal paper, Baker (1995: 243) puts forward the idea of *universal features of translation* or *translation universals*, which are specific textual characteristics (e.g. lexical, grammatical or stylistic) typical of translated texts, irrespective of interference from languages involved in the translation process. Further, Baker (ibid.) posits a number of hypotheses on the differences between translational and non-translational language, e.g. that translations tend to be, among others, more explicit as regards lexis and syntax than non-translated texts, their content and form is simplified if compared with non-translated texts, and that language used in translations is more conventional and less creative than the one used in non-translated texts. As a result, translations exhibit distribution of lexical items that distinguishes them from original texts in the same language, which accounts for a symptom of specific translation strategies or tendencies, such as, among others, explicitation, simplification, normalization, sanitization and levelling-out Kenny (2001: 53-54). According to Olohan (2004: 92), these patterns are specific to translations and are seen to be more typical of translational language than of non-translational one. In addition, characteristics of translational language are a product of constraints inherent in the translation process and do not vary across different languages and cultures (ibid.). Thus, it is essential to study linguistic patterns which are specific to translated texts, irrespective of source and target languages involved (Laviosa-Braithwaite 1995: 153).

Laviosa (1998: 557-570), who studied distinctive features of translational English as compared with native English (represented by samples ellicited from the British National Corpus), found that translational English has four core patterns of lexical use: a relatively lower proportion of lexical words over function words, a relatively higher proportion of high-frequency words over low-frequency words, a relatively greater repetition of the most frequent words, and a smaller vocabulary (i.e. lower number of word types) frequently used. Further, Laviosa (2002: 60-62) adds that translational English texts have lower average sentence length and lower range of vocabulary than non-translational texts.

Consequently, a number of distinctive features of translational English in relation to native English have been uncovered. Nevertheless, if these patterns of lexical use in translational language identified by Laviosa (1998, 2002) are to be generalised as *translation universals*, the language pairs involved in the study must not be restricted to English. This observation provided motivation to undertake a project that examines features of translational Polish.

Therefore, in this article, two custom-designed reference corpora of translational and non-translational literary Polish will be compared with each other in order to verify the hypotheses on core patterns of lexical use in translational texts (Laviosa 1998, 2002) as well as to find traces, if any, of other translation universals.

For the purposes of this study, the typology of translation universals [TUs] proposed by Chesterman (2004: 6-7) was applied. Chesterman (ibid.) distinguished between two types of TUs: the S-universals, which are related to translation from the source to the target language, and the T-universals, which are related to comparisons of translational and non-translational texts (i.e. target-language texts, which are not translations). In this study, which deals with comparison of translational and non-translational texts, the search for T-universals will be pursued.

Methodology, research material, tools and stages of the analysis

In this study, a bottom-up corpus-driven methodology was applied. In contrast to the corpus-based approach, which always works within commonly accepted frameworks of theories of language, or – in other words – is theoretically-committed (which implies prior classification of linguistic data), the reference corpora of translational and non-translational texts were not adjusted to fit any predefined categories or theoretical schemata. Thus, the study questions were addressed through empirical analysis of frequency distributions of words as found in the corpus of translational (henceforth the PTT) and non-translational (henceforth the PNT) Polish texts.

When compiling these corpora, the most important criteria were representativeness and size. As regards the former, it was aimed that the texts represent contemporary literary Polish. As a result, the corpus of native texts (PNT) includes a collection of literary novels published in the years 1938-1998; in a similar vein, the corpus of translations (PTT) contains Polish renditions of selected British or American novels published in Poland in the years 1954-1996. These corpora are similar in terms of size: the PNT contains 482,728 running words, whereas the PTT includes 487,760 running words. Detailed information concerning make-up of the two corpora is presented in Table 1 and 2 below.

Table 19.1: Make-up of Polish Non-Translational Corpus (PNT)

No	Author	Title (Publication date)	Size (tokens)
1	Krystyna Siesicka	*Zapach rumianku* (1969)	30,517
2	Krystyna Siesicka	*Ludzie jak wiatr* (1970)	34,566
3	Jerzy Andrzejewski	*Ciemności kryją ziemię* (1957)	34,597
4	Jerzy Andrzejewski	*Bramy raju* (1960)	24,867
5	Witold Gombrowicz	*Ferdydurke* (1938)	71,265
6	Tadeusz Borowski	*Wybór opowiadań* (1951)	58,116
7	Stanisław Lem	*Pamiętnik znaleziony w wannie* (1961)	57,576
8	Olga Tokarczuk	*Prawiek i inne czasy* (1996)	55,155
9	Dorota Terakowska	*Poczwarka* (1988)	68,810
10	Jerzy Pilch	*Bezpowrotnie utracona leworęczność* (1998)	46,606
	TOTAL		482,728

Table 19.2: Make-up of Polish Translational Corpus (PTT)

No	Author	Title, (Publication date)	Size (tokens)
1	William S. Burroughs	*Pedał (Queer)* (1985)	25,521
2	Jerzy Kosiński	*Malowany Ptak (The Painted Bird)* (1965)	59,602
3	Jerzy Kosiński	*Wystarczy Być (Being There)* (1971)	21,976
4	Salman Rushdie	*Wschód, Zachód (East, West)* (1994)	30,183
5	Wilbur Smith	*Katanga (The Dark of the Sun)* (1965)	67,913

6	Wharton William	*Dom na Sekwanie (Houseboat on Seine)* (1996)	62,065
7	William Golding	*Wieża (The Spire)* (1964)	50,699
8	William Golding	*Władca Much (Lord of the Flies)* (1954)	48,997
9	Winston Groom	*Forrest Gump* (1986)	58,456
10	William Gibson	*Neuromancer* (1984) (1992)	62,348
	TOTAL		487,760

Subsequently, the quantitative corpus-driven analysis was completed with the use of WordSmith Tools 4.0 (Scott 2004), which is a suite of programs custom-designed for text analysis. According to Hoover (2007: 517-533), the aim of quantitative approaches to literature is to represent elements or characteristics of literary texts numerically, applying the powerful, accurate, and widely accepted methods of mathematics to measurement, classification, and analysis. Furthermore, the availability of texts in electronic format has increased the attractiveness of quantitative approaches as innovative ways of reading amounts of text that overwhelm traditional modes of reading.

The study was broken down into the following stages: the corpora were compared in terms of descriptive statistics, followed by comparisons of word length, frequency profiles and frequency spectra. As a result, the corpus-driven research procedures were used in order to verify the hypothesis on core patterns of lexical use as applied to Polish translational texts.

Corpus-driven analyses

Descriptive statistics

Descriptive statistics describe linguistic data in quantitative terms, which is commonly accepted in corpus linguistics as basic indicators of style and lexical richness (Olohan 2004, 78-81). Hence, it provides a holistic view of the two corpora of Polish texts (PNT and PTT), whose characteristics are presented in Table 3.

Table 19.3: Descriptive statistics for PNT (native texts) and PTT (translations)

Statistics	PNT	PTT
Number of tunning words	482,728	487,760
Number of word tokens (used for a wordlist)	478,504	487,362
Number of word types	70,722	65,412
Type/token ratio (TTR) (% or *x* per 1000 tokens)	**14.77**	13.42
Standardized TTR (STTR) (in % or *x* types per 1000 tokens)	60.40	**62.24**
STTR (mean across texts)	59.74	**62.19**

STTR standard deviation (STTRstd)	**39.75**	36.04
STTRstd (mean across texts)	**38.20**	36.03
Mean word length (in characters)	5.32	**5.36**
Number of sentences	42,936	50,183
Mean sentence length (in tokens)	**11.14**	9.71
Mean sentence length standard deviation (in tokens)	**23.37**	7.12

Table 3 shows that the two corpora are not of the same size, which is due to the fact that they contain full-texts of novels instead of their samples. Thus, the fact that PTT contains almost 10,000 more word tokens than PNT has to be taken into consideration while comparing lexical richness or lexical density with the use of either the TTR or the STTR. In general, these two indicators provide brief information as to the complexity/simplicity or specificity/generality of a particular text or corpus–lower TTR or STTR translates into narrow range of vocabulary and thus lower lexical richness in a text or corpus (Scott 2007: 157). However, the TTR is highly sensitive to differences in size of texts or corpora. As a rule, shorter texts have higher TTR value, and longer texts have lower TTR value (which is due, among others, to continuous repetition of grammatical words). As a result, although the TTR shows that non-translational texts are lexically richer, one must turn to the STTR, which is calculated on consecutive 1,000-token-long fragments of text and then averaged out, for more reliable information. Consequently, the STTR shows that translations (PTT) have, on average, 622 word types per 1,000 tokens, whereas in PNT there are only 604 word types per 1,000 tokens. The STTR calculated separately for each text in PTT and PNT and then averaged out yields similar results (622 and 597 in PTT and PNT, respectively). Summing up, this perfunctory measure of lexical richness shows that on the whole translational texts are more complex and specific lexically and have fewer lexical repetitions as compared with PNT. On the other hand, higher values of STTR standard deviation in the PNT show that some text fragments in non-translational texts are lexically richer than the ones in the PTT.

As regards the mean sentence length, there are differences between the PNT and PTT (11.14 and 9.71, respectively. This discrepancy enables one to formulate a number of hypotheses. Firstly, longer sentences in the native texts can show that their style is more explicit and precise as compared with concise and terse sentences in the PTT. Secondly, longer sentences may indicate that they are more lexically varied and that there is higher information load therein. Moreover, the mean sentence length standard deviation shows that the PNT has less uniform distribution of sentences. On the one hand, the mean sentence length is 11.14, but on the other hand, the high standard deviation of 23.37 signals that among these sentences one may identify very long ones. Overall, one may hypothesize that the style of the translations is more uniform in terms of length of sentences, while the style of typical literary texts (non-translational) is more varied, i.e. one is bound to find there both conspicuously short and long sentences.

To sum up the analysis and interpretation of descriptive statistics, one may hypothesize that the translational texts are, on average, lexically richer than non-translational texts, which is surprising with the view of the hypothesis of lexical simplification in translation. On the other hand, longer sentences in non-translational texts and their less uniform distribution there may show that they are more explicit and precise than the ones found in the translations. On the other hand, it may also mean that there is a tendency to use simple and concise sentences in the translations, which is in line with the hypothesis of syntactic simplification in translation. Nevertheless, it seems that further and more detailed qualitative research is essential to bring to life concrete illustrations of the above differences.

Word length

Although the data on the mean word (i.e. 5.32 and 5.36 for PNT and PTT, respectively) provide no conclusive evidence of conspicuous differences between translational and non-translational texts, the issue of distribution of words of different lengths (henceforth 'n-letter words') has not been addressed yet. According to Kenny (2001: 127-134), creative and author-specific vocabulary is usually found among longer, multi-letter words rather than shorter ones, where usually grammatical (function) words prevail (i.e. they are repeated more often in a text). As the study conducted by Kenny (2001) was focused on German to English translations of contemporary literary texts, the claim on the length of creative vocabulary is relevant to these two languages. Nevertheless, since translation universals or universal tendencies in translation account for a rationale behind the present study, the said hypothesis can be extended to cover also Polish language material. As a result, comparison of word length may also constitute provisional means to study lexical richness in texts (provided that the observed differences are statistically significant)–more longer words will thus mean higher lexical richness. Thus, the following Figure 1 illustrates distribution of n-letter words (1-22 letters long) in the PNT and PTT.

In order to find whether different frequencies of n-letter words in PLLS and PLRC are only random or whether they are statistically significant (i.e. they are caused by some other factor than chance), Dunning's (1993) log-likelihood test at the probability value $p = 0.05$[1] was used. To that end, the modified LL calculator

1 The value of $p = 0.05$ suggests 5% danger of being wrong (1 chance in 20). As a 2x2 contingency table will be used to compare the frequencies of n-letter words in PNT and PTT, a degree of freedom (d.f.) equals 1, which means that according to chi-square distribution table (which is the same for log-likelihood test) one can reject the null hypothesis whereby there is no statistically significant difference between observed frequencies in PNT and PTT only if the critical value of log likelihood exceeds 3.84.

(after Rayson[2]) generated the LL scores for PNT and PTT, which are presented in Table 4 below.

Table 19.4: LL scores calculated for frequencies of n-letter words in PNT and PTT (p = 0.05, d.f. = 1, critical value = 3.84)

	Observed frequencies		**Expected frequencies**			
n-letter words	**PNT**	**PTT**	**PNT**	**PTT**	**LL score**	**Overused in**
1-letter words	41,462	40,863	40,785	41,540	**22.27**	PNT
2-letter words	49,581	50,985	49,821	50,744	2.31	
3-letter words	65,078	59,479	61,707	62,849	**364.94**	PNT
4-letter words	47,347	48,032	47,252	48,126	0.38	
5-letter words	62,882	66,840	64,266	65,455	**59.09**	**PTT**
6-letter words	55,651	58,126	56,366	57,410	**18.02**	**PTT**
7-letter words	45,251	48,469	46,430	47,289	**59.37**	**PTT**
8-letter words	37,924	41,127	39,163	39,887	**77.71**	**PTT**
9-letter words	28,023	29,082	28,290	28,814	**5.02**	**PTT**
10-letter words	19,712	20,699	20,020	20,390	**9.40**	**PTT**
11-letter words	12,433	11,404	11,809	12,027	**65.31**	PNT
12-letter words	6,822	6,639	6,668	6,792	**6.98**	PNT
13-letter words	3,287	2,985	3,107	3,164	**20.61**	PNT
14-letter words	1,562	1,380	1,457	1,484	**14.85**	PNT
15-letter words	832	666	742	755	**21.60**	PNT
16-letter words	354	308	327	334	**4.10**	PNT
17-letter words	174	133	152	154	**6.27**	PNT
18-letter words	72	90	80	81	1.69	
19-letter words	40	19	29	29	**8.03**	PNT
20-letter words	4	15	9	9	**6.58**	**PTT**
21-letter words	4	9	6	6	1.88	
22-letter words	3	4	3	3	0.13	
TOTAL						

2 The log-likelihood calculator developed by Dr Paul Rayson (UCREL University Centre for Computer Corpus Research on Language, Lancaster University, UK) is available at: http://lingo.lancs.ac.uk/llwizard.html. The said calculator was adapted for the purposes of this research in order to calculate a large number of results.

The results presented in Table 4 reveal that 1-letter-long, 3-letter-long as well as 11-17-letter-long and 19-letter-long words are significantly more common in non-translational texts, whereas shorter 5-10-letter words prevail in the translations. Since according to Kenny (2001: 127-134), creative vocabulary is usually found among longer words, one is made to conclude that the native texts are lexically richer than non-translated texts attested in PTT. Therefore, the T-universal related to lexical simplification typical of translated texts is validated in this study.

Frequency profiles

In order to determine whether translational texts (PTT) or non-translational Polish texts (PNT) have more repetitions and lower lexical variety among top-frequency words, a frequency profile proposed by Baroni (2009: 805-806) was used. As a rule, the frequency profile is obtained by a replacement of words in a frequency list (which was completed with the use of WordSmith Tools 4.0) with their frequency-based ranks, by assigning rank 1 to the most frequent word, rank 2 to the second frequent word, rank 3 to the third frequent word etc. It enables one to determine which frequency-based ranks (r) of words (tokens) have a particular frequency (f). However, a typical frequency profile was modified in that frequency information was substituted with information on cumulative percentage of the total word count (%cW) corresponding to frequency-based ranks. The results are presented in Table 5 below.

Table 19.5: Frequency profiles for top-frequency word types in PNT and PTT

Non-translational texts (PNT)		Translational texts (PTT)	
Rank	%cW	Rank	%cW
1	3.17	1	3.11
10	17.80	10	18.03
50	29.28	50	29.02
100	**35.16**	**100**	**34.68**
518	**50.01**	**546**	**50.01**

The data show that translational texts (PTT) feature no significantly different distribution of top-frequency words. As a rule, the higher the share of top-frequency words in the total word count (%cW), the less lexically varied and more repetitious a text or corpus. As a result, Table 5 shows that translational texts have fewer repetitions and higher lexical variety among top-frequency words (the words ranked 1-546 account for 50% of the total word count in PTT, while in the case of PNT there are only 518 words that reach this threshold).

In order to verify whether these differences are statistically significant or random in the case of words ranked 1-100, Dunning's (1993) log-likelihood test at the probability value p = 0.05 was used. As a matter of fact, the word types ranked

1-100 encompass 168,535 word tokens in PNT and 169,185 word tokens in PTT. The comparison of the two values conducted with the use of the said test yielded the LL-score of 17.73, which means that the differences between PNT and PTT are statistically significant[3]. Thus, one of the core patterns of lexical use in translational texts put forward by Laviosa (1998) that translations have a relatively higher proportion of high-frequency words over low-frequency words than native texts–a T-universal–was invalidated in the case of translational Polish literary texts.

Frequency spectra

According to Baroni (2009: 806), frequency spectra enable one to determine how many word types (w) in a frequency list have a particular frequency [w (f)]. As creative or author-specific vocabulary usually occurs in a text with low frequencies, frequency spectra can be used to study lexical variety and number of repetitions among bottom-frequency words. As a rule, a text is more varied lexically if proportion of bottom-frequency words in the total word count (%W) is higher. For the purposes of this study, the number of word types (w) corresponding to particular frequency (f) in the frequency spectra was substituted with information on the cumulative percentage of the total word count (%cW) corresponding to word types with frequencies 1-25. The results are presented in Table 6.

Table 19.6: Frequency spectra for PNT and PTT

PNT		**PTT**	
w (f)	%cW	w (f)	%cW
1-25	37.20%	1-25	36.29%

The data show that non-translational texts have higher lexical variety among bottom-frequency words, which account for 37.20% of the total word count. More specifically, there are 178,008 word tokens with frequencies 1-25 in PNT and 176,883 in PTT. In order to verify whether these differences are statistically significant or random, Dunning's (1993) log-likelihood test at the probability value $p = 0.05$ was used. The comparison of the numbers of words with frequencies 1-25 with the use of the said test yielded the LL-score of 54.05, which means that the difference between PNT and PTT is statistically significant. Overall, it means that

3 As a 2x2 contingency table was used to compare the frequencies of words ranked 1-100 in PNT and PTT, a degree of freedom (d.f.) equals 1, which means that according to chi-square distribution table (which is the same for the log-likelihood test) one can reject the null hypothesis whereby there is no statistically significant difference between observed frequencies in PNT and PTT only if the critical value of the log likelihood exceeds 3.84 (at $p = 0.05$).

Polish literary translations have lower lexical variety among bottom-frequency words than native texts. Such a T-universal can also mean that translators tend to use more conventional target language expressions while rendering creative vocabulary attested in the original novels. Nevertheless, further qualitative studies are required to validate this hypothesis.

Conclusions and future work

The results of this corpus-driven study reveal a number of similarities and differences between selected Polish translational and non-translational (native) literary texts. Firstly, descriptive statistics revealed that translated texts are, on average, more varied lexically and that shorter (and thus more concise and terse) sentences in the translations have more uniform distribution. Secondly, frequency profiles showed that non-translational texts have more repetitions and lower lexical variety among top-frequency words (1-100), which enables one to dismiss this characteristics as a potential T-universal. Thirdly, frequency spectra revealed that translations have lower lexical variety among bottom-frequency words (i.e. words with frequencies 1-25) than non-translated texts, which may be construed as a T-universal. Nevertheless, it seems that further qualitative research should be conducted to bring to life concrete illustrations of both typical and anomalous cases glossed over in this study.

All in all, the studies on translation universals account for unexplored research area, particularly in the case of Polish language material. Thus, more quantitative and qualitative studies (in line with the ones completed by Scarpa 2006; Corpas Pastor et al. 2008; Xiao 2009), including examination of other T- and S-universals (i.e. explicitation, simplification, normalization, sanitization and leveling out), should be pursued in the future. To that end, a compilation of a larger corpus of translational Polish–including texts representing different genres and produced by different translators–should be the step in the right direction.

References

Baker, M. (1993). "Corpus Linguistics and Translation Studies: Implications and Applications." In Text and Technology. In Honor of John Sinclair, Baker, M., Francis, G. and Tognini-Bonelli, E. (eds.), 233-250. Amsterdam: John Benjamins.

Baker, M. (1995). "Corpora in Translation Studies: An Overview and Some Suggestions for Future Research," Target 7(2): 223-243.

Baker, M. (1996). "Corpus-based Translation Studies: The Challenges that Lie Ahead." In Terminology, LSP and Translation: Studies in Language Engineering in Honour of Juan C. Sager, Somers, H. (ed.), 175-186. Amsterdam/Philadelphia: John Benjamins.

Baroni, M. (2009). "Distributions in Text." In Corpus linguistics: An international handbook Volume 2, Lüdeling, A. and Kytö, M. (eds.), 803-821. Berlin and New York: Walter de Gruyter.

Available at: http://clic.cimec.unitn.it/marco/publications/hsk_39_dist_rev2.pdf.
Chesterman, A. (2004). "Beyond the particular." In Translation Universals: Do They Exist?, Mauranen, A. and Kujamaki, P. (eds.), 33-49. Amsterdam: John Benjamins.
Corpas Pastor, G., Mitkov, R., Afzal, N., Garcia Moya, L. and V. Pekar (2008). "Translation universals: do they exist? A corpus-based NLP study of convergence and simplification." In Proceedings of the Eighth Conference of the Association for Machine Translation in the Americas (AMTA-08). Available at: http://www.mt-archive.info/AMTA-2008-Corpas.pdf
Dunning, T. (1993). "Accurate Methods for the Statistics of Surprise and Coincidence," Computational Linguistics 19(1): 61-74.
Hoover, D. (2004). "Testing Burrows's Delta," Literary and Linguistic Computing 19(4): 453-475. Oxford: Oxford University Press.
Kenny, D. (2001). Lexis and Creativity in Translation. London: Routledge.
Laviosa-Braithwaite, S. (1995). "Comparable Corpora: Towards a Corpus Linguistic Methodology for the Empirical Study of Translation." In Translation and Meaning Part 3, Thelen, M. and Lewandowska-Tomaszczyk, B. (eds.), 153-163. Maastricht: UPM.
Laviosa, S. (1998). "Core Patterns of Lexical Use in a Comparable Corpus of English Narrative Prose," Meta 43(4): 557-570.
Laviosa, S. (2002). Corpus-based Translation Studies. Theory, Findings and Applications. Amsterdam and New York: Rodopi.
Olohan, M. (2004). Introducing Corpora in Translation Studies. London and New York: Routledge.
Scarpa, F. (2006). "Corpus-based Quality-Assessment of Specialist Translation: A Study Using Parallel and Comparable Corpora in English and Italian." In Insights Into Specialized Translation, Gotti, M. and Sarcevic,S. (eds.), 155-172. Bern: Peter Lang Verlag.
Scott, M. (2004). Wordsmith Tools Version 4. Oxford: Oxford University Press.
Scott, M. (2007). WordSmith Tools Help. Liverpool: Lexical Analysis Software.
Xiao, R. (2009). "How Different is Translated Chinese from Native Chinese? A Corpus-based Study of Translation Universals," International Journal of Corpus Linguistics 15(1): 5-35.

Analysis of the Translation of the Phraseological Units of Cien Años de Soledad into English: a Corpus-based Study

Natalia Quinteiro and Gabriel Quiroz

Abstract

Cien Años de Soledad (*One Hundred Years of Solitude*), the 1982 Nobel Prize winner, has been translated into many languages (in English by the renowned literary translator G. Rabassa). This literary work has a high sociocultural content, especially in the phraseological units, which may affect the equivalence in English. The achievement of an adequate translation of the phraseological units will keep the meaning of the text and transmit the sense to the reader in English.

In this article, a corpus-based contrastive analysis in Spanish and English is explained. First, 221 phraseological units were extracted in Spanish and its equivalents in English and then classified syntactically and according to the kind of equivalence level. Then, they were contrasted to several Colombian dictionaries in order to verify the authenticity of the phraseological units. After this, the translation procedures are identified to establish the most common procedures used by the translator. Finally, the level of adequacy is evaluated. The results of this study can be used to evaluate the translation of phraseological units using computational tools.

Keywords

Prepositional phraseological units, contrastive analysis, Spanish, English, translation, García Márquez.

Rationale

Regarding the election of the term, we will refer here to Phraseological Unit (PU), according to authors as García-Page (2008) and Corpas (1996). In short, it is very risky to choose any of the terms, due to the existing discussion among experts on this field. The main purpose of this study is not to discuss about the existing terms, as: *phraseological unit, phraseme, proverbial phrase, noun phrase, phraseoligism.* Certainly, we have adjusted to one of the classifications. However, this study is not intended to offer a new categorization, but analyzing the results of the PU English translation. We consider that only after the analysis, and not before, new conclusions can be reached.

The theoretical support will be basically based on the studies of Corpas (1996) and García-Page (2008). We will consider their taxonomy of the Phraseological Units as starting point. It is important to clarify that the classification of the PU will be based only on these studies, due to the fact that all the theorical proposals about phraseology vary deeply among them. Also, because the extent of this project requires only one organized and invariable classification to develop the analysis.

The following is an overall description of PU characteristics proposed by García-Page (2008: 23):

- Multiword: combination of two or more words
- Fixed expressions: unit that, during the course of the time, has tended to be fixed, stable, and invariable in usage.
- Idiomaticity: it refers to the obscure or untransparent meaning of a certain unit, which normally needs connotation.
- Institutionality: recognize and well-known among native speakers
- No sentence structure: there is no structure of a sentence syntactically complete.
- Frequency: constant use in the oral and writing communication of the unit.
- Irregularities: presence of any lexical, syntactic, or semantic anomaly.

As we said before, these characeristics correspond to a global clasification, in which the different discussions and disagreements from the different classifications and authors are omitted. Furthermore, we would like to clarify that, it is due to their general nature that not all PU correspond perfectly to all of the characteristics mentioned before (García-Page 2008: 23).

The author divides the phraseological units into four spheres: *collocations, locutions, phraseological statements (paremies), phraseological statements (routine formulas).* From all of them, this analysis will focus only on the second sphere*, i.e. locutions.*

Among the different types of locutions, their taxonomy includes nominal, adjectival, adverbial, verbal, prepositive, conjunctive, and clause. From all those cathegories, the purpose of this analysis is to study only the adverbial locutions, which grammatical pattern starts by a Preposition.

Methodology

Corpus and selection criteria

The corpus selected was *Cien Años de Soledad* by Noble Prize García Marquez with a total of 137.857 tokens. The English translation by Gregory Rabassa, *One Hundred Years of Solitude*, was 144.925 tokens.

322 phraseological units (PU) were extracted and 121 prepositional phraseological units (PPU) were extracted and validated. An automatic extraction was made by means of some Perl scripts in order to be sure there were no PPU missing from the analysis corpus.

The checking of the PU consisted in revising, once again, that they were phraseological units, using the following dictionaries: *Diccionario de uso del español de América y España* (2003) by Vox, *Diccionario de la lengua española* (2011) by the Spanish Royal Academy, and *Lexicón de fraseología del Español de*

Colombia (1996) by Mora. To do this, the classification criteria proposed by the support author for this study, as García-Page (2008) and Corpas (1996), were strictly considered. In the checking process, some particular cases were eliminated, as they corresponded to the patterns as well as to the criteria, but their context did not support them as PU. For instance, the PU *por la fuerza*. It follows all the criteria (i.e. idiomaticity, fixation, etc.) and it appears several times in the corpus in different contexts. However, in some of the contexts it does not have the function of PU but of a simple phrase within the sentence: "*...había encontrado la paz en aquella casa donde los recuerdos se materializaron **por la fuerza** de la evocación implacable...*" Here, its function is to link, but it does not have an own meaning within the sentence. Some other cases included some PU, which may present a variant in their structure, but in spite of this, they were indisputably PU. This is the case of the PU ***a pleno día,*** which corresponds to the pattern Prep + N + N. It appeared several times with variants in the last N, e.g. *a pleno sol, a plena salle,* etc. In this regard, it was determined that the variation in the last component corresponden either to the PU flexibility, or to its real structure was actually Prep + N. If this was the case, then, this PU will always be followed by an N, but this last N not being included as part of the PU. The other possibility is that each one of them is an independent PU, with a 70% of equivalence in their components, i. e. they all have as root the Prep and N *a pleno*, but the last N can vary (it may be *sol, calle, día*).

Search of the English translation

As the method used was not very precise, searching for the corresponding context fragment in English equivalent to the Spanish PU represented the most exhaustive step. To find the corresponding translation for each PU, we first read the PU Spanish context, then we translated key words or complete phrases, or sentences. We did all these with the option "Search" of the SCP concordance program.

Equivalence criteria definition

At this part of the analysis, we proceeded to study the categorization established by Mira (2011: 112-113) in his study about the translation into English of the PU existing in the Colombian novel *Rosario Tijeras*. Mira (2011) establishes 9 categories: total correspondence, correspondence in content but not in components, partial correspondence, regarding form and content, partial correspondence, regardind pragmatic-semantic value, calque, translation by paraphrase, translation by omission, case of wrong interpretation or PU not identified, and translation by a simple lexical unit. At first, we tried to follow the above categories, but we found they result ambiguos in most cases, due to the purpose of this study. Thus, we established new criteria, based on Mira categorization and in the object of study. Finally, the following classification was established: Phraseological Unit (PU), Equivalent but not PU, Paraphrase, Calque, Omission, and Error.

Results

Hereafter, we will describe the results obtained for the 121 PPU, according to the most frequent patterns in Spanish, English, and the classification for the English solutions. For each case, the most representative patterns and some examples are provided.

Most common patterns in Spanish

There are 21 different types of patterns, as shown in Table 1.

Table 20.1: Most common patterns in Spanish.

PU pattern	Frequency	Percentage
Prep N	40	32.52%
Prep Adj N	19	15.45%
Prep Det N	11	8.94%
Prep Det N Prep Det N	9	7.32%
Prep Det N Conj Prep Det N	8	6.50%
Prep N Adj	8	6.50%
Prep Det N Prep N	5	4.07%
Prep N Prep N	5	4.07%

As it can be observed in the former table, the most frequent PU pattern is Prep+N with 40 cases (32.52%), as shown in example 1.

1. a cañonazos, a culatazos, a tientas, al garete, de bruces, de pacotilla, en andas, en vela.

In the second place, it appears the pattern Prep+Adj+N, with 19 cases (15.45%), as shown in example 2.

2. a duras penas, a pleno día, de mala vida, de mala gana, de mala fe, de mal humor, a puros golpes.

The third most frequent pattern is Prep+Det+N, with 11 cases (8.94%), example 3.

3. a la deriva, a las volandas, hasta los huesos, por la fuerza, de un golpe.

The fourth most frequent pattern is Prep+Det+N+Prep+Det+N with 9 cases (7.32%), example 4.

4. al pie de la letra, con un nudo en la garganta, de la noche a la mañana, por los siglos de los siglos.

In the fifth place, there are two patterns, both with 8 cases, corresponding to the 6.5%. These patterns are (a) Prep+ Det+ N+ Conj+ Prep+ Det+ N, shown in example 5.

5. al derecho y al revés, al fin y al cabo.

And (b) Prep+N+Adj, shown in example 6.

6. a ciencia cierta, a fuego lento, en carne viva, en fila india.

In the last place, there are also two patterns, both with 5 cases, corresponding to the 4.07%. These patterns are (a) Prep Det N Prep N, shown in example 7:

7. a la buena de dios, al fin de cuentas, de una vez por todas.

And (b) Prep N Prep N, shown in example 8:

8. de mano en mano, sin cruces a cuestas, sin fórmula de juicio.

Most common patterns in English

There are 55 types of different patterns. Here are shown only those with more than 2 cases, shown in Table 2.

Table 20.2: Most common patterns in English.

PU pattern	Frequency	Percentage
Adv	23	18.70%
Prep Adj N	9	7.32%
Prep Det N	7	5.69%
No pattern	7	5.69%
Prep Det	6	4.88%
Prep N	6	4.88%
Adj N	4	3.25%

According to the former table, the pattern with more frequency in the English translation is Adv, with 23 cases, which represents the 18.70%. Example 9 shows some of these cases.

9. Exactly, secretly, slowly, adrift, overnight, grudgingly, endlessly, deeply.

The second most frequent pattern in English is Prep+Adj+N, with 9 cases, representing the 7.32%. Some of these cases are shown in example 10.

10. With great effort, in broad daylight, in good humor, with great joy.

In the third place, there are two patterns. Both of them with 7 cases, each one of them represents the 5.69%. The first of these patterns is Prep+Det+N, example 11.

11. In the tide, in one gulp, in a burst, on their knees.

The second pattern is omission, i. e. the PU was not translated as in example 12.

12. A fuego vivo, al fin y al cabo, en plena calle, sin tregua.

In the fourth place, there are also two patterns, each one with 6 cases. They represent the 4.88%. The first of these patterns is Prep+Det, shown in example 13.

13. After all.

The second of these patterns is Prep+N, shown in example 14.

14. With cannons, by feel, at will, with joy, by ear.

The fifth and most frequent pattern is Adj+N, with 4 cases, representing the 3.25% in example 15.

15. Slow fire, bad people, evil mother, bad women.

Classification of English solutions

There are 7 types of different solutions in English. They can be observed in Table 3.

Table 20.3: Classification of English solutions.

Type of ENG solution	Frequency	Percentage
Phraseological Unit (PU)	39	31.71%
Equivalent but not PU	36	29.27%
Paraphrase	32	26.02%
Calque	7	5.69%
Omission	6	4.88%
Error	3	2.44%

This table shows clearly that the most frequent ENG solution was PU, with 39 cases and representing 31.71%. Example 16 shows one of these cases.

16. **SPA**
    [...] la única que podía determinar ***a ojos cerrados*** cuándo se servía el vino blanco, y de qué lado y en qué copa [...]
    ENG
    [...] the only one who could tell ***with her eyes closed*** when the white wine was served and on what side and in which glass [...]

The second most frequent solution is Equivalent but not PU, with 36 cases, and corresponding to the 29.27%. Example 17 shows one of these cases.

17. **SPA**
    Finalmente convencida, aunque ***a regañadientes***, dio el consentimiento para la coronación.
    ENG
    Finally convinced, even though ***reluctantly*,** she consented to the coronation.

Paraphrase is the third most frequent solution, with 32 cases, and corresponding to the 26.02%. An example of this solution can be seen in example 18.

18. **SPA**
    De emprendedor y limpio, José Arcadio Buendía se convirtió en un hombre de aspecto holgazán, descuidado en el vestir, con una barba salvaje que Úrsula lograba cuadrar ***a duras penas*** con un cuchillo de cocina.

ENG
From a clean and active man, José Arcadio Buendía changed into a man lazy in appearance, careless in his dress, with a wild beard that Úrsula managed to trim ***with great effort*** and a kitchen knife.

Calque is the fourth most frequent solution, representing the 5.69%. Example 19 illustrates this type of solution.

19. **SPA**
Por la época en que se le ocurrió la lotería de adivinanzas, Aureliano Segundo despertaba ***con un nudo en la garganta***, como si estuviera reprimiendo las ganas de llorar.
ENG
Around the time of the riddle lottery, Aureliano Segundo began waking up ***with a knot in his throat***[1], as ifhe were repressing a desire to weep.
(with a knot in his stomach)

Omission was the sixth most frequent solution, with 6 cases, and corresponding to the 4.88%. Example 20 shows one of these cases, where the PU was just omitted, and its sense and meaning is totally absent in the English version.

20. **SPA**
Puso a hervir todo ***a fuego vivo*** en un caldero de aceite de ricino hasta obtener un jarabe espeso y pestilente más parecido al caramelo vulgar que al oro magnífico.
ENG
He put it all to boil in a pot of castor oil until he got a thick and pestilential syrup which was more like common caramel than valuable gold.

Error was the less frequent solution in the English translation, with 3 cases (2.44%). Example 21 shows one of these cases, where the sense of the Spanish translation was misunderstood in English.

21. **SPA**
A pesar de que el coronel Aureliano Buendía seguía creyendo y repitiendo que Remedios, la bella, era en realidad el ser más lúcido que había conocido jamás, y que lo demostraba a cada momento con su asombrosa habilidad para burlarse de todos, la abandonaron ***a la buena de Dios*.**

1 The solution should be with a knot in his stomach.

ENG

In spite of the fact that Colonel Aureliano Buendía kept on believing and repeating that Remedios the Beauty was in reality the most lucid being that he had ever known and that she showed it at every moment with her startling ability to put things over on everyone, they let her go ***her own way***.

Conclusions

Though the majority of the solutions were a PU, this majority does not even represent the half of the total of PPU and may affect readers' understanding of the literary work not only in the authors's intention but also on the the readers' effect. Omission and error cases represent a minimun percentage, which means that in general terms, the quality of the translation is acceptable.

The most frequent solutions were PU, paraphrase, or equivalent but not PU. Sometimes, criteria are difficult to apply due to lack of linguistic resources.

References

Corpas Pastor, G. (1996). Manual de fraseología española. Madrid: Gredos.

Diccionario de uso del español de América y España. (2003). [CD-ROM]. Barcelona: Editorial Spes –Vox.

Diccionario de la lengua española. (2011). [Online]. Madrid: Real Academia de la Lengua.

García Márquez, G. ([1967] 2002). Cien Años de Soledad. Bogotá: Norma.

García Márquez, G. (1970). One Hundred Years of Solitude. English Translation by Gregory Rabassa. USA: Avon Books.

García-Page Sánchez, M. (2008). Introducción a la fraseología española. Estudio de las locuciones. Barcelona: Anthropos.

Lingüística Española Actual. (2001). Vol. 23 (1).

Mira, G. (2011). "La equivalencia en la traducción de las unidades fraseológicas. Un estudio empirico," Ikala 16: 105-131.

Mora Monroy, S. (1996). Lexicón de fraseología del Español de Colombia. Bogotá: Instituto Caro y Cuervo. Series Minor. XXXVII.

Solano Rodríguez, M. Á. (2004). Unidades fraseológicas francesas. Estudio en un corpus: la Pentalogía de. Belleville de Daniel Pennac. Planteamiento didáctico. In Biblioteca virtual de Miguel de Cervantes.
Available at: http://bvc.s3.dev.cervantesvirtual.com/pdf_parser/003caa3a-82b2-11df-acc7-002185ce6064.pdf [August 2011].

Travalia, C. (2006). "Las colocaciones implícitas," Estudios de lingüística Universidad de Alicante. 20: 317-332.

Zuluaga, A. (1980). Introducción al estudio de las expresiones fijas. Frankfurt: Peter Lang.

Zuluaga, A. (1998). "Análisis y traducción de unidades fraseológicas desautomatizadas," Lingüística y Literatura 19-20 (34-35): 203-220.

Zuluaga Gómez, F. (2005). "Locuciones, dichos y refranes sobre el lenguaje: unidades fraseológicas fijas e interacción verbal," Forma y Función 18: 250-282.

CAT Tools in the Work of Polish Translators of Specialised Texts

Monika Czarnecka

Abstract

The aim of the present paper is to examine the application of computer assisted/aided translation (CAT) tools, with particular attention given to web-based translation tools, in the work of Polish translators of specialised texts. Apart from the ordinary computer-based CAT tools, such as Trados and Wordfast, which are already widespread also in Poland, the author researches the field of web-based translation solutions, which seem to remain largely unknown by Polish translators, describes their operation, advantages and potential drawbacks. The author also presents the results of the survey in which she asked Polish translators about their familiarity with CAT tools, including web-based aids, the extent to which they use them, their attitude to and opinion about such solutions and their usefulness, etc. Based on the compiled results of the survey conclusions are presented.

Keywords

CAT tools, web-based translation tools, Polish translators, specialised texts

Introduction

The translation industry is developing rapidly nowadays: along with the growth in the volume of content to be translated the deadlines for delivering the target text are becoming shorter. This results in the creation of increasingly more computer and Internet translation aids with increasingly more functions for translators and their clients. Apart from the ordinary computer aided/assisted translation (CAT) tools, which are already widespread also in Poland, I decided to additionally research a relatively new field, namely web-based translation solutions, which seem to remain largely unknown among Polish translators. For the purpose of researching this field I prepared a survey questionnaire, which will be elaborated on in detail in a further part of the paper. Based on the results of the questionnaire, it can be concluded that the surveyed translators indicated familiarity with and use of two such web-based solutions, that is Google Translator Toolkit and Wordfast Anywhere, the description of which provided below will serve as an example of the applications operating in the so-called Software as a Service (SaaS) or the cloud-based technology.

Google Translator Toolkit and Wordfast Anywhere

Google Translator Toolkit (see Figure 1) is a free personalised tool for translators, which was developed in mid-2009. It uses the Google Translate technology consisting in machine translation (MT)[1]. An uploaded document may not be larger than 1 MB, whereas translation memories (TMs) can have the maximum size of 50 MB per upload, and it is possible to upload up to 1 GB of both TMs and glossaries a year[2]. In order to start translating, one has to first upload one's source file. There are three options: a document from one's computer, a website, or an article from Wikipedia. First, the source and target languages of the text need to be provided. The next step is choosing the appropriate TM. If the translator does not have their own memory[3], they need to use the global Google memory, which replaces the segments in the file with the corresponding highest ranked segments found in the Google TM, and if no such segments are identified in the Google resources, MT is performed. If the translator has their own memory or wants to use the memory shared with them by their colleagues, Language Service Provider (LSP), or employer/client, the global memory will be adopted to translate only those segments of their text which are not found in their own or the shared memories. Generally, the aim of any TM is to store the translated segments and possibly use a ready piece of translation if the program recognises a segment which is similar to or identical with one available in the memory[4]. Using one's own private memory seems to be safer than the global memory in terms of security of the data entered while translating. The final product is a roughly translated target text divided into segments. The translator is then able to check the suggested translation of each segment and correct mistakes, if any. After finishing work, the translation can be shared as a Google Document or saved on one's computer. Of course the Toolkit provides multiple options and tools, such as merging or dividing segments, as usual in such translation tools[5].

The other web-based free translation tool known to a number of Polish translators is Wordfast Anywhere (see Figure 2), which is an even more recent development than Google Translator Toolkit: it was created in mid-2010. The

1 The history of the development of machine translation systems and the description of their operation, as well as their evaluation and forecasts for the future development of MT are to be found in Ł. Bogucki (2009).

2 The data obtained from the following website (accessed on 11 June 2011): http://translate.google.com/support/toolkit/bin/answer.py?answer=147829

3 There are certain web-based translation tools, such as Logoport or Lingotek, which do not provide their users with the possibility to add matches from their own TMs (Garcia 2007: 62-64).

4 A detailed description of how translation memories are created and employed is provided for instance by Ł. Bogucki (2009: 53-55).

5 A detailed description of the operation of CAT tools is to be found among others in Ł. Bogucki (2009: 52-66) or M. Eckstein and R. Sosnowski (2004: 62-73).

maximum number of 10 documents may be stored in the user's workspace at a given time, with a single upload size of 2 MB at the largest. The limitation of TMs on one's account is 1,000,000 Translation Units (TUs). The documents which have not been accessed for a longer period than 3 months and the accounts not accessed for more than 6 months are deleted the following month upon two notices[6]. In order to use Wordfast Anywhere, the translator has to first create an account and a TM for their purposes. It is also possible to use a memory shared by their partner or client. The first major difference from Google Translator Toolkit is that it is not possible to share one's TM with the general Internet public; it may be shared only with particular users of Wordfast Anywhere. It is also possible to connect to the Very Large Translation Memory (VLTM) from donated public TMs. Naturally, the source and target languages have to be provided and the decision whether to share one's memory with other users needs to be taken. The next step is uploading the file which is supposed to be translated. Then it may be chosen to perform MT based on the Google Translate technology, but this option can be disabled. The translation process is identical to that employed in the ordinary computer-based Wordfast Classic[7]: the translator may shrink and expand segments, search in glossaries, and find concordances of given words or phrases. The newly translated segments are stored in their TM, which may be shared with others. After finishing work the translator can download the translated file.

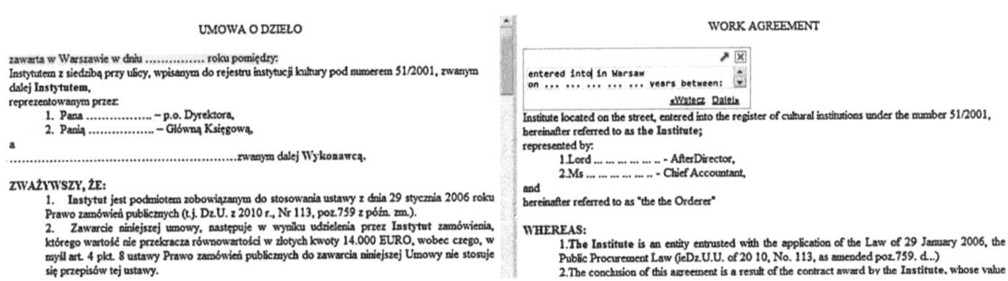

Figure 21.1: Google Translator Toolkit – screenshot

6 The data obtained from the following website (accessed on 11 June 2011): http://www.wordfast.net/anywhere/terms.html

7 Wordfast Anywhere is an online counterpart of Wordfast Classic in terms of available functions, while both of them have certain functional limitations in comparison to Wordfast Pro.

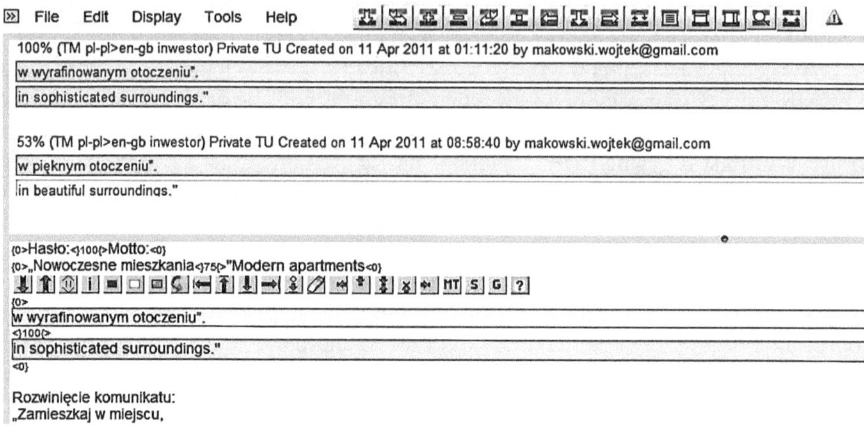

Figure 21.2: Wordfast Anywhere – screenshot

Web-based translation tools offer obvious advantages to the user in comparison to standard computer-based tools. First of all, there is no need to have any memory-intensive software installed on the computer – everything necessary is online. Secondly, the translator has the opportunity to do their job literally "anywhere" – on any computer and in any place since memories are always available: users do not have to remember to send TMs or take them to any workplace; they only need to have access to the Internet. Furthermore, sharing TMs is far easier online than with use of standard means of communication, particularly when translators cooperate with others on the same translation job, as it is possible to exchange TMs on real-time basis. Additionally, the option of MT can be useful, especially for small, standardised and popular chunks. As argued by R. Fiederer and S. O'Brien (2009: 52-69), a machine-translated and then post-edited target text may be clearer and more accurate, although of worse style, than one translated in a traditional manner. The type of online translation described above can perform a significant portion of work for the translator, obviously depending on the text type. The only task of the translator is to correct the provided rough translation.

This of course gives rise to such dilemmas as, for instance, whether the provided translation is accurate in terms of terminology or whether the translator should check any unfamiliar words; whether the time spent on correcting is considerably shorter than the time that would be spent translating the text; and probably the most crucial one: whether the information entered to global memories is safe. Sharing one's segments and memories constitutes the basis of cooperation of translators worldwide and provides access to the vast resources for free. This, however, may give rise to certain problems. Firstly, texts often contain confidential and sensitive (and hence vulnerable to abuse) information, which definitely should not be disclosed to anyone. Certain translators voice their suspicions on Internet forums that Google could use the data collected from anything that is uploaded to Google Translator Toolkit for unauthorised purposes. Although some point to the availability of the option to restrict the content of the translated texts, others are anxious about its being limited to other users only, and not Google, which may have access to it and make any use of it they like. Secondly, there is a threat or suspicion that Google could use the memories created for free by translators worldwide in order to later provide translation services for companies for a charge, or possibly for other commercial purposes. I. Garcia (2009: 203) points to four other drawbacks of employing web-based solutions:

> Firstly, it imposes the tool they must use: whereas the pre-translation mode allowed a translator to work using, say, a Trados-compatible tool rather than Trados itself, with web-based technology this is no longer feasible. Secondly, on anecdotal evidence it slows the respective response times for opening each segment, searching the data base(s) and returning results, and closing (uploading) completed segments (tool developers might dispute this point, but comments from translators suggest otherwise). Thirdly, it makes it difficult for translators to build up their own linguistic assets, although in some cases with extra effort they might perhaps circumvent this. Lastly, it clearly gives LSPs access to performance-related information that most self-employed professionals would like to keep confidential: hours spent, translation speed, work patterns.

The problems enumerated by Garcia refer to the situation where a particular translation is performed as a teamwork and the latter two are probably true about tools such as Logoport, which may be used only on the translation projects of Lionbridge (a TM vendor), and not about solutions such as the two described above. Despite the mentioned potential disadvantages, it can be concluded that in terms of easy use and availability web-based tools provide better solutions than those offered by standard computer-based tools.

Methodology of the research

Since programs such as Google Translator Toolkit and Wordfast Anywhere are relatively new on the market, I prepared a survey whose aim was, among others, to check whether CAT tools, including both the ordinary and web-based translation solutions, are recognisable and adopted by specialised translators in Poland. In order to gather the necessary data I prepared a survey questionnaire in which translators were able to specify the degree of their familiarity with particular CAT solutions and provide their comments on the ones which they employed in the past or were using at that time. I limited my interest to the group of specialised translators, since my assumption was that they deal with similar repeatable texts more often than those who translate non-specialised texts, and thus are most likely to find CAT tools helpful. The questionnaire was prepared in the Polish language as I was interested in Polish translators in general, regardless of the languages with which they work. Unsurprisingly, the vast majority of the respondents were the translators in the Polish-English language pair (76.6%), followed by those in the Polish-German language pair (27.4%), Polish-French (14.5%), Polish-Russian (7.3%), and there were single instances of translators who work with less popular languages. As many as 41.9% of the respondents translate from and into more than one foreign language. The survey questionnaire was conducted in January and February 2011. I created and published it on the Internet for the participants' convenience. I posted the link to the questionnaire in forums of several specialised Internet portals for translators, such as ProZ and GlobTra, as well as Goldenline, a portal for various professionals. I also sent the link to the survey to numerous LSPs asking them to disseminate it further among the translators with whom they cooperate. The total number of the persons who participated in the research amounted to 128, yet 4 of them proved to be non-specialised translators, and therefore had to be excluded from the analysis. The results of the research are obviously only fragmentary, as given no record of professional translators in Poland it is impossible to determine what percentage of them the final 124 respondents constitute, but they are hopefully representative enough to provide an outline of the situation of the use of CAT tools on the Polish translation market.

The number and profile of the Polish translators of specialised texts who use CAT tools

The fundamental issue to be established in the course of the research was the number of those Polish translators who employ CAT tools in their work. It turned out that nearly 81% of the respondents were adopting at least one CAT tool at that time. 8.9% of the total number of the respondents, being 11% of the CAT tools users, declared having completed training in the operation of CAT tools. Merely 1 person (0.8%) admitted not being familiar with any CAT tools even by the name. I had assumed that the translators with many years of professional experience might find it more difficult to change their working habits or that they are generally more reluctant to technological innovations and, on the other hand, that the beginners in the profession may find CAT aids too costly for them to purchase and therefore I expected them either to adopt free CAT tools[8] or not to adopt any. This assumption led me to investigate into the issue of the respondents' work experience in years and its correlation with the data on the application of CAT tools by the participants of the research. My guess proved to be only partially correct: it may be stated that a half of the translators with 25 and more years of professional

8 R. Sosnowski (2008: 199-212) provides a review of free CAT tools and compares them to commercial ones in terms of available functions and performance. His analysis proves that the former are nearly as successful as the latter and he forecasts their further improvement.

experience do not use CAT tools (being at the same time 25% of all those who reject CAT tools in their work), but the remaining translators are representatives of all possible lengths of professional career in similar proportions, with those having up to 5 years of work experience amounting to 12.5% of the total number of persons who do not employ CAT tools, and merely 6.4% of those falling into the category of the translators with up to 5 years of professional experience. For the sake of comparison, the research conducted among UK freelance translators[9] in 2004 showed that merely 28% of the respondents used CAT tools in their work at that time, and nearly half of the examined translators were completely unfamiliar with such solutions (Fulford and Granell-Zafra 2005: 10). This discrepancy in figures proves how fast the changes in the translator's workstation proceed.

Which CAT tools are popular among Polish translators of specialised texts

The next step was to determine with which CAT tools the translators are familiar. I enumerated 36 names of CAT tools in the survey and provided a possibility to add others to the list[10]. No one mentioned any additional CAT tools. The respondents were supposed to specify their familiarity with the listed tools by marking each of them either as one they were currently using, or one they had used in the past and no longer used, or one known from its name only, or one completely unknown to them. The list consisted of both ordinary CAT tools, which store TMs on one's computer, and web-based solutions, which enable storing TMs on external Internet servers. The respondents were currently employing 21 of all CAT tools provided in the survey (see Figure 3)[11].

9 My research did not intend to focus on freelance translators only, but it nonetheless turned out that as many as 86.3% of the respondents were freelancers, and 4% of them were freelance and in-house translators at the same time, whereas only 9.7% of the respondents were solely in-house translators. Therefore, I find the quoted research relevant for such a comparison.

10 My list of CAT tools was compiled based on the selection thereof provided by ProZ and supplemented with the names of CAT solutions mentioned by translators on various Internet forums for translators. It needs to be noted that Translation Workspace was developed in 2010 based on Logoport, its predecessor, which was launched in 2004. Both of these CAT tools were listed separately in my questionnaire.

11 The CAT tools included in the questionnaire yet not currently used by any respondents are as follows: Alchemy Publisher, Fusion, Heartsome, IBM CAT tool, J-CAT, Kartouche, Lingotek, LogiTerm, MEMOrg, Multicorpora, Multilizer, Pootle, Snowball, TransSuite 2000, Uniscape CAT tool.

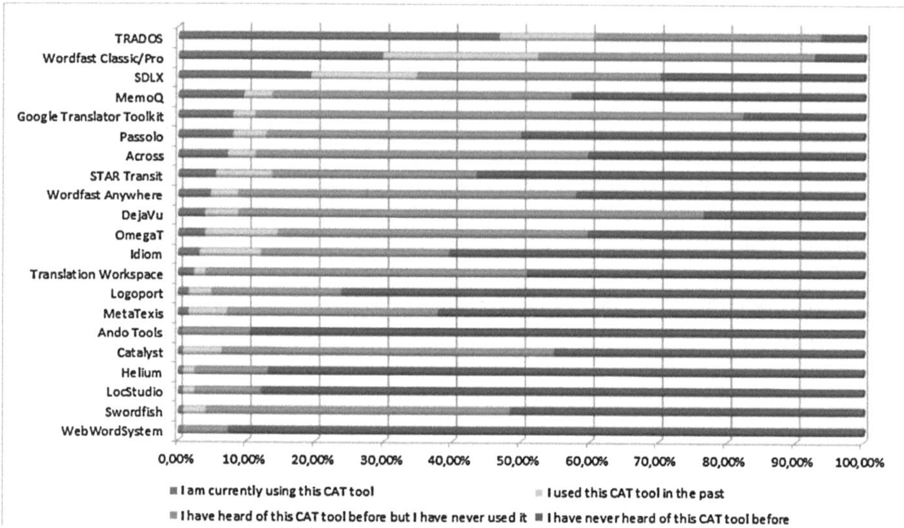

Figure 21.3: The familiarity of Polish translators of specialised texts with selected CAT tools (source: own work based on the results of the conducted survey).

The unquestionable leader among such solutions is Trados with 46.8% of the respondents currently using it and 13.7% of them having used it in the past, while only 6.5% of the translators declared not having even heard this name before. The second most popular CAT tool is Wordfast: 29.8% of the translators participating in the research are using it at present, 22.6% of them used to employ it, and merely 7.3% of the respondents do not even know its name. SDLX is the following CAT tool in terms of popularity with 19.4% of the translators using it at the moment, 15.3% of them using it in the past, and 29.8% not knowing it. From among the web-based CAT tools only two are recognisable enough among the participants of the research to deserve a comment. One is the above described Google Translator Toolkit, about which 71% of the translators had already heard, which was used in the past by 3.2% of the respondents, and which is presently employed by 8.1% of them. What is interesting, this solution is very popular among translators, giving it the 5th place in the provided list of CAT tools. The other web-based solution is the already discussed Wordfast Anywhere, which occupies the 9th place on the list, being now used by 4.8% of the examined translators, having been used by 4% of the respondents, and being familiar to 49.2% of them by its name.

Usefulness of CAT tools

The respondents were also asked to specify how often they used CAT tools and how they evaluated them in terms of usefulness. Interestingly, the results proved that the frequency of applying CAT tools and the opinion thereof do not depend on the particular solution employed. The vast majority of the translators using CAT tools adopt them to most of their translation jobs, and only several of them take advantage of CAT tools with all the translated texts or with only some of them. As many as 50% of the translators employing CAT tools in their work use more than one of them, motivating the situation with their clients' preferences, that is some clients require one CAT tool to be employed and others a different one, while some of them do not have any preferences. Therefore, many translators need to have two or more CAT tools at their disposal. When it comes to the translators' own preferences, again no clear pattern can be observed, as there seems to be an equal number of those who give priority to Trados over Wordfast, for instance, and those who declare the reverse. The reasons for using a particular CAT tool are again identical regardless of the tool mentioned.

Not all translators decided to enumerate advantages of using CAT tools but the most often repeated merit of all CAT solutions is the fact that they are time-efficient (39% of all CAT tool users): in the case of repetitive texts they save the translator's time by substituting the fragments of the original text that have been entered into the TM with their target language equivalents, which at the same time ensures terminological consistency (emphasised by 11% of those who employ CAT tools in their work), and by copying personal names or numbers to the target text. What is more, CAT tools usually suggest concordances, which is considered useful by some translators (4%). Another advantage provided by CAT solutions which the respondents emphasised is that they help preserve the original format of the translated file (6%) and spot the translator's mistakes (3%), for example spelling ones. The possibility to create one's own glossaries within certain CAT tools was also praised by the translators (3%). The translators appreciated the simplicity of using a given CAT tool (7%) and its pleasant interface (4%). Some of the mentioned advantages of CAT tools confirm what Bogucki (2009: 59-61) considers their most important qualities: they make the translator's work faster, they help preserve terminological consistency, and enable terminology database management. Also, an interesting study of CAT tools confirming their productivity was conducted by F. Vallianatou (2005) based on her personal experience and calculations.

Disadvantages of CAT tools

The examined translators seemed to perceive more advantages than disadvantages in employing CAT tools in their work, which resulted in the fact that all the problems enumerated below were mentioned by single respondents only. However, what certain translators complained about was above all the fact that there are only some file formats that a particular CAT tool supports and that many of them are not successful with handling for example Excel, Powerpoint or PDF files (4%). Another problem indicated by the respondents was the high price of certain CAT tools (2%). They observed also occasional problems with preserving the format of the original file (2%), mainly in the case of tables, and with slowing down the computer (2%). The translators pointed to instances of unexpected errors (5%), instability (2%), some file formats being incompatible and inconvertible (2%), difficult operation of some CAT tools (2%), and their limited functions (1%).

The reasons for resigning from a particular CAT tool

The survey revealed that 49.2% of the respondents used to adopt at least one CAT tool and now they employ either different solutions or no longer need to use any such tools (5.6%). Two major reasons why the translators stopped using particular CAT tools were repeatedly mentioned: one was the fact that the clients with whom the translators cooperate no longer require this particular CAT tool, or that the cooperation with those clients ended (52.5% of those who resigned from particular CAT tools), and the other was that the tools did not live up to the respondents' expectations by being prone to failures and therefore they willingly replaced them with new and better solutions (47.5% of such translators). Since the respondents were allowed to enumerate more than one reason for abandoning the application of a particular CAT tool, a problem which reoccurred in the comments of several persons was the fact that CAT tools are not compatible with each other by not supporting the same range of file formats. This is also related to the predominance of SDL Trados[12] (a bundle including Trados and SDLX), which was named by one respondent as "the only proper choice", since translators are sometimes forced by their clients to purchase this particular CAT tool and resign from other solutions. The issue of interoperability of various CAT tools is addressed, for instance, by J. Gough (2010) and Ł. Bogucki (2009: 57-58).

Conclusions

In conclusion, it may be stated that a significant number of Polish translators of specialised texts employ CAT tools in their work nowadays, and it seems that along with the increase in the number of such solutions on the market, in their functions and in the demand for them among clients, this number is likely to grow further in the future. The results of the survey prove that translators in Poland prefer the

12 A detailed description of the operation of this currently most popular CAT tool is provided by A. Mańkowska (2008: 147-159).

standard CAT tools, but it cannot be stated that they are unfamiliar with the web-based tools. The fact that the latter are a novelty on the market seems to be a sufficient explanation for the lower popularity of such solutions in comparison with the traditional CAT tools. It may be also speculated that the preference of the ordinary CAT tools is a result of the translators' habit or distrust for online solutions as such. When more translators decide to give the new web-based tools a chance, more conclusive evaluation of their usefulness will be possible. For the time being, the number of the translators who agreed to participate in the research and, more importantly, the number of the translators who declared familiarity with web-based tools, appears to be too scarce to allow decisive judgements.

References

Bogucki, Ł. (2009). Tłumaczenie wspomagane komputerowo, "Przekład – mity i rzeczywistość". Wydawnictwo Naukowe PWN, Warszawa.

Eckstein, M. and R. Sosnowski (2004). Komputer w pracy tłumacza. Praktyczny poradnik. Tertium, Kraków.

Fiederer, R. and S. O'Brien (2009). "Quality and Machine Translation: A Realistic Objective?," Journal of Specialised Translation 11: 52-74.

Fulford, H. and J. Granell-Zafra (2005). "Translation and Technology: a Study of UK Freelance Translators," Journal of Specialised Translation 4: 2-17.

Garcia, I. (2007). "Power Shifts in Web-based Translation Memory," Machine Translation 21(1): 55-68.

Garcia, I. (2009). "Beyond Translation Memory: Computers and the Professional Translator," Journal of Specialised Translation 12: 199-214.

Gough, J. (2010). "A Troubled Relationship: the Compatibility of CAT Tools". Accessed on 14 June 2011 Available at: http://translationautomation.com/technology/a-troubled-relationship-the-compatibility-of-cat-tools.html

Mańkowska, A. (2008). "Pakiet SDL Trados – narzędzia pomocne w pracy tłumaczy". In Rocznik Przekładoznawczy, Kościałkowska-Okońska, E. and Zieliński, L. (eds), 147-159. Toruń 2008.

Sosnowski, R. (2008). "Wolne oprogramowanie dla tłumacza – mit czy rzeczywistość?" In Rocznik Przekładoznawczy, Kościałkowska-Okońska, E. and Zieliński, L. (eds), 199-212. Toruń 2008

Vallianatou, F. (2005). "CAT Tools and Productivity: Tracking Words and Hours," Translation Journal 9 (4).

Language and Power in Multimodal Audiovisual Translation

Anna Bączkowska

Abstract

This paper investigates the problem of how signals of power (both verbal and nonverbal) are translated in feature films. Based on some glimpses from *The Proposal* (2009, starring Sandra Bullock and Ryan Reynolds), a preliminary analysis is presented of (1) the correlation between verbal expression of power and its gestural-aural encoding in the original version, and (2) the rendition of power in several languages (Polish, Swedish, Italian, Spanish, Portuguese and French). This cross-linguistic preliminary research is immersed in the theoretical framework of multimodality (Kress 2010), which enjoys a growing popularity in discourse analysis and recently has gained increasing attention in audiovisual translation. The study demonstrates that depending on the target language, power expressed in subtitles (1) varies in degree (it is either attenuated or augmented relative to the original version) and (2) seems to be dependent on and restricted by distinct language conventions typical of Romance, Germanic and Slavic languages.

Keywords

Multimodality, audiovisual translation, power, cross-linguistic analysis, subtitles

Introduction

The aim of the analysis presented in this paper is to investigate the problem of multimodal subtitling of power across several languages. The key words for our research are thus multimodality and power, and the overall field of analysis is a subtype of audiovisual translation. Theoretically, a multimodal approach to communication, initiated over a decade ago by Kress and Leeuwen (1996), is promoted in our research. Multimodality is currently gaining popularity in studies into natural discourse, yet in translation studies it is still in gestation, and thus not much debated, despite some interesting pioneering works conducted by Taylor (2003, 2004, 2009), infused with Baldry's (2000) study of the media, which were highly insightful and spurred further research that spread well beyond the initial seat of this novel approach to subtitles, i.e. the University of Trieste. While multimodality *per se* is receiving increasing interest in AVT, a multimodal approach to power in subtitles, to the best of our knowledge, is an under-investigated topic, and thus it will be addressed in the present paper. Probing into this topic, we shall discuss contexts limited to situations where interlocutors display power, either linguistically or in a visual-gestural or paralinguistic fashion within the structure of a feature film.

Power

Power research has a long tradition in linguistic-oriented studies of the language used by interlocutors (Fairclough 1995, 2005), where it is largely seen as creating asymmetries between discourse participants. Over the decades, linguistic expression of power has been investigated from several perspectives, which may be generally subsumed under the rubric of either behaviourist or non-behaviourist perspectives (Locher 2004). The behaviourist (Dahl 1957) approach is marked for having a focus placed on the effect of exerting power, which is supposed to occur only when there is an actual alteration in behaviour of the person who is the target of power exertion. Bachrach and Baratz (1970) are at odds with Dahl's proposal; they consider power in terms of conflict and permit not only non action (change in behaviour) but also no decision. A conflict over values is a sufficient factor to treat a situation as an example of power exertion, if it requires that A comply with B's wishes (due to fear). Thus power can occur in a non-decision-making situation, which means that, as opposed to the behaviourist approach, non-action does not preclude power. Lukes (1974) criticises Bachrach and Baratz's proposal on the grounds that it deals solely with individuals and relies too much on visible grievances. With this caveat in mind, Lukes puts forward his own theory known as a three-dimensional approach to power, which is not based on *observable change*, or *conflict*, but on another key word – *interest*, understood as a clash of expectations. As a consequence, it drifts away from behaviouristic to non-behaviouristic power research. Luke assumes that acting against the interlocutor's interest spurs *latent conflict*. In a similar vein, Watts et al. (1992) merge the concept of *power-to* with *power-over* achievable if the person with power has *freedom of action* in regard to perceived interests. A more interdisciplinary approach to power is represented by Locher (2004), who sees power markers both in language and in contextual information (social context) in which language is immersed and without which language cannot be sufficiently informative in terms of power display. There is more to it than just linguistic expression of asymmetry, as he claims; signaling power is a dynamic process and is contestable (interactants of lower status can also exercise power), and unfolds as a conversation progresses. Therefore, some signals of power-driven conflict may not be immediately discernible, they may remain latent, with the viewer witnessing at a specific moment only exacerbating relationships.

In sum, a shift can be noticed over the years of the development of power research from a focus on behaviouristic, observable power display to concentration on latent and contextualised markers of power seen in terms of impoliteness and disagreement rather than just asymmetry in the current exchange. In the interim, recent research geared at interdisciplinary investigation gathers momentum in the field of linguistic-cum-nonlinguistic analysis of interaction, which shall be expounded in what follows.

Very importantly for the present discussion, it must be admitted that the linguistic standpoint, even though it is one-sided, provides us with a powerful insight into the nature of talk in connection with status, expressing domination and hierarchy. However, as Berger (1994: 493) stresses, other – nonlinguistic – aspects of communication have been persistently avoided or unnoticed as factors contributing to power making, within which he mentions gaze patterns, proxemics, body orientation and posture, as well as paralinguistic signals (speech rate, intonation, etc.).

It is worth mentioning perhaps that on a more general note, the need to subsume nonverbal communication under the rubric of the study of linguistic communication, traditionally cultivated almost exclusively by pragmatics, has been explicitly expressed by Wharton (2009). This view harks back to the early studies conducted by Mehrabian (1972), who, as we recall, estimated the range of nonverbal communication within the overall act of communication at around 55% and paralinguistic signals at c. 38%, thus leaving only a very small portion of the cake (only 7%) to verbal signals. Given the portion of nonverbal signs participating in the overall act of communication, it would not be politic to ignore them, even when verbal communication is under inspection. Where a description of communication enjoyed so far largely in pragmatics centering solely on the linguistic level falls short is in the Mehrabian's 55%. It seems impossible to fully address an account deprived of the lion's share of the communication pie. This would make for a highly restrictive study, which could not do justice to a communicative event. Echoes of Mehrabian's thesis reverberate both in Wharton and Berger. Following on from the theses elaborated by Mehrabian, Wharton and Berger, as well as Kress (elaborated in the next section), the account presented in this research strongly adheres to the view offered by these authors that communication engages a number of modes, being thus by definition multimodal.

As in the present analysis the aim is to investigate power displays captured (verbally and visually) by single frames rather than an evolution of power-driven conflict presented in the plot, by necessity the description will revolve around cropped fragments, limited to single scenes which along with linguistic markers, also contain visual markers of power. Our analysis is thus primarily language- and context-driven, with socio-cultural convention-driven aspects ignored.

Multimodality

The theory of multimodality is a relatively new approach to communication, which draws on Halliday's (1978, 1994) systemic-functional theory, later extended to a socio-semiotic theory of communication. Originally proposed by Kress and Leeuwen (1996) for the analysis of static visual images, and recently refined by Kress (2010), and applied to natural communication and the theory of conceptual metaphor (Cienki and Muller 2008), discourse analysis (O'Halloran 2006), education (Unsworth 2001), film analysis (Bateman and Schmidt, forthcoming) and other fields of research (Ventola et al. 2004), multimodality acknowledges that while language is a valuable and highly important mode of communication, other modes, extralinguistic semiotic resources, are equally valid in message transmission and therefore, definitely deserve attention in academic investigations. Multimodality thus marks a major shift in scholarly research from language-oriented to multi-modal, all-encompassing scrutiny of human communication, where focus on sheer words and language envisaged as an isolated phenomenon is superseded by broadened look at a combination of verbal and pictorial information, and where language is contextualised in a wider range of signs, none of which is downplayed in the process of signs integration and meaning making. A multimodal approach to communication expediently signposts expansion of the scope of carriers of meaning that contribute to message construal by stressing the importance of the so far largely neglected visual elements, enriching thus the previously impoverished, as it seems, pool of meaning resources. Following this, the solely linguistic, *in vitro* to use Baldry's (2000) notion, analysis should perhaps not be set aside completely, but certainly phased out by a polysemiotic (see Gottlieb 2000: 15), or *in vivo*, analysis, which captures much more than what a printed text can convey. It traces manifestations of meaning in an unrestricted fashion. Discourse analysis is no longer a solely textual enterprise; multimodality dictates a joint venture approach spawning a visual-cum-verbal-toting tools and methodologies. This promising avenue of research better parallels spatial and temporal dimensions of communication and unveils in detail movement and change, transition points in discourse and interdependence of and viewers' shuttling between linguistic and pervasive extralinguistic resources, making the analysis of meaning a study into the dynamics of multifaceted communication. The dynamic aspect of communication seems to be of prime importance for an analysis of films, where moving images constitute the basic units for research.

Analysis

A film allows us to analyse only a semi-natural discourse, as it provides us with data which are scripted and edited for the purpose of film production. Despite this restriction, it is believed that the data are a rich resource of information which discloses important features about the nature of discourse in flux. In the study which follows, examples are culled from a feature film, a romantic comedy entitled *The Proposal*, produced in 2009, starred by Sandra Bullock (Margaret) and Ryan Reynolds (Andrew) and directed by Anne Fletcher. Three scenes will be presented and analysed both linguistically and multimodally with a view to showing the mutual interaction of these types of signals and their contribution to the overall interpretation of a message as either powerful or powerless. The languages we shall investigate in the subtitles are: Polish (professional and nonprofessional), and nonprofessional versions of French, Italian, Swedish, Spanish and German[1]. All the nonprofessional versions were downloaded from the Internet and their authors remain anonymous. As the purpose of our investigation is to trace some correlation between verbal and nonverbal semiotic resources in different languages in the context of power display, the analysis primarily focuses on cross-linguistic comparison rather than on evaluative intralinguistic description. The fact that most of the subtitles exemplify nonprofessional translations, therefore, is not of primary importance. Each scene will be presented in a table with the original soundtrack in English and their subtitled version in the six target languages, together with their back translations. In the tables the following symbols are used: "M" to indicate "man", "W" to indicate "woman", "NP" stands for nonprofessional version and "P" for professional.

Scene 1: "Praise"

On the extralinguistic level, we are exposed to a picture of a boss (Margaret) sitting at a desk in her office and shuffling her papers while conversing with her secretary (Andrew). There is no eye contact during this conversation; at the end of the exchange the boss turns around to face her computer and her office window, with her back turned to the man. Her voice is unpleasant, with a firm tone. On a linguistic level, the woman is scolding her secretary for praising her, as he is not empowered to compliment a person of higher rank.

Scene 1	PRAISE 3:51:04
M: Wow, nicely done. W: If I want your praise I'll ask you for it.	Fr: -Bien joué. Je vous dispense de vos compliments. *BT: - Nicely arranged.* *I excuse you from paying compliments.*
Pol NP: - Dobra robota. - Jak będę chciała, żebyś mnie chwalił to ci powiem. *BT: Good Job.* *- If I want you to praise me I'll tell you.*	Ger: - Gut gemacht. Wenn ich ein Lob will, sage ich es. *BT: - Good job.* *When I want praise, I say it.*

1 The back translations of subtitles in Spanish, Italian, German and Swedish were provided by colleagues specialising in these languages from our research group Multimodality Lab, Pamela Stoll Dougall, Raffaella Panizzon and Marek Kieś. The French translations were conducted by Monika Szuba (PWSH in Gdynia).

Pol P: - Brawo.
Jeśli zechcę twoich pochwał, poproszę o nie.
BT: - Bravo.
- If I want your praise I'll ask for it.

It: - Wow, bel colpo.
Quando vorrò i tuoi complimenti, te li chiererò.
BT: - Wow, great move.
When I want your compliments, I'll ask you for them.

Sw: - Snyggt gjort.
Vill jag ha beröm ber jag om det.
BT: - Nice job.
If I want to get praise then I ask for it.

Sp: - Caramba. Te felicito.
Si quiero elogios, te los pido.
BT: - Great. Congratulations.
If I want praise, I'll ask you for it.

In the Polish NP and P versions the verbal message reflects its original script in terms of retaining the personal pronoun *you* and the direct manner of expression (*I'll tell you*). Impersonal expression, on the other hand, is visible in the German and the Swedish version (*When I want praise, I say it*, and *If I want to get praise then I ask for it*), where the utterances do not address the man as such, but rather make reference to similar situations regardless of who the sender of the information is. By making reference to an imaginary and general situation the utterance loses a personal tone, and more distance is introduced. Moreover, both translations are impersonal due to the use of present tense and the notion of iterativeness coded in this way in the main clause, which signals that no reference is being made to this particular scene (and to Andrew) even indirectly; instead there is an imaginary unidentified person, who could stand for any addressee and a recurring behaviour of the woman in similar situations. As a result, the German and Swedish texts seem to be more firm and robust than their original English counterpart. In the Spanish rendition a single situation is triggered by the utterance due to the use of future simple tense and the use of personal pronoun *you*, and thus a hint at the secretary may be sensed. The French translator is most polite of all the subtitles tabulated above. The burden of inappropriateness of the secretary praising his boss is in a way taken off his shoulders and justified by the addressee when she says *I excuse you from paying compliments*. This is implicative of the boss, by and large, having nothing against being complimented by a person under her control while at the same time indicating that it is unnecessary rather than inappropriate. Finally, the Spanish subtitler is not only direct but also emotional, similarly to the Italian version and Polish professional; all use interjections, and in this respect they follow the English soundtrack (*Caramba, Wow, Brawo*). In the Polish nonprofessional version, as well as the German, French and Swedish texts, emotional language is obviated.

In sum, on the linguistic plane power is best discernable in the Swedish and German versions, with Polish and Spanish occupying the mid ground, and to the least extent it is encoded by the French text. Power sensed in this scene stems from the use of impersonal language, the use of present tense and distance imposed on the interlocutor.

Multimodally speaking, the linguistic plane reflects the extralinguistic information encoded by gestures, kinesics, eye contact and proxemics to a varying degree in the translations. While the visual image shows a woman who is cold, unfriendly or even stern, principled and serious, these features are best reflected by the Swedish subtitle, whereas the other translations make this impression softer, with its extreme being expressed in French. The viewer may feel confused being faced with a stern voice and unfriendly behaviour (no eye contact throughout this exchange) and an excusing remark expressed by the serious boss in the translation. By resorting to unfriendly language, on the other hand, a subtitler emphasises the boss's character and behaviour, which plays a vital role in this scene, and allows the verbal expression to remain in harmony with the nonverbal signals.

Scene 2: "Prop"

In scene 2, the boss and her secretary walk along a corridor to the office of Bob, an employee under the supervision of Margaret, who is just about to dismiss him. This is how the scene opens. Margaret coldly and succinctly responds to her secretary's questions and requests concerned with a book that he wishes to publish (which is Andrew's book). The boss walks in a very decisive way, posture straight, spine tense and tight like a spring, high heels making her bob up and down and emphasise her springy gate. She holds her chin up, displays a confident and vigorous stride, and orients her body away from the interlocutor. A firm tone, unpleasant voice and short answers create an impression of her as a haughty, conceited and authoritarian person. The man in turn turns towards her, with only his profile captured by the camera most of the way down the corridor, struggling to catch her attention and establish eye contact with her, his shoulders directed towards Margaret, arm bent and hand directed towards his interactant, as if he wants to nudge her and make her notice him talking. Once they get to Bob's office, he opens the door for her, which only stresses his inferior position and his cajoling attitude towards his boss. The last straw is the line Margaret utters just before they enter Bob's office *Remember, you're a prop* and his agreement to this role encoded by his line *Won't say a word*. As for the linguistic level, the woman criticises the manuscript the man wants to publish, not realising who the author is. The secretary not only nonverbally but also linguistically expresses submissiveness. As they walk along the corridor, they exchange opinions about the value of the manuscript Andrew wrote, uttering the key words for our analysis towards the very end of the way. The nonverbal behaviour described above, then, does not accompany exactly the moment the lines in the table below are actually uttered, rather they occur in the flanking frames, but nevertheless they are assumed to play a key role in the scene analysed as they build up the background for the script examined below and unveil indirectly and nonverbally a great deal of information regarding the characters' personality, social status and position in the company as well as their mutual relations.

Scene 2 PROP 5:19:12

W: Remember, you're a prop.
M: Won't say a word.

Pol NP: - Pamiętaj, jesteś rekwizytem.
- Będę cicho.
BT: Remember, you're a prop.
- I will be quiet.
Pol P: - Pamiętaj, robisz za rekwizyt.
- Będę milczał.
BT: Remember, you act as a prop.
- I'll be silent.
Sw: - ø

Fr: Vous faites partie du décor.
- Je resterai muet.
BT: - You're a part of the scenery.
- I'll remain mute.
Ger: - Sie sind hier unwichtig.
- Ich sage nichts mehr.
BT: - You are unimportant here.
- I won't say anything else.
It: Ricorda che sei qui per assistere me.
- Sarò muto.
BT: Remember, you are here to help me.
- I'll remain mute.
Sp: - Recuerda, eres una decoración.
- No voy a abrir la boca.
BT: Remember, you're scenery.
- I won't open my mouth.

In the subtitled versions the power expressed by Margaret's verbal and nonverbal signals is reflected, however, to a different extent in each rendition. In the Polish nonprofessional version the man is identified as an object (the prop – *You are a prop*), while in the professional version he is temporarily treated as a prop (*You act as a prop* in the upcoming situation). The French and the Spanish translations are similar; they reduce the role of the man to an object (a decoration or scenery) yet, contrary to the Polish renditions, they do it by making reference to a more imprecise and blurred concept of *decoration* rather than a concrete single entity (a prop) which evokes definite pejorative connotations. Nevertheless, the Polish, French and Spanish versions are all blunt and austere. Equally, the German text is straightforward and unpleasant (*You are unimportant here*), yet without downgrading him to an object. Strangely enough, the Italian subtitle reverses the text by resorting to more positive aspects and emphasising the man's active role as an assistant and supporter (*You are here to help me*). This rendition is rather surprising and does not mirror the original pragmatic message, which seems to be much more destabilising or even destructive to their relationship. The Italian version is definitely the most polite one and, by the same token, it stresses the language of power most unsuccessfully, unless one takes into consideration the Swedish version, where these lines have been omitted altogether, thus conveying the whole burden of impoliteness solely to visual signals. Multimodally, bearing in mind the message conveyed by the nonverbal signals available on the screen, an impolite rendition which clearly demonstrates power is the expected option in this scene.

Scene 3: "Dismissal"

In the subsequent scene the boss and her secretary enter Bob's office. Margaret stands in front of Bob at some distance, propping her arm on a piece of furniture. Having exchanged some words on the furniture, which happens to be new to Bob's office, she shoots out unceremoniously and without a blink, *Bob, I'm letting you go*. Bob is astounded and furious, while Margaret remains calm, assertive and imperturbable, thus demonstrating power and superiority. The cup of coffee she is holding in her hand while talking to him only strengthens the impression of expressing irreverence towards her interlocutor.

In the subtitles, power has been reflected in the following way. While in the German and the Polish nonprofessional versions the translated texts do not diverge from the original line in English, in the Italian and Polish professional they sound stronger and firmer, stressing the superior position of Margaret over Bob (*I dismiss you* vs. weaker and less emphatic *I'm letting you go*), although this effect is achieved at the cost of a departure from the original, weaker form. The most straightforward and impolite variant is provided by the Swedish subtitler. Here, again, just as in the Polish and Italian renditions, the subtitler remains closer to the visual signals than to the English verbal expression. As in the previous scenes, a direct correlation between verbal and nonverbal signals seems to be the expected rendition, otherwise a viewer would be faced with powerful nonverbal signals and verbal signals which are powerless or powerful to a lesser extent.

Scene 3 DISMISSAL 5:43:03

Bob, I'm letting you go.

Pol NP: Bob, pozwalam ci odejść.
BT: Bob, I'm letting you go.

Pol P: Bob, zwalniam cię.
BT: Bob, I dismiss you.

Sw: Du får kicken, Bob.
BT: You are fired, Bob.

Fr: Je dois me séparer de toi.
BT: I have to part with you.

Ger: Ich lasse dich gehen.
BT: I'm letting you go.

It: Ti lascio andare.
BT: I dismiss you.

Sp: Bob, te voy a despedir.
BT: I'm going to dismiss you.

Discussion

In the scenes analysed, it is noticeable that the subtitlers rely on the verbal stratum, remaining close to the original English verbal expression to a great extent, yet at the same time they try to be faithful to the extralinguistic signs encoded largely by gestures and distance. In scenes 1 and 3, distance is physical; it divides the physical space into one belonging to the boss and another to an inferior employee. In scene 2, distance is disclosed through the lack of eye contact, asymmetrical body orientation, and paralinguistic features, such as impolite tone of voice.

Given the results of the above analysis, a question arises as to whether a multimodal translation is one which allows for the extralinguistic signals and thus (i) emphasises them in the subtitle or (ii) omits them by counting on the viewer's divided attention tracing both the textual and visual channels. Taylor (2004: 161) is of the opinion that a multimodal translation is one which refers a viewer to the visual elements on the screen and treats subtitles as solely complementary, relative to the overall interplay of many modes. This claim legitimises reduction techniques in subtitles, a practice which seems to be fully justifiable and in line with the theory of audiovisual translation recommending reduction as the main translation technique adequate for subtitles (due to technical restrictions of limited space and time).

However, subtitles may also be used to emphasise sundry aspects of the original message, in particular pragmatic and cultural aspects, such as irony, identity, compliments, humour, etc. (cf. Fernandes da Silva and Rodrigues Duarte, in press; Bączkowska and Kieś, in press). In the analysis presented in this paper, translations either complement the visual signals and thus reduce the emotional charge of power articulated by a subtitle and refer the viewer to the extralinguistic elements or stress the notion of power, authority and domination; the latter being more welcome than texts which attenuate the original verbal-gestural-vocal message and thus make the text more polite (and less powerful). While attenuation is demonstrated by the French and Italian versions, the Swedish and German seem to reinforce the notion of distance and impoliteness, and thus power.

Even bearing in mind the tendencies of, for example, Romance languages to use more polite constructions than German or Scandinavian languages (Lewandowska-Tomaszczyk, personal communication, House, 2011), it still seems that the French translator in scenes 1 and 3 and the Italian translator in scene 2 did not gauge power display appropriately and that they probably go too far in expressing politeness, to a degree which introduces discrepancies between the pictorial and verbal information, while the Swedish (scenes 1 and 3) and German (scenes 1 and 2) subtitles, encoding more impoliteness than expressed in the dialogue list, seem to remain more consistent with the overall message.

Any discussion of power is bound up, at least indirectly, with impoliteness and rudeness often accompanying power display actions (see Bousfield and Locher 2008). In connection with this thesis, an issue which is unresolved in this paper yet definitely deserves attention in future research is the question of language specificity and the construction-related restrictions a language dictates. As a consequence, what might sound impolite to non-native speakers of a language (and thus powerful in the scenes under scrutiny) may not necessarily be evaluated as impolite to the same extent by its native speakers. Language imposes, by its repertoire of constructions and conventions, how thoughts are verbalised. On the other hand, viewers from different socio-cultural contexts (representing different speech communities and countries) may not “share a common set of cultural expectations with respect to the social activity and the speech events” in which they partake, due to distinct past experiences of similar situations (Watts 1992: 51). These very important aspects of power display analysis (the linguistic restrictions and cultural expectations) cannot possibly receive due attention in this short paper, whose aim is first and foremost to signal the problem of linguistic-cum-nonlinguistic analysis of communication, including intercultural communication captured by subtitles. This problem being signalled will receive further attention in future endeavours. Nevertheless, it is interesting to note that the preliminary research presented in our analysis in regard to the German subtitles supports observations documented by a thorough study of im/politeness offered by House (2011), based on interactions of native speakers of German (academic teachers) with non-native students studying in Germany. In her investigation, House notices that most non-native students find German native academic teachers impolite in situations where impoliteness is not the intention of the speakers; rather, it results from linguistic conventions typical of the German language and perhaps also from socio-cultural conventions typical of teacher-student interaction rituals. Likewise, in our analysis, the German (together with Swedish) subtitles sound more straightforward, austere and impolite relative to the original soundtrack (and other languages at issue).

Clearly, theories of politeness and impoliteness provide an important backdrop for a study on power. The correlation between power display and impoliteness has also been visible and commented on in the analysis presented above. However, further research is needed to answer the question whether (1) impoliteness immediately entails power displays (and the other way round) and (2) to what degree an utterance classified in cross-linguistic comparisons as rude is qualified as rude on a politeness-impoliteness cline by natives speakers of the language at issue.

The present analysis, limited in the number of scenes under scrutiny, is meant to be a preliminary examination of the construal of power in subtitles, and thus the examples analysed spur solely initial questions and trigger tentative conclusions. Despite the preliminary nature of the research problem raised in this short paper, the question of signalling dis/alignment, dis/affiliation and generally membership categorisation seems to be not only an interesting but also an underdeveloped theme in audiovisual translation and thus worthy of further examination. It is also interesting to note that rendering power is not such an obvious and predictable matter. Even our initial examination allows one to notice a number of differences in the way power may possibly be translated for the target audience.

Conclusions

Power is observable not only in language but also in extralinguistic behaviour, it is signalled by an array of signs deployed in multiple semiotic resources that accompany language, rather than encoded solely by linguistic expression. In this respect, audiovisual translation, and subtitles in particular, should take into consideration the fact that, on the one hand, human communication is a polysemiotic and multimodal enterprise, which overarches linguistic and semiotic descriptions, and, on the other, the fact that audiovisual translation embeds translation in a dynamic environment, where moving images must be synchronised and correlated with verbal expression; of particular interest for a subtitler, therefore, should be kinesics (gestures) rather than a static image and isolated linguistic expression. As a result, what should be analysed (and translated) is a combination of verbal and nonverbal signals, which is known as a multimodal approach to discourse (translation).

Accommodating a multimodal approach to subtitles may lead to two possible solutions: a subtitler may either reinforce the verbal-visual-aural message by duplicating it in the translated text, or the visual-aural elements may be omitted in the subtitle, thus paring the text down, an approach in line with the common and prescribed subtitle technique of reduction. Regardless of which technique is employed, it is important that the overall message conveyed by a scene be sufficiently close to the original when it comes to power displays, yet at the same time subtitles should cater for the linguistic and socio-cultural expectations of the target audience. Excessive divergence from the source message, whether by resorting to over-politeness or over-straightforwardness, if not dictated by social conventions or structural restrictions, should be avoided, to secure pictorial-verbal convergence and contextual fidelity of the two elements integrated in an intersemiotic construal.

References

Bachrach, P. and M. S. Baratz (1970). Power and Poverty: Theory and Practice. Oxford: OUP.

Baldry, A. (ed.). (2000). Multimodality and Multimediality in the Distance Learning Age. Campobasso: Palladino Editore.

Bateman, J. and K-H. Schmidt (forthcoming). Multimodal Film Analysis: How Films Mean. London: Routledge.

Bączkowska, A. and M. Kieś. (in press). Multimodal Subtitling of Direct Compliments in Polish, Italian and Swedish.

Berger, C. (1994). "Power, Dominance, and Social Interaction." In Handbook of Interpersonal Communication, Knapp, M. I. and Miller, G. R. (eds), 450-507. Thousand Oaks: Sage.

Bousfield, D. and M. Locher (eds). (2008). Impoliteness in Language: Studies on its Interplay with Power in Theory and Practice. Berlin: Mouton de Gruyter.

Cienki, A. and M. Müller (eds.). (2008). Gesture and Metaphor. Amsterdam: John Benjamins.

Dahl, R. A. (1957). "The Concept of Power," Behavioral Science 2:201-215.

Fairclough, N. (1995). Critical Discourse Analysis: The Critical Study of Language. Harlow: Longman.

Fairclough, N. (2005). Language and Power. Harlow: Longman.

Fernandes da Silva, I. and J. Rodrigues Duarte. (in press). Compliments and Identity in What Women Want.

Gottlieb, H. (2000). "Texts, Translation and Subtitling." In Screen Translation, Gottlieb, H. (ed.), 1-40. Copenhagen: Center for Translation Studies.

Halliday, M. A. K. (1978). Language as a Social Semiotic: Social Interpretation of Language and Meaning. London: Hodder Arnold.

Halliday, M. A. K.(1994). An Introduction to Functional Grammar. London: Hodder Arnold.

House, J. (2011). "Impoliteness in Cross-Cultural Encounters." Plenary lecture, Cross-Cultural Pragmatics at a Crossroads: Linguistic and Cultural Representations across Media, Conference held in Norwich, UK, 29 June-1 July.

Kress, G. (2010). Multimodality a Social Semiotic Approach to Contemporary Communication. London: Routledge.

Kress, G. and T. van Leeuwen. (1996). Reading Images: the Grammar of Visual Design. London: Routledge.

Locher, M. A. (2004). Power and Politeness in Action. Berlin: Mouton de Gruyter.

Lukes, S. (1974). Power. A Radical View. London: Macmillan.

Mehrabian, A. (1972). Silent Messages: Implicit Communication of Emotions and Attitudes. Belmont: Wadsworth Publishing Company.

O'Halloran, K. L. (2006). Multimodal Discourse Analysis. New York: Continuum.

Taylor, C. (2003). "Multimodal Transcription in the Analysis, Translation and Subtitling of Italian Films," The Translator 9(2): 191-205.

Taylor, C. (2004). "Multimodal Text Analysis and Subtitling." In Perspectives on Multimodality, Ventola, E., Charles, C. and Kalternbacher, M. (eds), 153-172. Amsterdam: John Benjamins.

Taylor, C. (2009). "Pedagogical Tools for the Training of Subtitlers." In In So Many Words: Dubbing and Subtitling for the Screen, Anderman, G. and Díaz Cintas, J. (eds), 214-228.Clevedon: Multilingual Matters.

Unsworth, L. (2001). Teaching Multiliteracies Across the Curriculum: Changing Contexts of Text and Image in Classroom Practice. Buckingham: Open University Press.

Ventola, E., Charles, C., and M. Kaltenbacher (eds). (2004). Perspectives on Multimodality. Amsterdam: John Benjamins.

Watts, R. (1992). "Linguistic Politeness and Politic Verbal Behavior: Reconsidering Claims for Universality." In Politeness in Language: Studies in Its History, Theory and Practice, Watts, R., Ide, S. and Ehlich, K. (eds), 43-69. Berlin: Mouton de Gruyter.

ŁÓDŹ
Studies in Language

Edited by
Barbara Lewandowska-Tomaszczyk

Vol. 1 Barbara Lewandowska-Tomaszczyk / Patrick James Melia (eds.): PALC'99: Practical Applications in Language Corpora. Papers from the International Conference at the Universtiy of Łódź, 15–18 April 1999. 2000.

Vol. 2 Lou Burnard / Tony McEnery (eds.): Rethinking Language Pedagogy from a Corpus Perspective. Papers from the third international conference on Teaching and Language Corpora. 2000.

Vol. 3 Barbara Lewandowska-Tomaszczyk / John Osborne / Frits Schulte: Foreign Language Teaching and Information and Communication Technology. 2001.

Vol. 4 Piotr Cap: Explorations in Political Discourse. Methodological and Critical Perspectives. 2002.

Vol. 5 Ewa Waniek-Klimczak / Patrick James Melia (eds.): Accents and Speech in Teaching English Phonetics and Phonology. EFL perspective. 2002.

Vol. 6 Barbara Lewandowska-Tomaszczyk / Kamila Turewicz (eds.): Cognitive Linguistics Today. 2002.

Vol. 7 Barbara Lewandowska-Tomaszczyk (ed.): PALC 2001: Practical Applications in Language Corpora. 2003.

Vol. 8 Corpus Linguistics by the Lune. A Festschrift for Geoffrey Leech. Edited by Andrew Wilson, Paul Rayson and Tony McEnery. 2003.

Vol. 9 Barbara Lewandowska-Tomaszczyk (ed.): Practical Applications in Language and Computers. PALC 2003. 2004.

Vol. 10 Imagery in Language. Festschrift in Honour of Professor Ronald W. Langacker. Edited by Barbara Lewandowska-Tomaszczyk and Alina Kwiatkowska. 2004.

Vol. 11 Seana Coulson / Barbara Lewandowska-Tomaszczyk (eds.): The Literal and Nonliteral in Language and Thought. 2005.

Vol. 12 Piotr Cap (ed.): Pragmatics Today. 2005.

Vol. 13 Jacek Waliński / Krzysztof Kredens / Stanisław Goźdź-Roszkowski (eds.): Corpora and ICT in Language Studies. PALC 2005. 2007.

Vol 14 Krzysztof Kosecki (ed.): Perspectives on Metonymy. Proceedings of the International Conference "Perspectives on Metonymy", held in Łódź, Poland, May 6–7, 2005. 2007.

Vol. 15 Barbara Lewandowska-Tomaszczyk / Tomasz Płudowski / Dolores Valencia Tanno (eds.): The Media and International Communication. 2007.

Vol. 16 Krzysztof Kredens / Stanisław Goźdź-Roszkowski (eds.): Language and the Law: International Outlooks. 2007.

Vol. 17 Barbara Lewandowska-Tomaszczyk (ed.): Corpus Linguistics, Computer Tools, and Applications – State of the Art. PALC 2007. 2008.

Vol. 18 Barbara Lewandowska-Tomaszczyk / Katarzyna Dziwirek (eds.): Studies in Cognitive Corpus Linguistics. 2009.

Vol. 19 Barbara Lewandowska-Tomaszczyk / Marcel Thelen (eds.): Meaning in Translation. 2010.

Vol. 20 Łukasz Bogucki / Krzysztof Kredens (eds.): Perspectives on Audiovisual Translation. 2010.

Vol. 21 Piotr Stalmaszczyk (ed.): Turning Points in the Philosophy of Language and Linguistics. 2011.

Vol. 22 Stanisław Goźdź-Roszkowski: Patterns of Linguistic Variation in American Legal English. A Corpus-Based Study. 2011.

Vol. 23 Kamila Ciepiela (ed.): Identity through a Language Lens. 2011.

Vol. 24 Stanisław Goźdź-Roszkowski (ed.): Explorations across Languages and Corpora. PALC 2009. 2011.

Vol. 25 Krzysztof Kosecki / Janusz Badio (eds.): Cognitive Processes in Language. 2012.

Vol. 26 Alina Kwiatkowska (ed.): Texts and Minds. Papers in Cognitive Poetics and Rhetoric. 2012.

Vol. 27 Paul A. Wilson (ed.): Dynamicity in Emotion Concepts. 2012.

Vol. 28 Piotr Pęzik (ed.): Corpus Data across Languages and Disciplines. 2012.

www.peterlang.de

Kolibri 360 GmbH
Ferdinand-Jühlke-Straße 7
99095 Erfurt, Deutschland
produktsicherheit@kolibri360.de